A
Certain
Respect
for
Tradition

To Kat,
with warmest wishes
Enjoy,
Mark Miller
November 23/2006

OTHER BOOKS BY MARK MILLER

Some Hustling This!
Taking Jazz to the World, 1914-1929 (2005)

The Miller Companion to Jazz in Canada
and Canadians in Jazz (2001)

Such Melodious Racket:
The Lost History of Jazz in Canada, 1914-1949
(1997)

Cool Blues:
Charlie Parker in Canada, 1953
(1989)

Boogie, Pete & The Senator:
Canadian Musicians in Jazz, the Eighties
(1987)

Jazz in Canada:
Fourteen Lives
(1982)

A Certain Respect for Tradition

MARK MILLER ON JAZZ

Selected Writings 1980-2005

THE MERCURY PRESS

The publisher gratefully acknowledges the financial assistance of the Canada Council for the Arts, the Ontario Arts Council, the Ontario Media Development Corporation, and the Ontario Book Publishing Tax Credit Program. The publisher further acknowledges the financial support of the Government of Canada through the Department of Canadian Heritage's Book Publishing Industry Development Program (BPIDP) for our publishing activities.

 Canada Council for the Arts   Conseil des Arts du Canada   Canadä

Editor: Beverley Daurio
Cover, composition and page design: Beverley Daurio
Cover image: Joe Henderson, Montreal, 1986. Photograph by Mark Miller
Printed and bound in Canada
Printed on acid-free paper

1 2 3 4 5   10 09 08 07 06

Library and Archives Canada Cataloguing in Publication

Miller, Mark, 1951-
A certain respect for tradition : Mark Miller on jazz : selected writings, 1980-2005 / Mark Miller.
Essays previously published as articles, chiefly in The globe and mail.
ISBN 1-55128-125-2
1. Jazz--History and criticism. 2. Jazz musicians. I. Title.
ML3507.M649 2006   781.65   C2006-904324-8

The Mercury Press
Box 672, Station P, Toronto, Ontario Canada M5S 2Y4
www.themercurypress.ca

Table of Contents

Preface

I've been listening to jazz for about 40 years, writing about it for more than 30. It was a Gil Evans recording — I'm not sure which at this late date, possibly *La Nevada* — that first caught my ear one night on CJRT-FM's *The Jazz Scene*, very early in Ted O'Reilly's long and distinguished career as the voice of jazz in Toronto. At a time when my contemporaries were drawn to the Beatles and the Rolling Stones, something about Evans' music, and about jazz more generally, was to me equally beckoning.

My local library in Toronto, the Richview branch, had a small but well-chosen jazz collection that included LPs by Charles Mingus, Ornette Coleman, Django Reinhardt and even Charlie Parker and Dizzy Gillespie at Massey Hall in 1953 — the same Massey Hall where, at 14, I would hear my very first concert in May 1966. (Well, it was the Lovin' Spoonful, but everyone has to start somewhere, right? And *Do You Believe in Magic?* is still good for a little thrill whenever I hear it again on the radio.)

I started to read the American magazine *Down Beat* in 1967, beginning with the June 29 issue, which I bought in Montreal while visiting Expo '67 with my parents. I also followed the columns that Jack Batten wrote locally for *The Globe and Mail* — "Wouldn't *that* be a nice gig to have," I said to myself more than once — and I watched for Richard Williams' byline in Britain's *Melody Maker*.

At the same time, I discovered that Canada had a fine jazz publication of its own, *Coda Magazine*, which was edited by John Norris and Bill Smith in the book room of The Jazz and Blues Centre, then a second-floor walk-up on Yonge Street, south of Bloor. John and Bill — both firm, persuasive and progressive in their views — were influential in shaping my thoughts about jazz and in 1973 welcomed my first efforts, as they welcomed so many others' first efforts, to write about it in a respected forum. Moreover, it was on Bill's recommendation that I was called to do my first review for *The Globe and Mail* in November 1977. By then, I was also contributing to *Down Beat* and the International Jazz Federation's *Jazz Forum*.

Some months would pass before I did my second review for the *Globe*, but from that point, March 1978, I wrote on a regular freelance basis about jazz for the newspaper until I decided to stop at the end of 2005, completing more than 4,000 articles in the course of 27 years — shorter and longer reviews, interviews, overviews and news items.

And yes, it *was* a nice gig to have, though not forever. The business of jazz, the media in general and the *Globe* in particular have all moved in new directions. Their various interests, and mine, simply diverged.

Some 80 of those articles from the last 25 of those years are included in *A Certain Respect for Tradition*, along with a few from other sources, including the longest piece here, a 4,000-word piece about Cecil Taylor from *Banff Letters*, and a few more not previously published. All have been selected according to the simplest and most subjective of criteria: they are pieces I like about musicians whose work — for the most part — I appreciate. Accordingly, the general tone of this collection is sympathetic, even admiring.

I have been known, of course, to take a harder line at times. But *A Certain Respect for Tradition* is as much a celebration of jazz as it is a survey of my work as a journalist; the world will be none the richer for reading once again what I may have thought at one point or another about Ramsey Lewis, Larry Coryell, Stanley Jordan, Jamie Cullum or Randy Bachman.

These pieces were not intended, and are not offered now, as definitive portraits. In keeping with their origins as newspaper articles, and subject as such to practical constraints of time and space, they are the product of brief encounters — reviews of a concert or of a set or two at a club, interviews by telephone, conversations in hotel rooms and coffee shops, quick chats at the bar or the band table. By and large, they are also quite immediate to that encounter — to the performance that is under review, or to the engagement, tour or recording that has occasioned the interview.

[Red Richards] is an unassumingly adept showman, the easy entertainer who is comfortable enough in his work that he can let a note drop here and there without instinctively pausing to watch it roll under the piano. (The Globe and Mail, March 7, 1985)

With one exception, they have been ordered here chronologically by the date of the encounter in question (see footnote, p. 16); the interviews with Cecil Taylor in July 1985 and November 1986 seem entirely too complementary to be set apart.

Altogether, they reflect the changing face of jazz as it was heard in Toronto, and more broadly in Canada, between 1980 and 2005. Some of the music's pioneers were still active in the early 1980s, including Benny Carter and Jimmy McPartland; many women instrumentalists emerged during the 1980s and 1990s, among them JoAnne Brackeen, Myra Melford and Maria Schneider; several important European modernists and postmodernists were increasingly a presence at the turn of the new century, not least Peter Brötzmann, Willem Breuker and Misha Mengelberg.

Finally, these pieces have undergone some adjustment since they first appeared in print, whether a word, a phrase, a sentence that might have been better turned in the first place, or an assertion that the passing years have turned cryptic. (Two portraits, Stéphane Grappelli in 1981 and Jimmy Hamilton in 1986, have been entirely redrawn from interviews originally done for the *Globe*.) And, inevitably, there are corrections, not least to the given name of a very young Marsalis, which on first hearing — back in November 1980 at the Rising Sun in Montreal — sounded like Quinton.

As the title of this collection would have it, the reviews and interviews here reflect a certain respect for tradition. That is, a respect for the jazz tradition as qualified by the belief that one of its defining traits is the essential role that change, and more specifically synthesis, has played in its development. Jazz began as a synthesis of African folk and European classical music and has continued to evolve through its assimilation, or re-assimilation as the case may be, of outside elements, be they from classical music, the classical avant-garde, rock or the many folk idioms now collectively known as World Music. (See "Rivers," page 168.)

Pat Metheny put it very well in a interview I did with him in 1997: "To me," he suggested, "if jazz is anything, it's a process and maybe a verb, but it's not a thing. It's a form that demands that you bring to it things that are valuable to *you*, that are personal to you. That, for me, is a pretty serious distinction that doesn't have anything to do with blues, or swing, or any of these other things that tend to be listed as essentials in order for music to be jazz with a capital J."

Mine, moreover, is a view of jazz from the vantage point of Toronto, and of Canada more generally. It's not a view concentrated on, or by, those neo-conservative, jazz-with-a-capital-"J" considerations, cf. Wynton Marsalis, that shaped the music in New York and, by extension the rest of the United States, during the 1980s and 1990s. Nor is it a view swayed by the corporate-minded commodification of jazz, cf. Diana Krall, undertaken by the recording industry with the co-operation of a suggestible media during the 1990s and early 2000s.

The photo count on Diana Krall's new CD [The Look of Love] stands at 11, including one shot by Bruce Weber that should appeal to ankle and foot fetishists, a niche market that jazz has ignored for far too long. (The Globe and Mail, September 20, 2001)

Mine, I would like to think, has been a longer view of jazz, both geographically and historically — a view expressed with a degree of skepticism, perhaps a trace of humour, a fondness for the play of words, an aversion to writing in the first person — book prefaces aside — and, more than even a certain respect for tradition, a great affection for the music.

Acknowledgements

Inasmuch as most of the pieces in *A Certain Respect for Tradition* were original-ly written for *The Globe and Mail*, I must thank the arts editors during my 27 years with the newspaper — successively, Donn Downey, Karen York, James Adams and Andrew Gorham — for the freedom that they allowed me, particularly as a free-lance writer, to determine my own course as a critic and for the trust that they showed in the choices I made and the opinions I expressed.

My thanks also to other friends and colleagues at the *Globe* over those 27 years — among them, alphabetically, Suzanne Buhasz, Rebecca Caldwell, Warren Clements, Beppi Croisariol, Celia Donnelly, Robert Everett-Green, Christopher Harris, Susanne Jones, Elaine Knapp, David Lancashire, Eric Nelson, Elizabeth Renzetti and Trish Wilson — for their moral and logistical support. Without it, I surely would not have stayed as long as I did.

My debt to John Norris and Bill Smith of *Coda* has been noted in the preface; I must also acknowledge the early encouragement I received at York University from Don Rubin, who saw some potential in the assignments I did for his theatre criticism course and encouraged me to consider arts journalism as a career.

My debt to Beverley Daurio has been noted in my previous three books pub-lished by The Mercury Press on her watch, but I must express my gratitude again for her immediate interest in taking on a selected writings collection and, as ever, for her customary understanding, amity and judgement in seeing it into print.

Finally, my thanks to all of the musicians included in *A Certain Respect for Tradition* — for what they said and what they played.

Mark Miller, April 2006

"Short"

Art Blakey and Guy Nadon (1980)

Jazz drummers come in a variety of packages. Art Blakey and Guy Nadon, the two drummers who have had Montreal swinging this week, come in small ones: Blakey is short, stout, American and powerful; Nadon, short, funny, French-Canadian and fast.

Blakey, at the Rising Sun on *rue* Ste-Catherine until Sunday, is one of the recognized greats. At 61, the Pittsburgh-born musician was one of the first into the bebop game, and for the past 25 years has led the Jazz Messengers, a finishing school for a host of important hard-bop players. This year's class has a remarkable young trumpeter, Wynton Marsalis of New Orleans, and two fine saxophonists, altoist Bobby Watson and tenorman Billy Pierce.

Nadon, on the other hand, is barely known outside of his native Montreal. At 46, and after more than 30 years in the business, he plays jazz at the beginning of the week in little rooms like the Bar Emery/Chez Dumas just off *rue* St-Denis, where he was co-leader with alto saxophonist Maurice Mayer of a loose quintet that closed on Wednesday, and at l'Imprévu in Old Montreal, where he leads his own septet next Monday. On weekends, he makes his living with dance and wedding bands.

Blakey's strength is, to coin a phrase, his strength. There's something volcanic about his playing as it erupts momentarily in the least expected places — the middle of a ballad, for example — and then pours forth continuously at hotter tempos. He's a natural wonder; he makes his exertions look easy, usually with a smile on his face and always with a certain simplicity to his movements at the drums. His rhythms are basic, even primitive at times, but their power is undeniable, spurring his musicians on from behind and below to performances that may cover only a limited area of jazz, stylistically, but touch all of its passions.

Like Blakey, Nadon is an original. His technique comes in Buddy Rich proportions. But he's a spontaneous Buddy Rich, or perhaps a French-Canadian Phil Seaman; either way, his playing is simply ridiculous — *that* good and *that* possessed. With his small kit set up at the front corner of the stage, he leads the musicians with a glance over the shoulder and a "forward-ho" gesture. When the tempo is fast — and Nadon's fast is *fast*; even the ballads sometimes hit quadruple time for a chorus or two — he inevitably leaves the others well behind, choking on his dust, but all smiles and laughter at the sheer absurdity of whatever he has just played. He hasn't the looseness of the Americans who have defined jazz drumming, Blakey among them — Nadon cuts razor-sharp corners on the tempo shifts and swings intricately in a clipped, almost staccato manner — but he makes it clear in conversation that he doesn't want to play like anyone but himself. In that he has succeeded: he is an original in a country where originals are few.

Both drummers end the night with *The Theme*. Blakey announces, "We'll be black tomorrow," no doubt a standard line. Nadon begins a similar *dénouement*, and then pandemonium breaks out. Now he's singing — country tunes, *Arriva Derce Roma* and *Hey Ba Ba Re Bop*, in a variety of voices and languages, with microphone in one hand, drum stick in the other. It all comes to a crashing end 25 minutes later. The man's irrepressible. The best jazz drummers generally are.

November 14, 1980★

"Gossamer strings"
Stéphane Grappelli (1981)

Stéphane Grappelli arrives a little late for lunch at Stop 33. "I have been acting like a star today," the Parisien violinist and pianist announces lightly, sounding more pleased with himself than apologetic as he settles in with his guests for the occasion. He's the gentlest of souls, though, and no offence is — or ever could be — taken.

His jeans and his blue turtleneck sweater immediately set him apart from most of the other patrons at the Sutton Place restaurant, businessmen whose sense of themselves is complemented by the grand, if cloudy vista that the room offers over the city in which they conduct their affairs. But something about Grappelli in their midst marks him if not as a star, then as someone nevertheless very important.

Which, of course, he is — one of the first great European jazz musicians, a distinction that he shares with the Belgian gypsy guitarist Django Reinhardt, dating back to the 1930s when the two men, together with their accomplices in the Quintette of the Hot Club of France, made music of remarkable verve, virtuosity and lyricism. It was jazz. It was not, however, *American* jazz.

The businessmen at Stop 33 could know nothing of this, but there had still been a slight hush in their conversations when Grappelli first made his way softly into the room.

The party at his table includes two members of the Toronto press, but he has a question of his own to ask. "I understand there is a new Massey Hall," he wonders, tangential to his latest appearance two nights hence at the old one. "Where is it?"

* Unless otherwise indicated, the date following each piece in *A Certain Respect for Tradition* is the date on which that piece first appeared in *The Globe and Mail*.

He seems disappointed to learn that "it" — the future Roy Thomson Hall — is still under construction. "Oh well," he responds, "I prefer to see it when it is completed."★

He brightens at the prospect. "I suppose it will be *moderne*? With everything for the benefit of the sound? Because, you know, the sound of a *théâtre*, or a concert hall, is like a violin; you take three, four, five violins — they've all got the same shape, but not the same sound... So I really wish this new Massey Hall will be as good as the *actuel* one. I am very happy at Massey Hall; it is an old building, and that goes with my age."

Massey Hall, for the record, is in its 88th year. Grappelli is 73 — 73, and still curious about this, that and the other, including some of the buildings that he can see on the western Toronto horizon through the rain that is now trailing down Stop 33's windows.

His sense of curiosity has served him well throughout his career, indeed as early as his first encounter with jazz — a raucous, raggy recording of *Stumbling* made in 1922 by the most popular American band in Paris at the time, Mitchell's Jazz Kings. "I was attracted immediately," he remembers, of what in every respect would have been foreign music to a young Frenchman. "I don't know how to explain that. I was hypnotized."

Another dozen years would pass before Grappelli and Django Reinhardt established the Quintette of the Hot Club of France. And in truth it was really the guitarist's evocative melodic and rhythmic *élan*, both unprecedented and unsurpassed by American standards, that gave the ensemble its unique identity. Grappelli, for his part, had taken his lead from violinist Joe Venuti, tempering the New Yorker's jocosity to suit his own, more delicate sensibilities, a process of refinement that would continue over the years — though with no loss of authority — to the point where he often plays now as if on gossamer strings.

Grappelli and Reinhardt were an unlikely and often uneasy match, one fastidious and the other the freest of spirits. Caught together in London at the outbreak of the war in September 1939, they remained in character. Grappelli stayed safely put, while Reinhardt dashed back to Paris and continued to work in France and Belgium throughout the German occupation.

It was in London that Grappelli began to speak English. More than 40 years later, he still fishes for compliments about his command of his second language; he laughs coyly when they come. "To be a bit pretentious, I am very pleased with myself. I learned English [from] the musicians. I was obliged: I had an orchestra, a combo, so I must speak their language. That's the best way to learn, to be involved. Like someone who starts to swim — somebody pushes him into the water. That's the best way to do it."

★ Grappelli would perform at Thomson Hall in 1983.

He had become a musician in much the same manner. "I never had any teachers," he explains, "because my father could not afford that. And in any case, he had no idea for me to be a violinist. My father was a dreamer — a marvellous one, I must admit — but he was not thinking about what I would do in my life when he was not there any more. So I must find my way myself."

Grappelli and Reinhardt were reunited soon after the war and recorded together for the last time in 1949, four years before Reinhardt's death. The guitarist's legacy, and Grappelli's contribution to it, has followed the violinist ever since. For a time — nearly 20 years all told — Grappelli largely ignored it, working instead with pianists and in orchestral settings. In 1973, however, he revived the Quintette's old sound with a succession of guitarists — Diz Disley first and again currently, Martin Taylor most notably — and found himself with a new and enthusiastic audience in North America.

And yet he reveals some ambivalence about his change of course when he speaks of his work lately with the American bluegrass mandolinist David Grisman, as represented on the LP *Hot Dawg* (Horizon) in 1978 and by a live recording from 1979. Never mind that they reprise the old Quintette's favourites *Tiger Rag*, *Sweet Georgia Brown* and *Minor Swing*; that's apparently not the point of their partnership.

"He has such a big range of ideas," Grappelli suggests. "And that's what I like: I like to play with people who bring something to me. I like to go out of what I used to do with Django Reinhardt 40 years ago."

To that end, he continues to record with pianists, most recently the American Hank Jones and the Frenchman Martial Solal.★ Chick Corea is on his wish list — "I have great *envie* to play with him" — as are Herbie Hancock and McCoy Tyner.

Nor does his search for fresh challenges end with pianists. Lately he has taken possession of an electric violin, one that offers him an additional lower octave with which to work. His rationale for the acquisition? "Because it's unusual," he responds, quite in character. "I like something new." But there's something more to it than either novelty or curiosity. "It's between the violin and the cello," he continues, describing its range, "with the same fingering as the violin, but the strings are bigger and they hurt your fingers."

He's talking like an artist now, not a star. "I'm ready for anything to please the people who come to hear me. You must suffer a bit. For them."

Previously unpublished; October 1981

★ The LPs *London Meeting* (String) and *Happy Reunion* (Owl), respectively.

"Dues"
Benny Carter (1982)

It was early one night, late last week, and Benny Carter had no sooner taken the stage at Lytes in Toronto, alto saxophone in one hand and trumpet in the other, when a voice from the audience made it known that someone in the house was celebrating a birthday.

Now Benny Carter is the fellow who wrote for and played in the great Fletcher Henderson band at the turn of the 1930s, the fellow who was one of the first major American jazzmen to live and travel in Europe during the mid-1930s, the fellow who was the leader of several distinguished bands in New York into the early 1940s, who subsequently became a significant figure in the Hollywood music industry, who recently was the recipient of an honourary doctorate from Princeton University, and the fellow who has been, throughout, one of the pre-eminent alto saxophonists in jazz.

But Benny Carter, who is all of those things, is also very gracious. And so he sang *Happy Birthday* to "whoever you are." It was, he noted immediately after, the only time he had ever started a performance by singing. Even at the age of 74, there is still room for yet another first.

Those who interpret jazz history have suggested that Carter has never quite enjoyed the popular success or recognition that he deserved — that he has always been a musician's musician. Recent history at Lytes seems to reinforce both theories: a few nights after Carter had sung *Happy Birthday* for someone who should have known better than to ask, he was honoured by visits from clarinetist Peanuts Hucko, vibraphonist Peter Appleyard and Boss Brass boss Rob McConnell, the last with valve trombone in hand, ready to sit in.

Carter himself is not given to pointed observations about his own importance, his career, or his music. He does admit that a chronological discussion of his career "would take quite a little while," but he demurs when it is suggested that he has influenced the course of jazz. "That," he suggests simply, "is for someone else to say."

It is only when he speaks of his own orchestras — his studio groups in the early 1930s and his touring bands that followed his return from England in 1938 — and begins without prompting to list some of his former sidemen that he seems prepared to acknowledge his significance.

"In all the bands I had, I had great musicians, great people, all of whom I love dearly. And I'd like to think it's reciprocated. Gee, I had J.J. Johnson, Max Roach, Miles Davis, Dizzy Gillespie, Eddie Heywood Jr., Teddy Wilson, Cozy Cole, Sidney Catlett, Chu Berry..."

Otherwise, Carter is philosophical about his considerable achievements. "Most of what I've done has just come to me. Only for very short periods have I had an agent, so I wasn't often submitted for anything. I was of course loath to submit myself. I'm not shy, or modest, but if things are going well enough, I'd say, 'What the hell,' and relax. And I've been very fortunate: many things have come my way."

As it happened the trumpet came first, when Carter was growing up in New York City. Bubber Miley was the inspiration, but the trumpet "lasted one week-end" before Carter traded it in for a C-melody sax. Here, his model was Frankie Trumbauer. It was only when the C-melody went the way of the unicorn that Carter turned to the alto. "Some years later, I returned to — or should I say I added — the trumpet, with encouragement from Doc Cheatham, who gave me a mouth-piece in 1929 that I still use today."

Despite his eloquence with the alto, and despite the fact that he is playing a limited amount of trumpet at Lytes, Carter concedes that the trumpet is "sort of my favourite instrument, but I don't get to play it very much. And it's the kind of instrument that, as they say, 'If you don't play, you're gonna pay.'"

He notes that he'd have to give the the alto and trumpet equal time to get as comfortable with the latter as he would like. But again he grows philosophical. "At this point, there are a lot of things that I would like to do, and shall probably never do, so I just won't talk about them... There are things I may still be able to do, but if I don't, life won't owe me anything."

It has been, instead, as much with the pen as with the alto that Carter has made his name in music, beginning with his first records — the band, drawn from the Fletcher Henderson outfit, had the unfortunate name of the Chocolate Dandies — and continuing in Hollywood with film and TV scores. The balance between writing and playing has been artistically satisfying, he admits, but as his studio assignments grew in number — from *Stormy Weather* in 1943 through *The Snows of Kilimanjaro*, *Night without Sleep* and *An American in Paris* — he has played less, emerging only from time to time to teach, to tour, or to do a club date like this one at Lytes.

"I'm still paying my dues," he says, back briefly on the road, 40 years on. "But I'm also collecting."

January 14, 1982

"Cocky"
Jimmy McPartland (1982)

It is with steady hand, practised hand, that Jimmy McPartland dashes off yet another autograph: "To... Best Always..." He doesn't simply oblige, he offers, and provides for the purpose a small photograph xeroxed from his own collection — a photo not found in many of the history books.

There are eight musicians sitting or standing under McPartland's "Best Always." The photocopy has left Frank Teschemacher, Dave North and Dick McPartland virtually faceless, and Jim Lanigan and Floyd O'Brien mere ghosts. Bud Freeman is scarcely recognizable, but Jimmy McPartland stands as bold as life left of centre, and a dark, brooding Dave Tough sits behind him, a small man partially hidden by a large bass drum.

These are The Wolverines, sometimes known as Husk O'Hare's Wolverines, although McPartland, who claims the band as his own, scoffs at the memory of the Chicago agent. "*He* didn't organize *anything!*"

They played Des Moines in 1925, where a photographer captured the likeness that McPartland would autograph so freely years later, and they took over the White City Ballroom on Chicago's south side in 1926. Jitney dancing — 10¢ a dance — was the order of the night. Freeman, Tough and the others made $90 a week; McPartland, who says he was 17 but was certainly a year or two older, drew $350 — "pretty good loot."

These are not, however, *The* Wolverines — not the Wolverine Orchestra, with Dick Voynow its nominal leader and cornetist Bix Beiderbecke its undisputed star soloist. Not the Wolverines whose recordings of *Jazz Me Blues* and *Riverboat Shuffle* for Gennett in 1924 made jazz history. The violins at the McPartlands' feet are the giveaway: you wouldn't catch Bix anywhere near a violinist, at least not until 1927.

This is, in reality, the Austin High Gang in a kind of graduation photo, if indeed any of its members had really graduated. McPartland, for one, left school in October 1924 to take Beiderbecke's place with *The* Wolverines in New York. By the time McPartland had assumed the Wolverine name from Voynow, one breakup in Florida and one re-formation in Chicago later, Bix was near the peak of his career. His demise would come all too soon, all too quickly. His association with the Paul Whiteman Orchestra, which some jazz musicians thought a fate worse than death, was two years away; death itself was six.

For a few years in the 1920s, Jimmy McPartland followed Beiderbecke. For the next 50, Bix would haunt McPartland. The younger man doesn't seem to mind. The nightly requests for "some Bix" are handled cheerfully, prefaced by a reminiscence that usually ends "but he drank terribly." Privately, McPartland adds, "I did too, but I was athletic."

He might comply with *Davenport Blues*: softening his tone and quoting Bix directly in uncanny emulation. But ultimately the tribute would serve to put McPartland's own style in context.

"Do you think I copy him?" he asks, rhetorically. "I don't think so. He knew that; I knew it myself. A lot of people think I copied him. I don't. The only time I copied anything from him was on the *Shades of Bix* record, and I did that intentionally."

Shades of Bix — not quite as catchy as the "Sons of Bix's" that Eddie Condon once proposed as the name of something or other — was recorded for Brunswick in 1953, a collection of tunes with Beiderbecke associations. McPartland carries copies with him when he travels, selling them along with *Jazzmeeting in Holland* (Riff), which found him reunited in 1975 with Bud Freeman in the company of drummer Ted Easton's Jazzband. With their six Dutch friends, the two former Chicagoans played *Jazz Me Blues*, either the third or fourth tune that the Austin High kids learned note for note from *The* Wolverines' Gennett recording.

Shades of Bix, *Jazzmeeting in Holland* and several LPs by his former wife, the British pianist Marian McPartland, form a top-heavy pile of records on the coffee table of McPartland's Toronto hotel room. There is fruit on the night table, and food on the overhead shelf of the clothes closet. Photos of recent and not-so-recent McPartland — and of course those Wolverines — are spread on the dresser, hiding worn and graying typewritten lyric sheets. *Cherry* is one.

Onstage and off, apparently, McPartland dresses for comfort: a paisley ascot at one end, running shoes at the other, and a belt with a cornet on the buckle holding everything tight in the middle. He chain smokes as he talks, and in an hour-and-a-half he covers the first 23 years of his life. Then, of his own accord, he stops. In 1930. "There are a lot of aside things," he says, summarily, "but they don't matter. These are the high points."

"My brother always called me 'Cocky,'" he begins. "I was fresh, brash — a punk." He was also the fighter of the two McPartland boys. Dick, two years older, had survived rheumatic fever as a child and suffered from a heart condition; it usually kept him out of trouble as a boy, but it also curtailed his career in the 1930s and took his life in 1957.

Their father, a music teacher who at one time had also played third base for Anson's Colts (forerunner to the Chicago Cubs), showed the boys how to box and to play the violin. The younger McPartland took particularly to boxing, and to related aggressive activities. At 13 or 14, armed with .45 calibre pistol that he had stolen from a Cadillac parked outside a Chicago nightspot, he shot it out in Cicero,

Illinois, with a farmer whose chicken coop the McPartland gang had raided. Jazz legend suggests that a more innocent firearms offence a few years earlier had sent an 11-year-old Louis Armstrong on his way — to a waifs' home, where he received his first cornet lessons. And so it was with McPartland: he was put on probation with the recommendation that the McPartland family find a quieter neighbourhood than the tough "near west side."

Jeanne McPartland, now divorced, took her children farther west to Austin. The boys went to Austin High. Frank Teschemacher was there, as was Jim Lanigan. "We were all violinists — Teschemacher, my brother and Jim Lanigan, who was an *excellent* violinist. And I played, but I wasn't too good." Bud Freeman, meanwhile, was "just another guy in the neighbourhood."

They all gathered after school at a nearby soda shop, The Spoon and Straw, to listen to the newest records. It was inevitable that the New Orleans Rhythm Kings and King Oliver's Creole Jazz Band with Louis Armstrong would turn up sooner or later on the juke box — the bands themselves had arrived in Chicago from the South by 1922.

It all happened very quickly. The Austin High boys chose up instruments — McPartland, in character, took the cornet "because it was the loudest instrument" — and began the arduous process of copying the records note for note. The NORK's *Farewell Blues* was first, a tune recorded on August 29, 1922. The band was listed as the Friar's Society Orchestra under the direction of one Husk O'Hara [sic], and it wasn't long before the boys found the Friar's Inn on Wabash Avenue and heard the band first hand — at least whenever someone opened the front door.

The Creole Jazz Band made its first records seven months later. *Chimes Blues* was a favourite with the young Chicagoans, who found their way in due course to Oliver's feet at Lincoln Gardens on E. 31st Street. The first records by *The Wolverines* followed in February 1924. McPartland, initially enamoured of Oliver, Armstrong and the NORK's Paul Mares, was won over by Bix. "His tone was the thing that floored me — that round, full, lovely tone." Before the year was out, and less than two years after he had taken up the cornet to learn *Farewell Blues*, McPartland himself would be playing with the Wolverines in New York.

He had matured quickly. The boys took occasional jobs almost immediately as the Blue Friars, although history remembers them more readily as the Austin High Gang, a name that was never used in a commercial context. "The reason they called us a gang, is because we were," McPartland explains. "I was the frontman. If anything happened, my brother would always say, 'Go ahead, Cocky.'" After one such incident at a fraternity dance, the word went out: "'Forget 'musicians,' that's a gang — those guys are all fighters.'"

McPartland took his first professional job at 15 with a violinist, Al Haid, at a summer spot on Fox Lake for $35 a week, a room and all the corny music he could take. "I didn't like the band, but I liked the money... and the girls. The older ones thought I was so cute." He stayed six weeks.

He spent the next summer with the Maroon Five, a University of Chicago outfit that worked at Lost Lake in Wisconsin. Already a student of ixeology — "your basses, *pomoxes salmoides*," he recites "and your muskies: *esox esox*, the tiger muskie, and *esox lucious*, the silver muskie" — McPartland worked during the day as a fishing guide. "I was a spot caster, a good one. I've been very fortunate, I guess, because anything I want to do, or love to do, I go all the way. Boxing, fishing, music — all the way."

On New Year's Eve, 1923, he took a society booking with Charles "Murph" Podolsky's orchestra. Vic Moore, once and future Wolverine, was the drummer. Ten months later, on Moore's recommendation, McPartland joined *The* Wolverines, appropriately enough at the Cinderella Ballroom in New York. He spent several days at Bix Beiderbecke's side learning the tunes that the Wolverines had not recorded — McPartland, of course, already knew the ones they had. Within two months, he would appear on a Wolverines record. His first, their last.

The band was on the wane. Without Bix's unswerving influence, McPartland declares, Dick Voynow "went commercial," recording stock orchestrations of *When My Baby Walks down the Street* and *Prince of Wails* that half the Wolverines couldn't read. So it was that McPartland would have to wait three more years to make a record of lasting value — three years divided between Des Moines, Chicago and Detroit with the Wolverines and between Chicago and New York with Ben Pollack.

The historic session, December 8, 1927 for OKeh, was issued in the name of McKenzie and Condon's Chicagoans, although McPartland — true to form — insists, "It was *my* band, McKenzie and Condon just got the recording contract."

Circumstantial evidence might just support the claim: Teschemacher, Freeman and Lanigan from Austin High were present; Dave Tough was in Europe, so the upstart Gene Krupa played drums. Joe Sullivan was the pianist. Condon drank and played banjo, while Red McKenzie stood by and did a Husk O'Hare.

They recorded two tunes that day, *Sugar* and *China Boy*, and two more eight days later, *Nobody's Sweetheart* and *Liza*. All in the key of F, which may say something about the limits of homemade musicianship. Those four tunes nevertheless defined the Chicago style for all to hear — based on New Orleans jazz before it, clearly, but with allowance for the headstrong urges and individuality of the young Chicagoans.

"I charge more money now, work when I want to, with whom I want." McPartland is no longer a young Chicagoan, no longer talking about times past. He has jumped 55 years to times present; *good* times, it seems. "Not that I'm rich," he continues, "but I own my own house. It's paid for — it's worth between $90,000 and

$100,000 — and I've got maybe $22,000 in savings accounts and chequing accounts. So I'm not hurting.

"I have no bills. I don't drink. I even eat in the room here. I've got what I need: oatmeal, peanut butter, honey, fresh fruit... I don't eat meat any more. I eat fish, chicken — I had a good one last night downstairs. Vegetables — I've got some fresh carrots up here. I use cream cheese on my bran bread instead of butter. I put wheat germ in my orange juice.

"I pray to the Lord and ask for guidance. The guidance I got was that I must get in good health. I've been swimming practically every day, or playing golf, since last February. I went from 186 pounds to 168, and I'm 75 years old. I'll be 76 next March 15."

The Ides of March?

"Yeah, that's me."

Previously unpublished; September 1982

"Next year"
Betty Carter (1983)

Betty Carter is talking about jazz singers, or rather about *jazz* singers. "There's lots of voices out there, good strong voices," she admits, "but when it comes to improvising, the *spontaneous* stuff, I'm not worried about anyone out there now. When it comes to voice, well, I never really had a voice. I had a *sound*...

"Right now," she continues, "more people are improvising, taking a chance. Everybody is putting little phrases here and little phrases there in the songs that they do. That's not really *it*, but they figure, 'Somebody might make a mistake and call me a jazz singer.'"

The Carter sound, all syllables and swoons, has been out there, unmistakeably, since 1946 — since a teenaged Lillie Mae Jones won an amateur contest in Detroit singing *The Man I Love*. But it would take her another 30 years and another three names — Lorraine Carter, Betty Bebop and finally Betty Carter — before she began to reach a major audience. Sure, she was noticed in the late 1940s with Lionel Hampton's band, and briefly in the early 1960s with Ray Charles, but there were also as many, indeed more, quiet periods when the record companies were not prepared to deal with her on her own terms and she, as a result, would not deal with them at all.

Even now, over chips and a Coke during a sound check at Lytes, where she is singing for the next two weeks, Carter contends, "I'm not a star — not yet. All I've done is really by word-of-mouth. There hasn't been a heavy campaign, no real television exposure — *if* you notice — and no hit records — *if* you notice."

So not yet a star. But Carter is, at 52, enjoying some recognition as the most vital jazz singer in the tradition today. She sets up her own lineage: "There's your basic three — Billie Holiday, Sarah Vaughan and Ella Fitzgerald. If you've got those three girls in front of you, what else are you going to do? There was Dinah Washington, too, and countless other singers all over the country in their own home towns who sang good — because everybody was allowed to sing good. You didn't have to be like anybody. All you had to be was good."

She declines to add herself to a specific place in the lineage. "I don't know, let somebody else tell that story. I came up on the tail end of all that beauty in music, trying to develop Betty Carter, because I knew I couldn't be Sarah Vaughan, Ella Fitzgerald or Dinah Washington."

It has been her personal strength, but also her professional limitation, that she would always remain true to the search for her own identity. Eventually it pushed her to form her own record company, Bet-Car, in 1971, and now, as both an artist and a businesswoman, she cannot talk long about music without talking also about the music industry.

She decries the record companies' attitudes toward today's performers — toward "the kids who had the potential, but the potential was not immediate; it had to be developed. You can spot a diamond. You can tell when somebody's going to be *somebody*. If you can spot it, it seems to me, you set it aside, and you say, 'Well, I'm going to *work* with that.'

"But the young kids today don't have that opportunity, for someone to sit down and work with them. In the '50s, we did have that chance: a lot of musicians grew up with the record companies — Blue Note, Prestige — and they were recorded because they had potential. Miles Davis definitely wasn't a great trumpet player when he first started, but the potential was there."

While her own successes with Bet-Car have included a Grammy nomination in 1981 for *The Audience with Betty Carter*, they have not brought her renewed interest from the majors. "Nah," she says dismissively. "They wouldn't know what to do with me. Don't forget that most of the executives of the large companies are at least 15 years younger than I am. At *least*. They think they know best for the record company, so they want to produce me. But what do they know about me? The younger they are, what can they tell me about *me*?"

Satisfied, then, with the state of her recording career, she sees the growth of her audience just as a matter of time. But she's realistically philosophical. "Each year that I've been in the business, something spectacular happens that makes you think you're going to be a star next year. But no, it doesn't happen, and the next year comes along; something else happens that makes you think, 'Next year's the year.'"

Later, with chips and Coke finished, she returns to the proverbial "next" year. "Well, maybe it's not supposed to happen. Maybe I'm going to be one of those singers that people will talk about forever, but never really..."

She leaves the thought uncompleted, then brightens. "But I've raised my kids. I'm not going to be on welfare. I've got property. I've never done anything I didn't want to. I'm happy the way I've done it."

January 19, 1983

"Roundabout"
Carla Bley (1983)

How's this for a disclaimer: "If you're a musician," Carla Bley observed earlier this week, speaking from distinguished personal experience, "I don't think not thinking is dangerous. If I were a scientist and didn't think, it might be very dangerous. But musicians don't have to be self-consciously objective, if that's not the way they are. A lot of them just make things up... but I don't know if they believe what they say."

Or this, put more simply to a *Down Beat* writer in 1978: "I like to lie, it's so creative. I like to make mistakes, it makes me think up ways to correct them."

Carla Bley in conversation is much like Carla Bley in performance, a mixture of the leg-pull and the profound. The trick is to figure out which is which. Her flat delivery and distracted train of thought make communication seem like a real effort for the 44-year-old keyboard player and composer. At the same time, they belie one of the keenest minds and slyest wits in contemporary jazz.

"I think" she ventured, evidently lost in the middle of an answer, "I'm not a thinking-type person."

Uh-huh.

"I don't have *time* to think," she scoffed.

It was in fact a rare day off for Bley, just returned to her home in upstate New York after a week spent in Europe attending to the score of a French film and the mixing of a new album by Charlie Haden's long-dormant Liberation Music Orchestra.★ A day later, her own band would begin brief rehearsals for a tour that

★ Released as *The Ballad of the Fallen* by ECM Records.

will find the 10 musicians stopping at the Spectrum in Montreal and the El Mocambo in Toronto.

It was the Liberation Music Orchestra's celebrated first LP for Impulse! in 1969, following hard on Gary Burton's recording of her *Genuine Tong Funeral* (RCA) in 1967, that firmly established Bley as a force among the composers and arrangers of jazz. Previously, her name had been attached to several widely recorded, if quizzical melodies, and to the widely recorded if quizzical pianist Paul Bley.

Thirteen years later she returns to the Liberation Music Orchestra's new incarnation as the dominant figure in her field, a position gained on the basis of her three-LP "chronotransduction" (read: opera) *Escalator over the Hill* (JCOA) and several recordings by her own unique ensemble, including *Dinner Music, European Tour 1977, Musique Mécanique* and *Social Studies* (all WATT).

The years between Liberation Music Orchestra recordings have done more than boost her personal stock; they have apparently dated the LMO's devotion to revolutionary causes rather badly. The music for its recent European tour was new, she notes, but not unlike that of the original, and now classic, recording. "We did another song from the Spanish Civil War, a song from El Salvador, a song from Chile, and a song from Portugal — all related to the kind of movements that Charlie Haden is interested in."

But the revival, it seems, was not a particular success. "Success?" she asked, weighing the word carefully, and then added in an "oh-well" voice, "The critics did not like it; the audiences didn't like it either."

The subject of the political overtones of her own performances — she did, after all, write *Spangled Banner Minor and Other Patriotic Songs*, the suite of subverted anthems heard on *European Tour 1977* — brought a typically roundabout but ultimately revealing response. "I don't know, I'll have to think about it for 10 years... I do something, and it occurs to me later on why I did it. I don't even know now why I did things 10 years ago...

"Okay" — back to the subject — "five years ago, when I used anthems in *Spangled Banner Minor*, I did that because it was irreverent, and irreverence has always been a thread going through my musical life. If you're not supposed to do something, I do it. So it was a nervy thing to do; I don't think it went much beyond that. No, I don't think music can change the world."

Later, she returned to her supposed irreverence, by way of explaining why, only now, will she be touring jazz-enlightened Japan for just the first time in her band's six-year history. "I've got internal problems in the jazz community, as well as outside the jazz community. Through my own fault, I think, a lot of people in the community have decided that I'm not true blue, because my records have always included something outrageous, and the community is very conservative. So, I've been becoming more conservative."

There followed a mischievous change of voice. "You'll find out," she warns. "*This* is how it's going to be: we're going to wear tuxedos and never blow our noses onstage... We've always tried to stifle ourselves" — she's laughing now — "but we usually failed. We're going to try it again, and maybe we won't succeed this time either. Maybe it will be just as bad as before."

Ironically, Bley has been very good to the jazz community, however she interprets its feelings toward her. Parallel to her own rise, she has watched the growth of the New Music Distribution Service, a company that she formed with her husband, trumpeter Michael Mantler, to handle small record labels, including their own WATT and other musician-produced albums.

Initially just a family project, NMDS is now a six-person operation, having undergone what she described as "negative growth." She elaborates: "The record companies are closing their doors a little quicker and a little harder now, so musicians, instead of just disappearing, are making their own records and having us distribute them. Every year, the record industry says 'No' more often than it says 'Yes,' so we get bigger and bigger."

It was, of course, Bley's own, early experiences with that same recording industry that inspired NMDS. "For a long time I found 'No' was always the answer."

Even now, she said, it still wouldn't be "Yes."

"But now," she added, with something between satisfaction and finality, "I would never ask."

And of those who would belabour the fact that she is woman in a man's field, she had this to say: "I still do run into that, but not as much. When I do, it makes me sad, but I try not to be angry — as I used to be. I try to understand that it's something that's always going to come up. If I had only one leg, they'd ask me what it's like to play the Hammond organ with only one leg. So I try to be gracious and say I've not had any problems being a woman... There might be problems, but I haven't really thought about it. As I said before, I don't really think about much. I don't have the time..."

February 19, 1983

"Intermission's over"
Tony Collacott (1983)

"When I hear a pianist," Tony Collacott begins, referring to those with whom he shares a job description, "and if I'm going to like him, I want to hear the total boy — I want to hear him throw everything in but the kitchen sink. That's just my personal appetite for music. There's so much fine piano playing that you can call tasty, that's good time-keeping, that's 'marvellous this' and 'marvellous that.' But there are just a handful of people I want to sit down and listen to — Art Tatum, McCoy Tyner, Oscar Peterson, Horowitz — just a handful who don't hold anything back, who've gone all the way to the other end of the world to play."

Collacott could be talking about himself, as he relaxes prior to his current week of work at George's Spaghetti House in Toronto. It was just such piano playing that made him the toast of the local jazz scene in 1963, when he was merely 16 — fiery, extravagant, everything-*and*-the-kitchen-sink piano playing.

But Collacott didn't stop there. He approached life in the same way he approached the piano — all the way to end of the world, holding nothing back — and he turned himself into a living legend, one lost first in action, then inaction.

And now found — alive and well after a year at the Queen Street Mental Health Centre, and living in a government-run group home in the Broadview/Danforth area. He sits back, but he does not sit still, in his new, renovated surroundings, and he continues to withhold nothing, speaking more openly than discretion might advise of a star-crossed career that could easily be sensationalized. The words come in a rush — there are parallels again with his piano playing — as ideas are punctuated by bursts of excited laughter and full statements come to rest on the quick turn of a phrase.

He is 36, and looks alternately much older and much younger. He talks a lot about survival; fame and fortune are not without interest to him at this point — he can talk enthusiastically, if unrealistically, about approaching a "major" record company with a tape that's available for "world-wide release" — but they're not uppermost in his mind.

"My prime consideration," he declares, "is that I'd like to stay alive. I've lived through two suicide attempts, I've lived through years of narcotics and now I'd really like to see my years out. And I don't see any value in making it to the top of the business unless you're going to be happy, alive and on the good side of the law."

He is, he says, a "habitually happy man," although he acknowledges this wasn't always so. "I did my years as a suffering artist. I did my years as a pain-in-the-ass to everyone, intense and miserable. I've seen all those years and I've learned to be happy. I've worked at it."

In his teens, Collacott was a driven man — intensely competitive and, in his own words, "terribly vicious." Music, he recalls, "was a life and death business... If I didn't win the fight, it wouldn't be a question of a loss of self-esteem, it would be death by exposure."

Jazz brought him his early notice — one so young and so gifted is always good copy — but jazz, he notes, wasn't his first choice. "Jazz was one type of music out of every type, and I tried to bite the whole thing off. In the last 10 years I've decided I'd like to be a jazz pianist, but when I was younger I wanted to do everything. I just couldn't find enough time — enough time for Beethoven, enough for my Tatum records, my Carmen Cavallaro records, my Eddie Duchin records, my Roger Williams records. I was trying to do it all, and at the same time my major consideration was simply survival — I had to eat, and anything went.

"I didn't have an artistic direction. I'd listen to other musicians talk about this piano player and that one, and I'd think, 'Jive, my *stomach*.' Art never meant anything to me."

By the age of 20, he had moved on to rock music — to the Bossmen, fronted by singer David Clayton-Thomas, and then to Chimo. That's Collacott, exploding in the middle of the Bossmen's *Brainwashed*, one of the great Canadian rock singles of the 1960s. By 30, though, he had stopped working for a living altogether and, at the advice of a psychiatrist, gone on welfare.

"He said, 'Well, you're wasted, so we're going to look after you — you don't have to worry about working any more.' I said, 'Fine, I won't argue...

"Then one day I was running around the heart of the psychiatric civilization down on Queen Street and I thought, 'Well, I better get back to work. Intermission's over.'"

After an eight-year hiatus, he played George's twice last year with his trio, and he performed in January for CJRT-FM's Sound of Toronto Jazz series at the Ontario Science Centre — a brave booking for the series, all things considered, and a triumph for the pianist.★

He returns to the hospital every day at the "crack of dawn" to practise on the piano. "You have to put so much time in to get anywhere, to get even a little bit of music out of yourself. Where I want to go I'm not going to get there any faster than one day's practising at a time. There's an old saying, 'It's one per cent inspiration, 99 per cent perspiration,' right? My commitment to music is the perspiration... The inspiration? Well, that's arbitrary personal taste."

May 27, 1983

★ Collacott was not active in music after the mid-1980s.

"Blythe"
Sammy Price (1983)

"That's all," announced Sammy Price at the end of Saturday night's second set at the Café des Copains in Toronto, hitting the final note, rising from the piano bench and scooping up his watch from its place above middle "C" on the piano itself — all in one practised, business-like motion.

Between sets, he sat quietly, biding his time and holding court with a succession of charmed young women. They were wide-eyed, but Price — whose middle name just happens to be Blythe — was cool. "You're jaded," they teased. "Faded," he replied with wonderful timing, "not jaded."

At 74, Price — originally from Honey Grove, northeast of Dallas — has had a long, well-travelled career in jazz as a blues and boogie-woogie stylist whose significance rests in no small part on his work as a studio musician for the Decca label in New York, where he accompanied such illustriously named singers as Bea Booze, Blue Lu Barker and Cow Cow Davenport during the late 1930s, and led his own Texas Bluesicians in the early 1940s.

His music remains bluesily full-bodied, and his piano style continues to be of the basic, two-handed school — a product of those older days when melody was supreme, when improvisation really meant embellishment and when rhythm was subject to just the slightest flirtation.

In Saturday's third set, he played fundamental blues and boogie-woogie for about a quarter of the time, and pop songs with blue tinges for the rest, the kind of familiar standards that — regrettably — often move members of an audience to sing along quietly.

Price is not that sort of entertainer, however. His version of *As Time Goes By*, for example, was as level-headed and measured as that old chestnut comes. No ghosts of Sam and Miss Ilsa here. It nevertheless brought him a kiss on the forehead from one of his admirers; still cool, he muttered an "Oh, brother" as he turned away and launched quickly into his next tune.

To close the set, Price pieced together a medley of Ellington songs that took on overtones of self-commentary: *Don't Get around much Anymore, (In My) Solitude* and *It Don't Mean a Thing (If It Ain't Got That Swing)*. His music works like that — on more than one level. Lightly in any case, but nicely.

July 18, 1983

"Edgewise"
Jay McShann, Big Miller
and Buddy Tate (1983)

They started on Monday night, sitting around a bottle backstage at Edmonton's Shoctor Theatre after their Jazz City International Jazz Festival concert and telling stories about two Kansas City alto saxophonists of some legend, John Jackson and Charlie Parker.

Jay McShann, Buddy Tate and Big Miller gathered again at the Centennial Library Theatre during the dinner hour on Tuesday and told a few more, publicly, for a Jazz City workshop titled "Kansas City Revisited." They talked on for another hour after that on their own.

None, ironically, is Kansas City born — not the ageless Oklahoman McShann,★ not the Texan Tate, 68, nor the Iowan Miller, 59 — but Kansas City was a meeting point for musicians in the U.S. midwest and southwest during the '30s. It had to do with the trains, observed Miller early on at the library; Kansas City was a terminal for several important lines and, he said, "everybody stopped off."

Miller, now an Edmonton resident, immediately took up the role of master of ceremonies for the workshop, despite his billing as a "special guest" of the two visiting musicians. Nevertheless, amid much laughter and some music, McShann — warm and modest with a high, sweet voice ringing still of Muskogee — and Tate — suave and modest, with the voice and bearing of a leading man — managed a few words edgewise.

"First time I heard Charlie Parker," McShann recalled, well into the workshop, and after several of Miller's familiar raps, "he was playing the same [way] that he was playing before he passed on. I happened to be coming through the streets in Kansas City — in that time they used to pipe the music out, you know, in the street — and I'd thought I'd met all the musicians in Kansas City, but I heard a different sound, so I went inside to see what was happening...That was our first meeting. He had it all together then."

Parker — or Bird, as he was known — joined McShann's small band in 1937 and later worked in the pianist's big band as well.

"It was a right funny thing," noted McShann, "Also in that big band was [tenor saxophonist] Jimmy Forrest. We'd be in New York — different places and whatnot — and Bird would play *everything* there is to play on that horn, and then Jimmy

<hr>

★ McShann's age was a mystery to all in 1983; his year of birth was later revealed to be 1916, making him 67 at the time of these recollections.

Forrest would come up right behind him and *he'd* [be the one to] tear the house down. I never could understand that; it used to frustrate me.

"People wasn't ready for Bird. Twenty years later, 25 years later, they were ready to accept it. Even the musicians, during the time we went to New York [in 1942] — they used to come up to the Savoy, where we were playing, and all these guys, the top musicians, they didn't want nobody to know they were there listening to some guy from Kansas City called Charlie Parker. So they'd come in and hide over in all the corners — until Ben Webster came through and pulled the covers off of all of them."

Parker, of course, was not McShann's only discovery. A young Big Miller worked with the pianist from 1949 to 1954. "I was supposed to be a saviour of souls," Miller remembered. "My father was a preacher and, if your father was a preacher, they said the son will follow... Then I met McShann, and *that* solved *that*."

Miller was McShann's singer and, in short order, his bassist. "At the time," McShann recalled, "we were in Kansas City, and we went on a job, and I don't think there was anyone there but Big Miller, myself and a drummer... So I finally said, 'Hey, Miller, have you ever tried to play bass?'

"'No.'

"I said, 'Do you know anything at all about a bass?'

"'No.'

"'Well, can you get a bass?'

"'I guess so.'

"'Well, just get one, bring on the stand, don't be worried about what you're hitting, just be sure you're hitting it on the beat.' So that's what he did. Later on, Miller was scaring the bass players around there."

McShann recreated another long-lost conversation by way of accounting for his band's admired reputation with the blues. "On our first recording date [1941 for Decca], we had all those tunes that the big band was playing, like *Yardbird Suite* — the things that Bird did later — so when we went to make our first records, oh, I guess we played an hour-and-a-half trying to get the [producer] to accept them, so, he finally says, 'We've been here two hours, and we haven't found anything we can use. I like what you guys are doing, but there's no way in the world we're going to sell that stuff.'

"We only had an hour to go — in those days, a session was only three hours — and we hadn't cut the first record yet. He said, 'You know a blues?'

"I said, 'Yeah.'

"'Just play it for me.'

"So we didn't realize — we played a blues, straight through, and he [recorded] it. He started smiling. Everybody was wondering: 'Why's he smiling?'

"He said, 'You know a boogie-woogie?'

"Said, 'Yeah.'

"'Let me hear it.'

"So we played a boogie-woogie, and another blues. By that time, he came out and said, 'I'll tell you what, we've got those three tunes now, so I'll take one of those other tunes you guys've got.' He took *Swingmatism*.

"In reality, the blues we played were impromptu things... That way, we got labelled as a blues band. When we played anywhere, the people would come in and see 12, 14 musicians, and they'd say, 'Man, I thought you had about four pieces; what are you doing with all the rest of the band?'"

Later, Miller again mentioned John Jackson, and McShann's recollections of Charlie Parker's section mate were clear. "Many times, people would hear some of the recordings J.J.'d be playing, and they'd think it was Bird. J.J. was really playing first [alto] in the band and seldom took a solo. When he felt like it, he'd turn loose... Whenever the whole reed section needed to be swung, we'd always put J.J. on first. I'd say we had 300, 350 'head tunes' and we had 300, 350 what we used to call 'skull busters' in the book. All those head tunes, Bird played first; all the written things, J.J. played first."

Miller remembered that the word went out for Jackson after Parker died in 1955. "It's no question that J.J. was the *man* at the time," agreed McShann, before alluding to some of the wilder stories that must have been circulating backstage at the Shoctor Theatre the night before. "Well, J.J. got married to a very Christian lady, and she changed all that. She had a tough job, though... J.J. did everything under the sun. But she finally brought him in."

August 18, 1983

"Diplomat"
Ruby Braff (1984)

Heads were shaking as soon as the word went out. Ruby Braff, the peppery, occasionally cantankerous, veteran cornetist, would be working this week at Bourbon Street with the young Toronto guitarist Reg Schwager, who is, even in his early 20s, the very picture of innocence.

Braff's partner on previous visits from New York has been the imperturbable Ed Bickert. Bickert, however, is occupied with Moe Koffman over at George's Spaghetti House this week. Thus, Schwager, Toronto's latest "coming" guitarist, is in the hot seat. Imagine the first time Wayne Gretzky went up against Gordie Howe. It promised to be a little like that.

So what's this? Ruby Braff, at the Bourbon Street piano during Monday's sparsely attended third set, amiably teaching Schwager some old tunes? "Do you know...?" he'd ask, rhyming off increasingly obscure titles. "Oh, you'll like this one," he'd say, as he laid out the chord changes, added the melody, occasionally sang the lyrics, and even doodled out a little improvisation. Schwager, catching on quickly, would play the first solo. Braff accompanied the guitarist for a time and then took up the cornet for a solo of his own. "Isn't that a nice tune?" he'd ask when the process was complete.

It wasn't great jazz. It wasn't bad jazz, either. But it was very much in the spirit of this music's oral traditions, a cross-generational encounter that could prove to be one of those important moments in the development of a young musician's personality.

Schwager could do much worse for a teacher. Braff, with his wonderful taffy-pull solos, is one of the purest improvisers around, a man to whom clichés seem to be of no practical value. For a long period of his career, he was caught out playing a classic style of jazz in a defiantly modern era; now, his playing seems surprisingly fresh, and very modern, despite the well-worn mainstream context in which he generally works.

His playing was no less fresh in the night's earlier, second set, although the collective efforts of the Braff quartet, completed by bassist Steve Wallace and drummer Jerry Fuller, were noticeably lacking in spark. The performance was all melodic ingenuity, with ample warmth but no real fire. Braff has a very personal sense of dynamics, and it gives his solos all the life in the world without necessarily having any effect whatsoever on his fellow musicians.

No one else on the bandstand presumed to take charge, of course, and it was only when Braff finally cranked up his cornet on the last choruses of *Easy Living* at the end of the set that the others in turn applied a little force of their own. After he thanked the few folks in the house, he made the usual introductions, concluding with a "Yours Truly, Henry Kissinger."

Ruby Braff, diplomat. Who'd have guessed?

January 18, 1984

"Sporty"
Milt Hilton (1984)

Milt Hinton carries his personal history of jazz in a soft black zip case, and a long black memory. The distinguished bassist and elder statesman of jazz, visiting Toronto to participate in the sixth annual Molson/Harbourfront Jazz Festival this weekend, was *there*, and he has the pictures to prove it.

The photos are in the zip case.

The Judge, as he's known, lays the case on one of the two beds in his Toronto hotel room — his wife, Mona, is napping on the other — and begins to turn the pages gingerly.

The first shot is of Louis Armstrong in a hotel room. The date is 1954, the second year Hinton travelled with the trumpeter's All Stars. Armstrong is listening intently to one of the three machines — two tape recorders and a record player — that he took with him on the road.

"Look, he's got a joint in his hand," Hinton begins, *sotto voce*. "He couldn't sleep at night. When he'd finish playing, he'd smoke a big joint to get him hungry, then he'd have a big Chinese meal and a bottle of beer. And he'd have a band boy to stay in the room to run the [recording] machines. The kid had to keep them going... As long as they were playing, Louis would be asleep, he'd be snoring. If they stopped, he'd wake right up. They were all *his* records, only his records... and Guy Lombardo's — that was his favourite band."

The second shot is of Billie Holiday, listening to a playback during her last recording session. Hinton was in the band. The year was 1959. Her eyes are mirrors of death. "She was dead three weeks after this," Hinton whispers, "I think she knew it was her last date."

Then there's a shot of Cab Calloway. "My musical father," Hinton comments, chuckling again. "He hired me in 1936 in Chicago to get him to New York where he could get a good bass player. I stayed in his band for 16 years." Calloway called Hinton "Fump." Fump called Calloway "Fess."

And there's a photo of the Calloway band in Atlanta in 1938, gathered in a doorway marked Colored Entrance. "There are generations of black kids who don't even know that existed," he notes, with obvious satisfaction.

In all, there are about two dozen pictures, a small sampling of the 500 that he hopes to see published soon in book form.★ These in turn have been culled from some 32,000 negatives shot over the last 40 or 50 years — on the road, at Beefsteak Charlie's in New York, on tenement steps in Harlem, at the White House...

★ *Bass Lines: The Stories and Photographs of Milt Hinton* was published in 1988, followed by *Over Time: The Jazz Photographs of Milt Hinton* in 1991.

As a history of jazz, however, they're a little misleading. A bit incomplete. For one thing, Milt Hinton isn't in *any* of them.

"Being 74 years old," he admits, "I was practically born into the music; jazz is about 75, 100 years old." He proceeds to offer a complex narrative that combines personal, musical and cultural history, and that starts by taking him from Vicksburg, Miss., his birthplace in 1910, to Chicago by 1919.

His mother, a church organist, bought the young Hinton a violin in Chicago, hoping that Sporty, as he was then known, might become a choir director. That would have been fine by Sporty, except...

"Except that I delivered newspapers in Chicago. I was 13, 14, 15, and I went through the South Side, which was the hotbed of jazz — all the clubs were there, the Sunset, the Entertainers, and they were right on my route! At 5:30 in the morning, when I'm going to deliver papers, I'd look in the window of the Entertainers Club — it was in a basement — and I'd see the waiters putting the chairs up on the tables, and I'd see the musicians in their tuxedos, having a nice taste, with their ladies waiting for them. I thought, 'Oh my God, *this* is the life!' That set my goals."

But Sporty was a violinist and violinists — with the rarest of exceptions — worked in the pit bands that would be rendered obsolete in 1929 by the advent of the talkies. "Al Capone opened a club in Cicero, Illinois, the Cotton Club, and all my high school peers got jobs in the band, making $75 a week. And *I'm* still delivering newspapers — $9.75 a week for 200 papers a morning. I'm seeing these guys getting off at four in the morning, buying Ford cars with disc wheels, and *I'm* stuck with this violin."

He tried trombone — "I could never figure that piping out" — then settled on bass, studying with Chicago's finest classical teacher. He worked with some of the great names of jazz — the huge pianist Tiny Parham, the legendary trumpeter Jabbo Smith, the crazed pianist Cassino Simpson, and the great New Orleans drummer Zutty Singleton. More reliably, he spent a few years with violinist Eddie South, one of those rarest of exceptions. "We used to call him the Dark Angel of the Violin," Hinton remembers. "He really *played*. He'd been to Europe, and he'd hung around with those gypsies. He could *sing* in Hungarian!"

Calloway took him on in 1936. Fump was in the band when Dizzy Gillespie was fired for allegedly throwing a spit ball on stage. Calloway's autobiography suggests Hinton was the real culprit; in fact, the bassist was closest to the spot where the projectile landed. And no, he hasn't a photo of *that*.

When Calloway went into *Porgy and Bess* in the early '50s, Hinton went into the New York studios. Jackie Gleason hired him for *The Honeymooners*; Percy Faith, Hugo Winterhalter and other studio leaders followed suit. Indeed, Hinton was one of the first black musicians to crack the studio world. "Music is the least prejudiced society you can belong to," he says now.

Thirty years in the studio, and The Judge has become one of the most recorded bassists in jazz. To his regret he did not record with either Duke Ellington or Louis Armstrong; he worked just one night with Ellington, at New York's Rainbow Grill, but he travelled widely with Armstrong.

He *did* record frequently with fellow Chicagoan Benny Goodman, though, often taking over anonymously in mid-session for Goodman's brother Harry. In 1955, Hinton remembers, he was called to play on the soundtrack for *The Benny Goodman Story* in Hollywood. "I said, 'Benny, you *know* I can't be your brother in the movie!'"

Now, he teaches and travels the festival circuit. He also works for Pearl Bailey when their schedules allow; he will miss an engagement with the singer because of his Harbourfront appearance with the American All Stars — trumpeter Yank Lawson, trombonist Carl Fontana, pianist Ralph Sutton and drummer Butch Miles.

Photography, meanwhile, is simply a hobby. "But because I've been playing around for such a long time," he suggests, "it has become historically important. I've got photos that go back numbers of years and that depict some of the happenings of jazz — what we were like, where we came from, where we were going..."

And with that "we," he finally puts himself in the picture.

August 4, 1984

"Class"
Barry Harris (1985)

They were lined up two and three deep at the bar for Barry Harris Tuesday night at the Café des Copains. Class was in session.

As the three-piece suits went on about their businesses, sitting in the $3 seats out in the room, the young Toronto musicians and the real jazz fans paid rapt attention and not a penny more at Harris's elbow. The Detroit-born, New York-based pianist knew exactly what was going on, and his long, second set of the night was an extended lesson, much of it played at demonstration tempo. Call it piano slow hands.

Harris, 56, is one of the great teachers in jazz. He cannot play without revealing something to someone. On Tuesday he touched on subjects as specific as chord voicings and as general as repertoire. He would begin a tune by laying out all of its harmonic options — "You could go this way," he seemed to be saying to his charges. "Or this. Or this. Or maybe that." Finally, he'd choose one option for himself and follow it through just far enough to sneak out of the tune altogether.

Now and then he would play a little bebop up to tempo — in the manner of one of his influences, Bud Powell — as if to say, "You figure this out for yourself." And somewhere in the middle of the performance he essayed a medley of pieces by another of his inspirations, Thelonious Monk. Harris's interpretations rolled on rounder wheels and along straighter lines than Monk's own, but were revealing in their clarity. Indeed, everything that Harris played was clearly and cleanly done. There's no confusion in this classroom.

Of course, what's instructive is not necessarily captivating. Harris tended to be ambivalent on the matter of interpretation, preferring to put more of his theories than his personality on display, as only a master teacher might.

March 28, 1985

"Mountains"
Cecil Taylor (1985)

It only takes a few groups of people who are possessed— and I think of music in terms of possession and trance — to frighten a great many, but also to keep the music alive and healthy. In my lifetime, it has been difficult, but it's getting better. It saved my life. I know that. — Cecil Taylor at 52, Banff 1985

Cecil Taylor, beach hat pulled low to the frame of dark glasses as a kind of theatrical mask that he would rarely remove, took a quick, gestural puff on his cigarette. The pianist had been talking for an hour or so on this Thursday afternoon in July about Duke Ellington and Billie Holiday, about the mythologies of jazz and the realities of the black experience, about Banff's mountains and New York's bridges, about poetry and ballet, about the fallacy of composition and the immediacy of performance, and particularly about the work at hand — the preparation of his orchestral music with students at the Banff Jazz Workshop for a concert the following night.

"Do you know what I saw this morning?" he asked, voice changing suddenly, tempo quickening. "I don't know *what* it was, I tell you. Just about, you know, a quarter of a block from where I'm going to turn into my little cabin, there's this animal with these *things*."

He seemed excited by the memory. "I don't know, was it an elk or something?"

Yes, he was told. There are many in the area.

"*Listen*," he replied sharply, resisting the notion that this revelation might be commonplace, "I've just come from New York which, after all, we know is the centre of the world. But it doesn't give us the centre of the world's information. *I'd* never seen an elk before. And that elk certainly had never seen *me* before, at that point, as it nibbled those greens.

"Instant recognition on both parts," he continued. "As far as that animal was concerned, I was from outer space. And from my point of view, 'What's this? *This* is from outer space.' So we looked each other in the eyes. We *both* backed up.

"I'm sure it thought, 'He's probably got a shotgun...'"

No, Taylor was corrected, this is national park. They are protected.

"And *I* thought," he pushed on, "he's probably going to charge at any moment. So I said, 'Wait a minute, it's *not* going to end *this* way... Listen, *you* got it... *I'll* walk over here...'"

Cecil Taylor in Banff was Cecil Taylor somewhat out of his element, a New Yorker spending a week in the great outdoors, yes, but also an iconoclast among those who would worship icons — moreover an iconoclast who is himself an icon to some, but not to most of the Banff Jazz Workshop's students. They looked in awe in another direction, "right down the hall there" as Taylor identified it just a little derisively, having heard them "playing those licks"— the same licks that are an extension of the very music, bebop, that he turned away from so dramatically 30 years ago.

Jazz was playing itself up a blind alley until Taylor and a few others around New York in the mid-to-late '50s headed over the walls of rhythm, harmony and structural concern that those musicians before them were building ever higher. In characteristic leaps and bounds Taylor, trained at the New York College of Music and the New England Conservatory and briefly apprenticed to swing musicians Oran (Hot Lips) Page, Johnny Hodges and other lesser figures, would eventually clear the obstructions altogether.

Once free he did not look back for a long time. He toughed out a career where he could find it — initially as an unknown leader in a few New York clubs and eventually as a celebrated musician on the international concert stage. In 30 years there would be just enough recordings of the Cecil Taylor Unit and of Cecil Taylor solo to document the evolution of his music, but hardly enough to suggest that he has been in any way a popular figure in jazz or any other sphere.

The intensity of Taylor's performances is taxing, intimidating — at times frightening. Moreover the energy, the fists and the forearms blur the links in his music to tradition. There are specific elements of Monk, and of Ellington before Monk, in Taylor's piano playing, and of Ellington in his ensembles. There are, generally, elements in his music of everything from the most fundamental of blues to the most advanced ideas of the conservatory.

But Taylor works at far enough of a distance from the known that the borders between idioms are blurred — not just within jazz, but in music, and then not simply in music but in pure performance. He works with dancers, taking commissions from Alvin Ayley and Mikhail Baryshnikov. He writes and reads poetry. He has made both dance and sound poetry a part of his own presentations. His concerts are ritualistic. They have a physical energy, a transcendent emotional power and a supporting intellectual rigour that is, in total, unmatched in jazz.

In the main, the jazz world did not move immediately to keep up with him. Far easier it was to dismiss or ignore his music than to come to terms with it. To a degree this has changed, but such early disdain might well have broken a lesser artist. Jazz is not a national park. The musicians are not protected.

"The same attitude that shaped the conservatory has shaped bebop," he commented, of the strain in his relationship with his peers in jazz. "I've been fortunate enough to continue. People now say hello, and I immediately acquiesce to their acknowledgement. That's when I talk about basketball and baseball and it's very effective just for that moment."

He had little need to talk sports in Banff, although boxing served him as a useful analogy on more than one occasion. Taylor was clearly enjoying both the setting and the project. *All* the world's a stage, only the scenery changes, and if Taylor isn't onstage, he is, by nature, watching closely from either the wings or the house. Generally at Banff the stage was his — informally, for three evening rehearsals with 22 of the workshop's musicians and for three noon-hour lectures with the workshop's full population, and formally, for a closing concert Friday at the Margaret Greenham Theatre. He played his several roles — musician, poet, dancer — and he played them in many moods.

"I love actors and actresses," he admitted, when the capricious nature of his own performance over the previous days had been duly noted, "so that's part of it. And it is also the totality of each day, because this is draining; you have to find ways to go back to your room and pull it together."

Draining, indeed. Taylor's daily routine included three to four hours alone at the piano to prepare for the solo half of his concert, and another four-and-a-half hours with the workshop's musicians to create the orchestra music that would complete the program.

He taught the ensemble his music "from the ground up," as one participant, Texas guitarist David Phelps, put it; "not going around with mimeographed lead sheets, but giving us our notes — serving us our notes," as another guitarist, Ohioan Rick Peckham, suggested, sounding a little awed by the humility of the process.

Taylor worked from a sheaf of dog-eared papers wrapped in torn plastic and carried around in a leather, draw-stringed bag. The process went like this...

"Okay, saxes, will you add these notes please: E, down to B; A down to G.

"Trombones — C#, up to B, down to G, up to F#.

"Basses — E up to A, up to D, up to C# B natural..."

And so it went, dictated line by line until every section had its part — reeds (four), brasses (three trumpets, two trombones), strings (four guitars, three basses), percussion (three) and voices (three). The musicians wrote the score in their own hands, notating the rhythmic values of each short, teetering phrase as Taylor played it over at the piano a few times. He might offer additional verbal instruction, something like "Saxes, play that first phrase like a rollercoaster" or, "I want you to create a mountain of thought in just one sound."

The process was repeated frequently, painstakingly, and not without some confusion, and the piece grew little by little, episode by episode, unit by unit. Ultimately, he would ask for xeroxes of each part as the musician had written it — this, together with a personal statement of what the musician felt to be his or her own "most outstanding personality trait."

No real sense of the music's larger shape was apparent until well into the rehearsals. As the sun set slowly behind the mountains late each night, the light gradually dawned on the musicians: Taylor wasn't really giving the music shape at all, just the merest of outline, leaving it to them to fill in the missing dimensions. He was working at two levels simultaneously, handing around his notes and, with each and every one of them, delegating a little piece of creative responsibility.

"Once you have the material, you can adjust it [according to] how you feel about it," he advised at one point.

And, "You've got all that material, so use it. You can switch the order — just don't hesitate."

And, again, "There are only four real notes in what you have; you'll have to find out which ones they are."

Taylor's terms of reference were intentionally vague, and initially they brought him skepticism. In the absence of a clear direction, he asked implicitly for his musicians' trust. But the focus of that trust shifted gradually: as the proffered responsibility was assumed — by an emboldened few at first, and then by the rest, following their peers' lead — it became a question of whether the musicians trusted themselves.

Taylor had taken Duke Ellington one further. The orchestra is my instrument, Ellington used to say. The orchestra is *their* instrument, Taylor now seemed to be suggesting.

The Vancouver bassist Lyle Lansall-Ellis[*] later observed, "The beautiful thing about the way he works is that he presents a situation and then says, 'Okay, what are you going to do with it? It's *your* music.'"

* L.S. Lansall-Ellis later performed as Lisle or L.S. Ellis.

Another participant, New York saxophonist Andy Middleton, spoke of Taylor's "landscapes of colour, " adding, "The way I see it, he never knows how it's going to come out, he just gives us the map."

A third, the Vancouver vocalist D.B. Boyko, commented, "You don't distrust him, you just keep in mind that he's always curious about what he's doing..."

At first Taylor played the observer. His instructions delivered, he moved outside the oval formed by the instrumentalists and singers in the rehearsal room and took his place by the door or — back to the world, figuratively speaking — by a southerly window, smoking continuously and moving interpretively from time to time. He was, by turns throughout the rehearsals, quiet and talkative, intense and relaxed, excited and reserved, wry and serious.

Slowly he let the music out of his control. As it began to carry itself, he joined in at the piano, playing a sketchy sort of accompaniment, stopping often to listen, but giving away nothing behind beach hat and dark glasses.

The formalities started to break down. The musicians were on their feet, making the first tentative, self-conscious moves out of their prescribed positions, just as Taylor requested.

"First you have to lose your inhibitions," he said, "and one way you do that is by starting to move." A trombonist used the bell of a tenor saxophonist's instrument as a mute; an alto saxophonist used the body of the trombonist for the same purpose. Full sections began to interact, physically at first and then musically. With each successive run-through, many of the musicians invariably wound up in a loose cluster around Taylor at the piano, as if pulled to him by some invisible force.

From one day to the next, the pieces seemed to change and grow — to transform — between rehearsals. Refinements were added, roles altered. Discussions continued among the musicians, Taylor now just an equal among them. By the sound check prior to the concert, the discussions were held almost oblivious to the pianist, who stepped forth only here and there with a word of arbitration.

The transfer of control was complete. Taylor retained only the element of surprise.

"You know," Taylor commented, with the rehearsals behind him and concert still ahead, "I don't think I'd ever want to be considered a composer."

It was one of several themes running through his conversations for the entire week. He would never quite complete a definitive statement on the subject in any single sitting; those who would follow his words, no less than those who would play his music, need be patient in the knowledge that, digressive though he may be, there is logic, there is direction, and there will be shape.

"You see," Taylor continued on this particular occasion, typically digressive, "the thing is this: even in those hallowed temples of Western Music, John Cage is thought of as a major contributor — I was in New York and went to a rehearsal at which he was admitted to the club: it was a Stravinsky festival at Philharmonic Hall when certain luminaries were asked to come and do certain things for little Igor, and John was included — and, you see, John says in *Silence*, [that] up through the 19th century, composers wrote what they heard. After that, they wrote to hear what they wrote...

"To sit down and write a piece of music," Taylor observed, "and to ask musicians to perform that music under the same directorial tutelage that Handel gave his musicians, seems to me to be rather questionable in concept. So that's why yesterday's rehearsal was so important. It was obvious — and this had been building up in two days, three days, right? — that everybody was not sure where the *stuff* was. They were getting a little cranky, you know. So, they were told certain things today. Specifics. '*This is...*' Because, once again, yesterday was very important for *me* in terms of what *I* learned about the nature of what I'm doing, you see. And you also learn that by seeing *where* it puts people in relation to *how* they function."

This is, in other words, the 20th century. The atom bomb, he would remark more than once, has been dropped; "The dynamic of the relationship between human beings has changed." Taylor thus chooses, as Ellington in his way chose before him, to celebrate rather than regiment the individuality of the creative spirit. To "compose" music, he would suggest, is to deny that individuality — "You write it for everybody, no matter what everybody's individual thing is."

He took up the argument again in one of his lectures. "If you sit down and write a piece of music, to say to people coming from different areas, 'Now look, you must play it this way,' seems to me to be an easy way out, a way to control the immensity of the different kinds of intelligences that are coming to spend some time with you."

His quarrel with composition went further, to the very concept of notation that he has rejected in favour of oral transmission — in the long, practical tradition of black folk music, sustained conceptually in modern jazz by Ellington and by those, like Charles Mingus, who followed his lead.

"What is that you're reading?" he asked rhetorically, during a lecture. "What *are* those notes? Does the music exist in those notes, and is that why you want to play it? Or does it exist because you *heard* somebody play something that touched you, and you *had* to go and find that instrument?

"When you're reading the note... how are you going to feel that note in direct relation to the making of sound — the making of sound just because you want to surrender to it, because you want to be *surrounded* by it. So, now, if you can read the note, is it pretty? I mean, don't they all look more or less alike? And you are told, 'You must be able to read the note.' What that does is takes your eye and puts it *there*; it decimates your ability to absorb sound, because of the unnatural position of your body. If you went to the idea of music because of the sound, then you're simply wasting your time and diminishing your spirit if you're going to start looking for notes to give you something more than the recapitulation of stuff that's been going on for a long, long, long time."

There can be, by the very nature of Taylor's methodology, no recapitulation in his orchestral music, although there is, he admits, recurrence. Indeed, the element of recurrence interests him greatly.

"You know — I said this to someone the other day— Somerset Maugham was reported to have said, 'If you're lucky you find one story and you rewrite it for the rest of your life.' Okay, I've been thinking about that for a number of years. And I have found one story that I have, but I have been consciously working on developing some others.

"That's why I want [the musicians] to write all that music. I have an idea. I'm really not into cataloguing each performance that I do, but I write a new version of the one piece, and you know, its development comes more or less in increments. After five years, you see, 'Oh, I've made this much ground.'"

"Like an inchworm," suggested Lyle Lansall-Ellis, who was in fact present five years before at another Taylor orchestra workshop in Woodstock, New York.

"Yeah, yeah, yeah," Taylor responded. "Exactly. *Exactly.*"

The sign was in a kind of free verse. Taylor might have seen a certain irony in its message, had he known the sign was posted in the lobby of the Margaret Greenham Theatre on the night of his concert.

It looked like this:

> Warning!!
> This concert will be loud.
> Extreme sound pressure levels may be
> injurious to your health.

He had chosen *Voices (Gun un un an)* as the title for the four pieces that he and the workshop developed together. The individual pieces, *Ymana (rayless ones), light (stilled)*, the sound poem *Owner of the Winds (voices)* and *Cun un un an*, would be presented as a suite.

And there was something else about *Voices*, mentioned almost as if an afterthought at the final, noon-hour rehearsal. "This is, for me, a very important piece," he advised, rather vaguely, "because it is in homage to certain aspects of my family background. All of the material, the specific material, is from the lore of Indians."

The allusions to his ancestry (maternal, one generation removed) would be much clearer the following night; the two versions of *Owner of the Winds* printed on the concert program, one for the three vocalists and one for voice and piano, sounded a pantheistic note appropriate to his material, and perhaps also to the glorious setting for his week's project.

The concert was neither the climax of, nor anti-climax to, Taylor's project. It was simply another part of the creative process that he had initiated five days before; it in fact signalled an arbitrary end to both process and project. Had there been a second performance, the music no doubt would have evolved still further.

So fully had he given the music over to his musicians that the concert could, and effectively did, start without him. As Lyle Lansall-Ellis led the bassists through the opening notes of *Ymana*, Taylor stood partially hidden behind the piano, beating on the raised lid. As the ensemble eased into its parts, he slipped onto the piano bench and began to play — not *with* the orchestra but against it, around it, above and below it. The figures that he had taught the musicians and that had blossomed, and continued to blossom, in their hands, were now the springboard for his improvisation: Cecil Taylor to the second power.

The solo performance that followed put the dimensions of the orchestra's achievement in perspective. Taylor reprised *light (stilled)*, reversing its transformation, taking it *back* to its modest origins before expanding it once more, this time with the keyboard as his orchestra — 88 voices to be selected, delineated and blended by a single mind.

His solos, however, were set in a different, far more specific context. Taylor had started offstage, as he often does in solo or Unit performances, with an extended vocalization: part chant, part song, part Indian ceremony, part Japanese theatre. The ritual was begun. He moved to, and around the stage, ankle bells accenting the graceful unorthodoxy of his movements; the brilliance of his dance was a revelation to the musicians who had worked at his side for the previous five days and now sat before him in the audience.

To the piano then, and Taylor offered five pieces and several playful encores, employing call and response patterns of calm motifs in alternation with pummeling, steel-fingered improvisations that blurred notes, clusters and lines into one compounded voice singing a soaring melody all of its own.

And what, he was asked on that Thursday afternoon in July, would he deem his *own* most outstanding personality trait?

"The belief," he said finally, and softly, after some deliberation, "that you must aspire to greatness, and that you must love the people who you recognize are great, because they touched you. And there are a lot of people who are very good. You respect them. But the mountains, the highest mountains — Duke Ellington, Billie Holiday, they're the highest mountains, you know, the *highest* mountains."

He was nearly whispering.

The years would seem to have changed Taylor. There was a time, a volatile and political period, when his music, then at its most intense — its most possessed — was seen to mirror Black anger at its deepest in America. Even now he would not let the absence of Black musicians in Banff go unremarked. Nor would he allow a suggestion that the passing years have moderated Black passions to go unchallenged.

"I wouldn't be so sure that there's less anger in the air," he cautioned. "The political climate would make the price for manifesting that anger much more costly than in 1968. A lot of people who got the publicity are either dead or in jail — or millionaires. So it is a different period now, but still there are things about this time that are, I think, an escalation of the more unfortunate aspects of that time."

Taylor is clearly a survivor, is vitally alive. He is free to travel the world, and now on the momentum of his own hard-won celebrity. And if not a millionaire, he is at least lately the owner of a brownstone in Brooklyn. He was panhandled on his doorstep recently. "I know now," he commented, thinking back on the incident, "that what I can do is do music, and write some poetry. Social worker, I'm not. But the larger ramifications of music mean that you can perhaps have a positive effect..."

And the larger ramifications appeal to Taylor, now philosophical, now almost reverent in his views. "The older I get," he observed during one of his lectures, "the more I understand that — and this is the point — music is just one of the manifestations celebrating the poetry as it exists all around us...

"Obviously," he said at another juncture, "music saved my life. Obviously, music has also made it possible for me to think that, if I should live to be 90, then *that* will be the time when I will be the most human... and also the most worthy... to look at these mountains."

Banff Letters, *Spring 1986*

"Metal has been tested"
Cecil Taylor (1986)

I'm totally anti-mechanical. I don't answer my phone. I have to be reminded that I have an answering service. But I like to meet other human beings. I'm lucky to be alive. The time has gone very fast. — Cecil Taylor in *The New Yorker*

His service answered on the second ring, just past ten o'clock one night this week, and Cecil Taylor picked up the phone in his New York brownstone almost immediately.

The celebrated pianist and composer, who in his 50s is one of only a few living musicians to hold an essential place in the 80-year course of jazz history, excused himself for what proved to be several minutes. A Donna Summer record playing near the telephone filled the silence.

Cecil Taylor listens to disco? Preconceptions about this magnetic, mysterious and, in some eyes, unapproachable figure were falling like leaves on a blustery November day.

"We were just, ah, wrapping up the festivities," he averred on his return. The musician is a poet and a dancer, too, and he chooses his words with grace — shading, qualifying, scattering pronouns of all descriptions and constructing elaborate statements that move easily from the specific to the philosophical.

Taylor is very philosophical these days.

The party over, he turned to business — to his sextet's Toronto appearance Monday night at the Bamboo. The show kicks off the club's illustrious week-long lineup of contemporary jazz from New York and Toronto. Taylor's musicians for the engagement will be alto saxophonist Carlos Ward, bassoonist Karen Borca, marimba player Thurman Barker, bassist William Parker and drummer Frederick Waits. But the band, he noted, "is in transition right now," adding "This has been one of the most trying, emotional periods I've ever had."

The reference, clearly, was to the death in mid-May of Jimmy Lyons, Taylor's long-time friend and alto saxophonist. Lyons, just 52, had suffered from lung cancer.

The pianist had already emerged in the jazz avant-garde along the U.S. east coast when he and Lyons met in 1960. They worked together — at times with just a drummer as a third — through the lean, hard years when Taylor's musical vision was too overwhelming, too much of an emotional and kinetic blur, to be widely shared. At best it was puzzled over; at worst, dismissed, even vilified. But they persevered, and just as time has brought their music into some semblance of focus, it has brought Taylor some measure of recognition and relative security.

The years have not diminished the abstracted intensity of the Taylor perform-ance ritual, but perhaps they have made the man himself a little more accessible — just a phone call away, when he chooses to answer.

"My telephone is not listed," he admitted. "Up until recently, it had always been listed, but I don't think that many people were particularly interested in call-ing... Some of them might have been a bit fearful."

He is aware, then, of his power to intimidate? "Well, I mean ... the thought *has* been expressed... But it takes two to tango so, therefore, how one is perceived depends pretty much on the sense apparatus of the one doing the perceiving."

In any event, what others think is of no great concern to Taylor.

And, yes, he does listen to Donna Summer. He is a man of inexhaustible curios-ity. "I remember playing that record for Jimmy Lyons once after a rehearsal. And Lyons, he had this very wholesome grin, as if to say, 'What *is* [Cecil] up to now?'"

No longer — if ever — defensive, he admits to being "more involved with the joy of just learning about what I've decided is my life's work, of doing it every day and of becoming more aware of the journey one is taking and exulting in it.

"I don't think," he went on, "that the basic cultural attitudes have changed. It seems to me that those holding on to the firmament of the status quo are still pret-ty entrenched. My concern, therefore, is just to attempt to enrich the things *I* do.

"When one was 25 or so, one could get angry about a lot of things; one now appreciates the fact that 25 or more years later, we are still alive and have a good percentage of our faculties intact. We have to honour that. It doesn't maybe have as much to do with myself, as having been guided by some other force to make cer-tain choices, but I can see that the art form, the poetry form, the movement form — the *world* that I've chosen to participate in — is rewarding my search. As a con-sequence, I'm generally rather affable now."

Still, 1986 has found Taylor suffering the deep, personal loss of Jimmy Lyons during a period of professional advance. The experience, he said, has been "a kind of dynamic duality in opposites," a description that, in a different context, might well serve the pianist himself.

"Metal has been tested this year," he continued, his voice growing softer until, finally, it was barely audible, "and you find that having to pause and do whatever one does under those circumstances, you come to realize that you have a responsibility to keep moving, and the internal pondering means that you have pulled things together in a way, recognizing the development of life in its many vicissitudes.

"You begin to understand that your responsibility is to absorb and, in that attitude and that process, attempt to create beauty out of the responsibility given you by a life that has been shared with you. And so, in many ways, it is a very exciting period."

November 15, 1986

"Blacks and blues"
Mal Waldron (1985)

Mal Waldron has had "some luck." In jazz, that's often all there is to survival.
The New York pianist, now based in Munich, worked with Billie Holiday in the
two-and-a-half years before the great singer's death in 1959. "I remember her as my
big sister," he mused, sitting off in the wings of the Bibliothèque Nationale an hour
before his concert with bassist David Friesen on Sunday night in the Piano Plus series
of the Festival International de Jazz de Montréal. He's a dapper man of medium
height, animated in conversation and quick to add a laugh to most any statement.

"She was beautiful," he continued. "She loved to cook, and she used to invite
musicians to the house and feed them." When Waldron was on the scene, though,
it was a difficult time for Lady Day. Her career was in severe decline, beset by both
personal and professional problems, including the suspension of working privileges
in New York due to her narcotics convictions.

"She wanted to work there, because all her friends were there. She was very
unhappy about that. Now, I could work New York City, so she used to come by
the clubs where I was playing and sing a song when the police weren't looking."

And Waldron played for Eric Dolphy a few years before the influential reedman's death in 1964. "I remember Eric as a very driven person. He was like John
Coltrane in that sense — both were driven to produce something real fast, because
it seemed like the people who were going to die young knew it, so they had to get
it done in a hurry. Clifford Brown was like that, too. Billie was much more relaxed.
Well, Billie lived a little longer. She lived to 44, which was average — an average
age for a musician. In fact it was late for a musician..."

Indeed, Dolphy died at 36, Coltrane at 40, Brown at just 25. Brown's fellow
trumpeter Booker Little, with whom Waldron worked at Dolphy's side, made it
only to 23. And Waldron? According to the reference books, he's 58. "I'm 60," he
corrected, chuckling at his good fortune. "I've had some luck."*

Waldron was one of four notable pianists among the festival's performers on
Sunday night, three of them American veterans distinguishedly grey about the temples — Hank Jones and Ahmad Jamal were the other two — and the fourth a
bright young Canadian woman, Lorraine Desmarais. Jones lent his elegance and
gentle wit to drummer Louis Bellson's splendid all-star quintet (Pete Christlieb,
Barney Kessel, Michael Moore) in the early evening Grand Concerts series at the
Théâtre St- Denis, while the Desmarais trio polished off a concert of original material for the CBC's Jazz sur le vif series at the adjacent Théâtre St-Denis II. Later on,

* Waldron would live to the age of 77.

Jamal ran down a brisk, snappy set of personalized fusion jazz in the Jazz dans la nuit series, again at the smaller St-Denis theatre.

So much of piano jazz is in the touch. Jones' touch is refined but clear — his solos become chandeliers of melody. Desmarais' touch is confident and swift, and Jamal's touch is now hard and precise, part karate and part conservatory. Mal Waldron, he of the quick laugh in conversation, turns quite sombre at the keyboard. His touch hurts. His notes come in blacks and blues, like little bruises.

He's "basically" a bebop player, or so he contends, referring to the music that hit New York when he was about 20. He had already been introduced to jazz piano by Duke Ellington and Art Tatum; boppers Bud Powell and Thelonious Monk completed his initiation. ("No, I didn't dive right into bebop," he had said backstage, laughing at the very idea. "*Nobody* dived right into bebop. Everyone was shocked at first. We got into it gradually.")

His playing, however, concentrated as it is on the middle and bottom end of the piano, works according to a different design. His patterns repeat again and again, closely constructed ascending and descending lines that circle hypnotically around an idea until it all but disappears.

Tension is everything, and momentum very little, in Waldron's music. There were no shouts of satisfaction, and spontaneous applause only for some of Friesen's deft solos, in the course of the duo's single, 80-plus-minute improvisation. Much in Waldron's playing was Monk-like — his concentration at the piano, his fondness for dissonance, his punctuation of rhythms. But this was worried Monk. Monk without space.

Waldron and Friesen have worked together for the past three years, touring one month each in Europe and North America. The pianist has lived in Europe since 1966; the issue is still survival, but the terms are now entirely Waldron's own.

"I find over there that the accent is not so heavily on materialistic gain. It's not on what you have in your pocket, it's what you have in your head that counts a little bit, too... I still wouldn't live in America. It's not ready for me. My direction is not for material gain, my direction is to make music, you see, not to make money."

The irony, of course, is that the expatriate has done much better financially on the continent than he ever did in America. "Right, and I do better in America now that I live in Europe."

And how does the well-travelled Waldron view the Festival International de Jazz de Montréal which, it has been said, has a certain European flavour? This would be just a quick visit, but he had already noticed something.

"Yes, the streets remind me of Europe. And you have the cafés, too, which are not popular in America. People don't have time to be sitting in cafés in America; they have to be out making that dollar."

July 2, 1985

"A rainbow of overtones"
Ran Blake (1985)

The intermission was to last four minutes. Well, pianist Ran Blake, who performed a fascinating solo concert for Edmonton's Jazz City International Jazz Festival at the Centennial Library Theatre on Tuesday evening, does most everything else in miniature, so why not intermissions?

Actually, it ran seven-and-a-quarter minutes. There were extenuating circumstances. The pianist re-emerged at the four-minute mark to find two newspaper photographers on stage, in the best paparazzi tradition, awaiting his return. And Blake, who often seems pleasantly surprised that anyone would take an interest in him, obliged, shook hands all around and then asked for two minutes more.

Two minutes later, give or take ten seconds, the concert resumed — a most unusual concert altogether, titled *Third Stream Reflections* and grouped in five parts, as laid out in a two-page program under Blake's letterhead. (Third Stream Associates... Boston... Ran Blake... piano soloist from the New England Conservatory of Music, Department of Third Stream Studies... Owl/Soul Note Recording Artist...)

There were 29 tunes altogether, organized thusly: *Cinema, Five Miniatures by Thelonious Monk, Standards, Vertigo Suite* and *Seven Views of the United States*. His screening of these pieces — to use the metaphor provided by the cinematic context of a good deal of his music, as his last album, *Film Noir* (Arista Novus), and his next, for Owl, *Vertigo* (cf. Alfred Hitchcock) would suggest — is related to jazz more by the freedom to interpret than the freedom to improvise.

It is, at one level, very literate music in its references and it can be, at another, very pointed in its commentary — in the juxtaposition, for example, of *Silent Night*, Blake's own *Stockholm Syndrome* and *The Stars and Stripes Forever* that turned *Seven Views of the United States* into a kind of tragi-comic opera.

Blake played it all with an editor's sense of how few the absolute essentials often need be. Bars of melody would often disappear at a time, while other, full melodies — Bronislaw Kaper's *Invitation*, in Cinema, for example — were put together slowly and painstakingly, frame by frame, as it were. Melody became allusory, a mere reminder designed to evoke some sort of subliminal response. Blake's playing itself was not emotionally inclined; the associations that it called up, however, often were.

Pianistically, he was clean in dissonance and dark in suspense; his tensions sustained deliciously, breaking finally with dramatic, stabbed notes of melody that bled a rainbow of overtones. What else from a Hitchcock fan?

So, he asked a couple of Canadians lingering after the performance, who's doing the interesting films in *this* country? Jazz City was Ran Blake's third Canadian festival of 1985, following appearances in Ottawa and Montreal. In Edmonton he stayed an extra day to offer a workshop at the library on Wednesday afternoon.

A fair-haired 50, Blake sat crossed-legged on the edge of the stage, in sports jacket, slacks and a Billie Holiday T-shirt. What, he began by asking rhetorically, is third-stream music? It is, he suggested, elaborating on an answer from the house, the combination of classical music and jazz as identified in the 1950s by the American composer and scholar Gunther Schuller.

"I take the definition a step or two further," Blake added. "I feel it can be any kind of combination, it need not be exclusively European classical and Afro-American music of the U.S.A... I also conceive of it as a process: once a person has done it for a while, and is comfortable with two or more styles, then the music carries the name of the artist.

"I'm very honoured that I was invited here as a guest of the Edmonton jazz festival," he continued, "but I by no means consider myself a jazz musician. I respect Bud Powell and Charlie Parker too much to feel of that ilk, and I feel people like Charles Ives, Béla Bartók and Mahalia Jackson just too important to me."

Thus, a third-stream musician. A Ran Blake. It took him a long time to find himself, as he revealed later, offering the workshop audience his autobiography in quick, telegraphed sentences. He grew up, he said, "in a small Connecticut town loving Bartók, Debussy and black church music. I studied in Hartford. I could not find work. People kept saying, 'What kind of animal is Ran Blake? It's not jazz, it's not classical.'

"I went to New York, to the Lennox School of Jazz for four years. I got laughed at by one of my heroes, Stan Kenton, and found that the musician I thought would be most brutal to me, Oscar Peterson, was one of the most sympathetic. I don't sound at all like him, so I was expecting to be kicked to the other side of the room... I studied gospel piano in Harlem... I want to emphasize that I was not in a hurry, but I must also say that opportunity did not come around... I became a household fixture — or maybe irritant — at the Thelonious Monk family; I'm afraid I forced myself on them... I worked as a waiter at the Jazz Gallery on St. Mark's Place. I studied composition with Bill Russo. I did all kinds of work to stay alive. Then I met Gunther Schuller, who told me that I should settle down and not be in a hurry, that I need not take a one-way swim in the Hudson River, that I had talent, and that I was *not*, perhaps, jazz."

Now, the third-stream musician offers a third-stream education to a class of 35 at the New England Conservatory. He gave the Jazz City workshop a taste of its principles, among them a list of artists for close listening: Billie Holiday, Charles

Ives, Charles Mingus, Gunther Schuller, Max Roach, Béla Bartók, Igor Stravinsky and Thelonious Monk.

Holiday and Monk clearly are very close to his heart, as is — no doubt in some other way — music from Alfred Hitchcock's films. His fascination with cinema began with the movies of the '40s. "When anything was violent on the screen — and remember we're talking about 'violent' in the '40s, not the post-*Psycho* generation, so please don't think I'm sadistic — the music was very exciting." Blake eventually looked past the music to the very characterization and events on screen for his inspiration; the *Vertigo Suite* combines some of the original score by Bernard Herrmann and his own evocations of specific scenes in the film.

Holiday, Monk and Hitchcock. For Blake, the third stream runs wide; the pull of its currents is terrific.

August 16, 1985

"A difference in experience"
Reg Schwager (1985)

The sound of Einstürzende Neubauten, a frankly experimental German "scrap metal band," spills out into the fresh air as Reg Schwager opens the front door to his parent's home. The discord is unexpected: in his six or so years on the Toronto jazz scene, Schwager has established himself as one of those determined young Canadian guitarists who can bop with the best and play all the dusty old pop songs that anyone would care to request. To wit, a mainstream musician after his time and, in a sense, before. Either way, a traditionalist.

The small living/listening room holds a large record collection. The two albums on which Schwager has appeared should be here somewhere — *Lights of Burgundy* (Justin Time) by the Montreal pianist Oliver Jones, and a Canadian-European broadcast co-production saluting International Youth Year. Schwager and his younger sister Jeannette, a vocalist of no less promise, share the latter album with three European groups; the Canadians' four tunes include the pop standard *Star Eyes* and the jazz classic *Nuages*.

And yes, there the two LPs are, in a pile topped by The Clash, Billy Bragg and The Three Johns.

In his unassuming way, Schwager, 23, born in Holland and raised from the age of seven in Sudbury, has always been a source of surprise. He was scarcely 18 when he started playing in clubs around Toronto, looking years younger and sounding years older.

Suitably impressed, various veteran musicians took him under their wings. First, bassist Fred McHugh and drummer Spike McKendry, who broadened his awareness of the bop tradition and introduced Schwager to the Montreal jazz community. Then, vibraphonist Peter Appleyard, who added the guitarist to his jazz group at Toronto's Chelsea Inn. Lately, and briefly, the New York cornetist Ruby Braff, who coached Schwager through a week at Bourbon Street.

It *could* be a dizzying experience for an emerging musician. Schwager doesn't sound dizzied. "It's nice, but I don't ever let it really get to me, because I never felt that confident. I never felt, 'Well, those guys like me, so that's great, I'm cool.' I always felt that they didn't really know, or they did, and they were being nice. But I never took it seriously to mean that I was really good. I still don't."

Now Schwager is stepping out on his own in a variety of more contemporary situations. The most immediate of these concerns is a new trio with bassist David Piltch and drummer Michel Lambert. They began a six-night engagement at George's Spaghetti House last night and will travel next week to Montreal to record Schwager's first album under his own name.★

Piltch and Lambert are Schwager's peers; the jazz scene is finally beginning to catch up with the precocious guitarist. "That's really nice," he agrees. "I'm really excited about the trio. The thing that we have is a common experience. Geographically, it was quite different — Dave was here in Toronto, and Michel was in Quebec. But we've come up in a similar time period, with the same background of influences — the TV and radio — and in the same environment. Compare it to playing with guys who are 50. You can relate, it works, but there's such a difference in experience."

A second venture is the more or less free-improvisational Schwager/Lambert duo, which heads to Europe early in the New Year as the guitarist begins to explore his own cultural roots — "part of the growing process as a musician," he says.

Yet a third venture is Plectrum Spectrum, a unique ensemble completed by Lambert, Jeannette Schwager and three other guitarists, and inspired by the Schwagers' experiences with pianist Cecil Taylor at the Banff Jazz Workshop this past summer.

These of course are recent developments. Beginning in Sudbury as a teenager, one too small to join in his schoolmates' activities, Schwager dedicated himself to the study of jazz traditions — especially to matters of style and repertoire. Two Canadian musicians, the guitarists Ed Bickert and Sonny Greenwich, would be important influences, Bickert in particular on both Schwager's style *and* repertoire.

"At a certain point, I was obsessed with learning tunes," Schwager remembers, "so I was buying books and listening to records by people like Jerry Vale. I guess it

★ *Resonance* (Justin Time).

was because Ed Bickert was playing a lot of obscure tunes; I'd hear him doing something and I'd go looking for it."

By this time the Schwager family had moved to Toronto, and the inquisitive guitarist could be found in audiences for the most avant-garde of the city's jazz events. Clearly, he had something more than bebop in the works; clearly, he's not 25 years out-of-sync after all.

"I don't really think so," he responds to the suggestion. "I work bebop gigs, but the music that I play with Michel and Jeannette is *now*. We're using our influences, but our attitude when we're playing is of the moment."

And the issue now is attitude, not style. Those musicians who have recently caught the common ear are of little interest to Schwager — the Pat Methenys and the John McLaughlins. "I've never been into listening to the latest style or the latest trends," he admits. "I listen to what interests me, to what excites me."

The conversation returns to Einstürzende Neubauten. "They go from city to city and visit the local scrap yard to find 'instruments' to play at their concert that night," Schwager notes, sounding both impressed and amused by the ingenuity of the idea. "Their arms are just covered in cuts," he adds, now sounding only impressed. Such dedication — such determination — is not to be taken lightly.

November 26, 1985

"*Rasplendent*"
Sun Ra (1986)

What is it now, the Omniverse Jet Set Arkestra? It's always something different each time Sun Ra's Philadelphia collective travels to Toronto. Last time, if memory serves, it was the Cosmo-Ninth-Dimension Arkestra; before that, the Intergalactic Myth-Science Arkestra. Originally, 30-some years ago, it was simply the Space Trio.

Whatever — behind all the hyphens and adjectives, behind the *ra*splendent *ra*galia, behind the space-is-the-place routines and behind Herman (Sonny) Blount's claim to Saturn as place of birth, there is a jazz band that turns just slightly off axis.

The Omniverse Jet Set Arkestra turned quite smoothly, as Ra's arkestras turn, Thursday night at Larry's Hideaway, in two relatively straight-up, if loosely organized sets that alternated time-warped jazz history with African ritual. It should have been more fun than it was, but Ra's humility and sincerity tended to mute the colours of the performance.

By now, there is also a degree of familiarity to the Arkestra act, refreshed this time, however, by a shift in Ra's historical emphasis and by the contributions of a couple of newer members currently in his troupe. The 11 musicians make a fairly ragged ensemble in their recreation of the swing-band material of the '30s and '40s, but there has always been an approximate quality to a Ra performance that puts the right spirit before the right notes.

Ra has long been a devotee of the classic music of Fletcher Henderson, and now offers a healthy representation of Ellingtonia to boot. Stalwart Arkestra alto saxophonist Marshall Allen played a stunning Johnny-Hodges-with-a-head-cold to Ra's bemused Duke-in-a-fur-hat, while one of the newer faces, tenorman Ronald Wilson, took on the rousing role of Paul Gonsalves in a succession of solos that would make him, unexpectedly, the most prominent musician of the evening.

Wilson's high profile came at the expense of another Arkestra stalwart, the legendary saxophonist and percussionist John Gilmore, who seemed happy for most of the evening to play incidental drums, contribute to the ensembles and chip in some short, punchy tenor and clarinet solos. Later on, however, Gilmore and Ra teamed up for the most riveting music of the night, a long, improvised duet in which the tenorman worked entirely in shrill, whistling overtones to Ra's synthesized, *musique concrète* accompaniment.

Otherwise, the performance ranged far and wide through the jazz, and related pop, traditions, Ra setting up each tune with a dabbled sort of keyboard introduction. Gilmore sang *East of the Sun* while in fact standing west of the boss, the whole band stomped through *Mack the Knife*, Ra alone essayed a striking *Somewhere over the Rainbow*...

And on it went: a stronger performance than some past arkestras have given in Toronto, and yet not nearly the sum of its parts. Add the new and devilishly enthusiastic drummer Marvin "Boogaloo" Smith to a list of wonderful musicians that includes Gilmore, Allen, baritone saxophonist Pat Patrick and various others unnamed, and behind all the hyphens and adjectives, the garb and the rest, there could be a great band hidden in Sun Ra's considerable cosmic shadow.

February 8, 1986

"Lace work"
Jimmy Hamilton (1986)

It would have been easy to miss Jimmy Hamilton among the thousand or so musicians at the Festival International de Jazz de Montréal this year. It was hard enough to find the long-time Ellington clarinetist — at the end of a winding trail of elevators, escalators and right turns in the festival hotel. Or so the directions went. And then, yes, there it was — the gentle drift of *Creole Love Call* and the warm, dry sound of four clarinets...

Hamilton, John Carter, Alvin Batiste and bass clarinetist David Murray were preparing for the evening's Clarinet Summit concert. They had flown in from disparate points for this rare performance together — Hamilton, from the Virgin Islands, his home for the past 16 years — and they were well into a full afternoon's reunion/rehearsal. Theirs would be one of the festival's special presentations; it would also be one of the more than 125 concerts the festival would offer over its 10 days.

Hamilton went about his business in Montreal with quiet diffidence. ("He's a nice guy," wrote Ellington in his memoir *Music Is My Mistress*, "with patience and a dry sense of humor...") At 69, he was not the senior man at the festival. Benny Carter was there — the great altoist with whom Hamilton worked briefly before joining the Ellington band at the Hurricane Club on Broadway in 1942. And Woody Herman was also there, one of the few other surviving clarinetists of Hamilton's era. But so, too, in Montreal were the Gillespies and the Mangiones, the Hancocks and the Coreas, the Shorters and the Lacys, the Nascimentos and the Jobims, not to mention the James Browns and the Van Morrisons. Yes, it would have been easy enough to miss Jimmy Hamilton.

He has always been something of a hidden figure in jazz, first in the Ellington band, then in the Virgin Islands. His 26-year association with Ellington accounts for the better half of his career as a clarinetist and, secondarily, as an alto or — at Duke's request — tenor saxophonist.

The clarinet was one of several instruments to pass through the boy Hamilton's hands after his family moved from his birthplace, Dillon, South Carolina, to Philadelphia. "Youngsters like to play everything," he remembered over dinner, the Clarinet Summit rehearsal now behind him. "They don't know what they want, they'll try anything they can get their hands on. I was like that, too."

And there was something else. "I was also the type who liked a challenge. I didn't like anything that was too simple. The clarinet came to be a *real* challenge, so I put more time into it than most people who pick it up — I made a major study of it. The difficult things kind of came easy to me, but you'd really have to work for that, whereas you could pick up the sax and you wouldn't have to work so hard."

(Wrote Ellington of Hamilton: "He usually manages anything musical he sets his mind to... He has the capacity to discipline himself and the diligence to study in order to learn. He practises endlessly and scarcely ever gets away from the school rules.")

And there was something else again. "There's so much more that could be played on the clarinet than the saxophone. There's the range of the instrument, and the timbre of the tone is so expressive — from the softest to the loudest. You just get hooked on the sound."

Hamilton's sound is clean and singing, a cool pastel on the Ducal palette, as featured in a long list of Ellingtonia from *Air Conditioned Jungle* to *The Tattooed Bride*. Historians who already write about him in the past tense employ adjectives like "classical," "symphonic" and "legitimate." His models in this matter of tone were not the New Orleans personalities who preceded him but the Swing musicians who were more or less his peers, Benny Goodman foremost among them.

"I've always been the kind of person who likes pleasant sounds. I like quality. I don't like too much distorted sound. I'm not necessarily pushing to be a classical performer, either, although I've had a little training in that. I just want a good sound, and to get a decent sound you have to practise. There's a lot of clarinet players, they don't have the good sound — not to my taste. I like to have the good sound and still be able to play jazz, you know?"

It was Ellington, the clarinetist acknowledged, who played an important role in his development as a soloist. Hamilton became a member of the Ellington orchestra in 1942, with just a few years and a few bands — those of Carter, Teddy Wilson, Jimmy Mundy, Eddie Heywood — behind him.

"When I first joined the band, Duke didn't know *what* to write for me, because I was a different kind of player. He was used to somebody like [New Orleans clarinetist] Barney Bigard. And I really hadn't found my way, to be honest with you. Duke kinda found a way in which to use me, to play a lot of what he called 'lace work.' If a tune was going down easy, he'd say, 'Jimmy, you do the lacework.'"

Hamilton did the lace work until 1968. He was a company man but he would not be a lifer. "I had reached the pinnacle. I wasn't going any further, I wasn't going to make any more money. And Duke was getting older. He couldn't stand the rigours of the road as much as he used to. Where he used to work 40 weeks a year, those weeks weren't weeks any more — they'd just be days."

Don't misunderstand. It wasn't that Hamilton *liked* the road. Back in 1942, he was no more willing a traveller than he was a tenorman. Soon enough, he turned into a rough-and-ready saxophonist — quite the opposite of his approach to the clarinet — but he never quite settled with life on the road.

"To entertain people, and to go where they were to entertain them, you had to pay a lot of what we call 'dues' to get there. Many jobs we played we had to ride all night. You get there in the morning and all you can do is *look* at the bed because you had a TV show to do. You just couldn't rest...

"It's all great fun in the beginning. Going up, getting a raise here and there. But then you get up there, and you stay up there for a while — for 26 years. After a while you don't feel like paying those dues any more. If you were making more money at it, you could do it much easier — you could make yourself more comfortable mentally. But it wasn't that way."

Two years after Hamilton left Ellington, he made the Virgin Islands his mailing address — "Just put St. Croix on it and Jimmy Hamilton, Musician; they'll find me." He teaches in the schools there, plays in the night clubs and keeps in touch with the mainland by word of mouth with the musicians who work the cruise ships that ply the Caribbean; he has finally found the comfort that the road, and the Ellington orchestra, did not offer. "I stay in one place and everything happens to me within 15 minutes of home, 90 percent of the time."

Drawing on the other 10 percent, he was in New York in 1984 to perform with Clarinet Summit. The quartet's Public Theatre recording for India Navigation was, he suggested cautiously, "a bit popular with some people — that's how we got here [Montreal], I suppose."

Throughout the Montreal concert, his role in the quartet was clear. The Ellingtonia and the other classic material that he brought to the repertoire had the effect — as he had put it — of keeping the musicians' "feet on the ground." These touchstones, presented with Hamilton's characteristic clarity and simplicity, placed the more abstracted playing of the other three into perspective, and with it Clarinet Summit's review and reaffirmation of the instrument's place in jazz.

"We have our own world, you know," he had said before the concert. He was talking about clarinetists, of course, but he could have been speaking about Jimmy Hamilton, Musician, St. Croix. "We've been neglected a lot. But they finally got around to us, I suppose. It's been nice."

Previously unpublished; June 1986

"Dispatch"
Chet Baker and Paul Bley (1986)

Chet Baker was already on stage at the Théâtre St-Denis, sitting motionless in the dark, with trumpet in hand, as the audience found its place for his concert with pianist Paul Bley late Thursday evening. One of the most extraordinary moments of the seventh annual Festival International de Jazz de Montréal had begun.

The two musicians had previously worked together in the mid-1950s, when the Montreal-born pianist was new to the U.S. scene and when the trumpeter was a romantic, if rather star-crossed figure, popular for his soft-edged, boppish playing and wistful singing. Now in their 50s and among the most personal, and generally introspective, jazz musicians of the modern era, Bley and Baker have been lately reunited as partners on an album of duets, *Diane,* for the Steeplechase label in Copenhagen, which in turn led to this Montreal appearance.

Baker withdrew slowly to the wings of the theatre before the house lights went down, and it was Bley who made the first official entrance, alone. Beginning with several rolls of the left hand, he played his way through a relatively bold solo until the audience, which would be moving with more dispatch than either performer on this evening, cut him off during one pregnant pause with its applause. The ever congenial Bley seemed happy to go along with its decision.

Baker, gaunt and pained, reappeared a short way into Bley's second solo, found his high stool out of the spotlight and sat silent. So far, as a piece of theatre, it was wonderful. Not a word had been said — nor would be said — to the audience. The sense of anticipation was delicious.

The pace quickened. When, at the outset of the third piece, the spotlight hit Baker, he had the look of someone asleep. There was laughter. Bley, never less than gracious at any time during the next half-hour, called for silence. The two men began, Baker balancing precariously at the edge of his stool in order to bring the bell of his trumpet within range of the microphone. His solo was ghostly, full of phantom notes and cold air. There were boos, followed at the end of the piece by a shout of "C'mon Chet, wake up," more laughter, calls now from the house for silence, and the first signs of a walk-out.

Bley and Baker conferred *sotto voce* at centre stage. Baker would sing. He adjusted the microphone up just a little, and began *But Not for Me* in an off-key, tuneless voice, at one point bending almost double to the microphone, at another point just catching himself from falling as he sat back on the stool. The walk-outs continued, and Bley's characteristically poignant improvisation took on an added dimension as the accompanying score to this unfolding drama.

A technician twice scurried out from the wings to make further adjustments to the microphone as Baker essayed another trumpet solo, this one stronger than the first.

But it was too late. All was lost. Montreal audiences, so generous with their standing ovations, apparently can also be unforgiving. This audience was split. The walk-outs accelerated. There were shouts of "*Arrête!*" and "Off!" and there was more laughter. There was derisively rhythmic applause from some quarters; there was acute discomfort in others.

Another conference followed at centre stage. Both men left the stage. In time, Bley returned alone and played the tension out of the hall. Yesterday, a festival spokesman would say only: "Chet Baker wasn't feeling well, and it was impossible for him to continue. People who wanted to be reimbursed were reimbursed immediately."

Baker had been on stage for 30 minutes at most, a dramatic half-hour in which his mere presence had generated all the same bittersweet emotions that he once expressed so well in his music — a study of art as life, and life as art. He had offered just two solos and the refrain to *But Not for Me*.

"They're writing songs of love," he sang, "but not for me."

July 5, 1986

"Mindful"
Freddie Stone (1986)

It will be difficult to measure the considerable legacy of Fred (Freddie) Stone, the respected jazz flugelhorn player and composer who died Wednesday in Toronto of heart failure at the age of 51. His achievements were many — the various jazz and classical solos on record, the compositions, the professional affiliations as illustrious as the Duke Ellington Orchestra — but his personal influence will endure in a different and subtler way.

There was always something elusive even about Stone's most formal accomplishments. Those flugelhorn solos, for example — for Ellington, for the Ron Collier and Phil Nimmons big bands, for the early Boss Brass, for the rock band Lighthouse and for the Toronto and Winnipeg symphony orchestras in their premieres of Norman Symonds' third-stream concertos — had a darting, here-and-gone quality, a fast, evasive logic all of their own.

His compositions in turn were cut not from a single cloth but from the rough weave of folk music, the stiff drill of the classics (Stravinsky was a favourite) and the sporty patterns of jazz. Stone's melodic instincts made the seams magically invisible.

And the professional affiliations were always on his own terms. He matched his peers in Toronto's studio orchestras and jazz bands note for note, phrase for phrase, through the 1960s; otherwise he stood apart. He stayed with Ellington for less than a year, and just a single recording, *New Orleans Suite* (Atlantic), before leaving of his own accord when he felt the time was right.

He brought some of the unique Ellington tradition with him on his return to Toronto. Rather than taking up where he had left off two years before, he looked instead to the future. Mindful of his own formal and informal background in music — while a teenager hawking his father's band at the Casino Theatre, Stone became a protégé in passing of the St. Louis trumpeter Clark Terry who was in town with Count Basie — and mindful of lessons learned at Ellington's side, Stone began to teach. He worked first in local colleges and then opened his own studio, teaching on a private, one-to-one basis.

What Ellington had done as a composer, Stone took for his task as a teacher. "I look for the musical equivalent of personality," he explained two years ago. "Each individual is unique, or has unique potential, and I'm trying to find a way to represent that. Although I'm a big believer in studying history, I don't think we should emulate history."

In 15 years of teaching — of playing duets, of talking philosophies — he planted enough seeds in enough minds as a teacher, and touched enough hearts as a friend, to ensure that the principle would take hold. This is ultimately his legacy: a burgeoning wave of musicians, convinced of the "uniqueness of their statement," as he put it, prepared to speak in creative terms for themselves. His was a quiet revolution; Stone spoke in the softest of voices, and it made the message that much more compelling.

Of late, he had returned to the public eye. Though heart problems slowed him in 1982, he was able by November 1984 to introduce Freddie's Band, an exciting and fascinating improvising orchestra made up, of course, of pupils and former pupils — musicians so remarkably in tune with him and with each other that Stone could venture into performance with no planned material whatsoever and simply organize and "compose" on the spot.★

As he explained at the time, "I've gone through years of writing and orchestration with different ensembles — symphony orchestras, big bands — and I'm at the point now where I have musicians with whom I can bypass the writing process. Instead of writing a score, I work directly with the musicians."

His imagination thus fired, Stone branched out in the past two years with small, chamberish ensembles, brisk jazz sextets and even solo flugelhorn and piano

★ Stone's activities in this regard paralleled Butch Morris' practice of "conduction" in New York during the same period.

performances, the last heard on a cassette recording, *In Season,*★ the only published document of his music from this period of renewal. All of his work, from the orchestral constructions to the solo fantasies, reflected the same curiosity about, and wonder in, the creative process. In his gentle, quizzical way — eyebrows inevitably arched — he seemed as surprised and delighted by the results as anybody.

December 12, 1986

"A left-hand situation"
Ralph Sutton (1987)

Ralph Sutton was a boy of nine or 10 in Hamburg, Missouri, when he first heard recordings of the legendary stride pianist Thomas (Fats) Waller on a St. Louis radio station. The show was *Harlem Rhythm.* The boy was enthralled.

"That's amazing — to catch someone's ear at that age, and out in the country where I was living," Sutton remarks some 55 years later, more in recognition of Waller's greatness than in acknowledgement of his own youthful powers of musical appreciation. "I was taking piano lessons at the time. When I heard Fats, he made me feel so good — there was so much humour in his playing and he was such a great pianist, that I just latched on."

Waller died in 1943. Sutton never met him. But when Sutton himself began recording a few years later, it was clear — or so one of his fans was saying at Toronto's Café des Copains on Monday evening — that this was Waller's successor. Another fan put it more emphatically: "You've got a living legend here tonight."

Waller's successor or not — living legend or not — Sutton has done well by the piano. He was discovered at 19 by trombonist Jack Teagarden and soon followed the long, tall Texan to New York. He rejoined Teagarden's band on 52nd Street after the Second World War, then moved on in 1948 to work at Eddie Condon's, its namesake's dixieland saloon on West 3rd Street.

Sutton describes himself as the "intermission pianist" there, but adds — with reference to the raucous atmosphere that the guitarist enjoyed — "Eddie didn't call it the intermission, he called it the lull."

With Condon's still ringing in his ears, Sutton went west in 1955, first to California and then to Colorado, where he lives now, 8,000 feet above sea level, in a place called Bailey, southwest of Denver. For several years he was the pianist in the World's Greatest Jazz Band; for quite a few more years now he has been recognized as one of the world's greatest stride players.

★ Issued on CD under the same title by Unity Records in 1992.

The Waller legacy is never far from his performances — such stride staples as *Ain't Misbehavin'*, *Honeysuckle Rose* and *Keepin' out of Mischief Now*, among other classic jazz compositions. Naturally, there were some Waller tunes in Monday's first set, played not merely in imitation, but with great respect and affection.

"I got everything from Fats," Sutton was once quoted as saying, and quite reasonably so. But he qualified the acknowledgement with what seems like an uncharacteristically bold assessment of his own playing. "He was the greatest, but I think I might be second... as a stride pianist, that is."

Reminded of these words a dozen years later, he's quite taken aback. "I put myself second? Oh, no, I would never say that... That's real ego."

Ego? Not Ralph Sutton.

Not the Ralph Sutton who says he responded to the interest expressed by a Chicago writer, J.D. Shacter, in writing a Sutton biography — later published under the title *Piano Man* — with one simple question. "Why?" Not the Ralph Sutton who talks now about a fellow in Japan who has just completed the seventh edition of the Sutton discography. "The seventh edition," Sutton repeats, a little incredulous and a little more impressed as he carves out the book's dimensions in mid-air with his hands.

Indeed, as Sutton relaxes in sweater and jeans at the one-bedroom, Church Street apartment that the Café des Copains provides for its out-of-town pianists, it's hard to place him back 35 years among the Eddie Condon gang, possibly the most colourful collection of characters ever assembled in jazz on a nightly basis. In jacket and tie at the Café des Copains, he's equally hard to tell from his own fans.

He is, in short, a most reticent chap. Pressed for a definition of the stride piano style that he plays so conclusively, he proves inconclusive. "I don't know who put that label on it," he begins. He offers a few names — Waller, of course, and James P. Johnson — and a little stride pre-history. "It's a left-hand situation," he adds, helpfully.

A left-hand situation, yes: bass notes bounced on the first and third beat of every bar, alternating with middle-register chords dropped on the second and fourth. But Sutton's playing is no less a right-hand situation, no less melody than rhythm: there is delicacy to his touch and method to his attack. His stride figures are illusory and restrained as often as they're direct and driving, and he builds on them gradually through a set, winding up and backing off repeatedly before rollicking to a close. He can be incredibly powerful. He can also be remarkably gentle.

It might have been Jack Teagarden, his "godfather in music," who taught him that lesson. "He said something once," Sutton recalls. "You know how guys are always blowing so hard? Well, Jack always did it very easy. He told me, 'Remember one thing, Ralph, don't bruise yourself.'"

January 28, 1987

"Ad hoc"
Derek Bailey (1987)

"Would you prefer it if this were in French?" asked British guitarist Derek Bailey during another lull in a slow-moving press conference a few hours before his concert with Company on Saturday night at the Festival International de Musique Actuelle de Victoriaville.

Silence.

"Anyone here speak French?" he joked.

Laughter.

"Qu'est-ce qu'il a dit?" a mischievous French voice shot back — "What did he say?"

Bailey, Americans Sonny Sharrock, Fred Frith, Eugene Chadbourne and Arto Lindsay, and Montreal's René Lussier were all in town Saturday; a more distinguished gathering of free-thinking guitarists would be hard to imagine.

A panel with all six would have been interesting, a concert even more so, but the reticent Bailey faced his equally reticent inquisitors alone. At 57 the senior man of the six, he has been influential at various levels, the highest as the musician who, 20 or more years ago in London, began to draw guitar players toward free improvisation — away from the strict melodic and harmonic grids of jazz into the more abstract realms of sound and texture.

Other guitarists have taken it much further, among them any of his five fellow visitors to Victoriaville — Sharrock, for example, wildly intense with the German-American quartet Last Exit Friday night, and Chadbourne, irreverent and irrepressible with his hand saw, power drill, country songs and Dylan imitations in the company of Australian violinist and cellist Jon Rose on Saturday afternoon.

Nevertheless, it was Bailey's rather lighter hand that had eased open the door to the far side. Twenty-some years later, he presents himself as an unlikely revolutionary. With Company on Saturday night, he left the flamboyance entirely to cellist Tom Cora, drummer Gerry Hemingway and especially multi-instrumentalist Steve Beresford.

The four men had never played together before as a unit, which is, as Bailey noted earlier, more or less the point. Company, he suggested, "is an alternative to working solo, but not having a regular group — avoiding a regular group. I think it's better for this kind of music making not to have a regular group. The best results out of freely improvised music are arrived at out of a semi *ad hoc* situation. It's not totally *ad hoc*: the relationship between the musicians has reached a certain stage, but hasn't gone beyond that stage. At that point, it seems to me, you're likely to get better results."

The project began under the Company name in 1976 and at last count — some point in 1983 — more than 125 musicians had shared a stage with Bailey under its banner, usually for several days at a time, rather than this single Canadian concert. The guitarist plays his role of host in a dry, self-effacing manner, assembling an interesting guest list and then letting the party follow its own course. In Victoriaville, Company worked in twos and fours; "we thought of trying a trio," Bailey advised late in the performance, "but it seemed... *ambitious*."

Beresford was the life of this particular affair, playing piano, mini-trumpet and other oddities with a degree of humour and a certain theatrical flair that was far less apparent either in Cora's passionate bowing or in Hemingway's meticulous percussion. Beresford's musical lampshade routines had their limits, though, and by the concert's end he was repeating his earlier quips and one-liners to reduced effect.

Bailey's contribution was, typically, quite modest; what sounded so random appeared in fact to be carefully selected and given specific shape and size. There were no mere effects to his playing, in fact nothing very startling at all, just a musician long comfortable with his chosen unorthodoxy. The others, much younger, fell back from time to time on the tried, the true and the tricks; just as occasionally all four would, in their interplay, come up with something new.

Bailey had predicted as much earlier in the day. "We've never played before but there are all kinds of aspects and details of each other's playing that we're familiar with. Some things will happen tonight that I know will happen, but there's quite a lot I don't know will happen and there's other stuff I suspect might happen. I find that this is one of the big attractions about playing music. To remove those areas that are, at this point, either undefined or unknown would be to remove a lot of the attraction."

That attraction has its price, of course, one easily forgotten in Victoriaville where free improvisation and all the other avant approaches on display seem to make up a complete musical world, to scale, of their own. Bailey, however, reminded the festival audience of the larger reality when, in introducing Company's final quartet improvisation, he suggested, "So if when we've finished, you could do all that whooping and hollering you do for more popular musics..."

October 5, 1987

"Entirely mad"
Bobby McFerrin (1988)

It's hard to say which was more remarkable about Bobby McFerrin's solo performance at Massey Hall on Saturday night, the felicitous San Franciscan singer himself — *by* himself — or his eager Toronto audience. McFerrin characteristically leaves his inhibitions in the dressing room. A couple of thousand Torontonians stashed theirs under the seats for most of his one-and-three-quarter-hour concert.

A casual McFerrin — striped, button-down shirt, blue jeans and tennis shoes — appeared suddenly, and a little late, on an empty, baffled Massey Hall stage, carrying a cordless microphone in one hand and a bottle of Perrier in the other. He sang his first song from a sitting position at the top of the steps that led from the stage into the audience — steps that would see a lot of traffic before the night was over — and his trusting, two-way rapport with the audience was immediately in place.

McFerrin risks making a fool of himself every time he opens his mouth. He gets off safely about 98 per cent of the time, and the other two per cent slips by innocuously in the general pandemonium that he and his voices sustain.

Thus caught up in the spirit, some part of his Toronto audience bravely took the same risk. McFerrin had no shortage of volunteers when he needed them — someone to "do the hambone," two guys to sing scat choruses on *C-Jam Blues* (he got three, the third particularly fine), a woman dancer to interpret one of his improvisations, and "about 16 singers" for a choir (he got twice as many).

His volunteers were almost good enough, and quick enough, to seem like ringers. Almost. In fact, they were simply made to feel perfectly at ease. At McFerrin's side, who could be self-conscious? The rest of the audience, a little less nervy, was happy to just join in on the choruses whenever McFerrin beckoned.

This was not, then, a one-man show in the traditional sense. If its warmest moments were collective efforts, though, its breathtaking moments were McFerrin's doing alone.

Seven or eight years into solo performance, he now has his concert hits — his own song *Drive* among them, and lately Thelonious Monk's *Round Midnight*, which he sang on the soundtrack for the Bertrand Tavernier film of the same name.

He also has his routines. His two-register duets, for example, one operatic (for tenor voice and soprano) and the other gospel (for contralto-ish voice and bass), matched a novel idea with some spectacular singing that drew whistles of disbelief.

He made several forays into the audience, using those stair steps at one point as a visual melody to cue the willing Massey Hall choir, and relinquishing his microphone at another to a woman who volunteered to sing *Barney Google*. (She was pretty good, too. Of course.) And he offered his dazzling, if entirely mad re-creation of *The Wizard of Oz* as a closer, and the Mickey Mouse theme as his first encore.

These, in one form or another, were a part of his concerts at the Bluma Appel Theatre in 1986. New for 1988 are some songs from his latest album, *Simple Pleasures* (EMI), including the title tune (as a final encore) and *Susie Q*. Gone in 1988 for the most part is his mimicry of the trumpets, saxophones and other such instruments in jazz.

His ability to improvise is constant, although ultimately he improvises more like a comedian than a jazz musician. He has that ability to pull things together on the spot, to work out of the tough corners and to reverse direction on those tangents whose promise disappears as quickly as it appeared. However spontaneous the *musical* content of the performance may have seemed, it was obviously subject to tremendous self-discipline; if McFerrin regularly invited his audience's participation, he also discouraged it occasionally, summarily cutting off on-the-beat clapping when it did not serve his purpose.

No offence was meant or taken. No artistic egos were bruised. It may have been McFerrin's final triumph, in a night of triumphs, that he could send his audience out into the night feeling almost as pleased with its own musical abilities as it was with his.

May 2, 1988

"Miss D."
Dorothy Donegan (1988)

She started by parking her handbag inside the piano. She finished, when all but the encores had been played, by asking, "Did I get the job?" In between, Dorothy Donegan caused a small, happy riot Monday night in the Festival International de Jazz de Montréal's Piano Plus series at the Théâtre Port-Royal of Place des Arts.

Donegan, an irrepressible woman of 60 out of Chicago via Los Angeles, is Montreal's kind of piano player. She's of the same stylistic vintage as two of this city's favourite sons, Oscar Peterson and Oliver Jones — the 1940s, roughly, when Art Tatum's exacting, virtuoso influence ruled supreme.

That might have made her an odd match for the "Plus" component of this particular Piano Plus concert, the alto saxophonist Phil Woods, who is one of the great beboppers of this or any day. Set in historical sequence, Donegan stops precisely where Woods starts. Nevertheless, she leaned forward a little, and he leaned back a little more, and their duets together proved a second triumph for the pianist.

The first triumph was hers alone, a solo set that was great entertainment, great piano playing and occasionally great jazz — the sort of manic performance that has drawn Donegan a large popular following in Europe and a degree of critical dismissal in North America.

She's a tall, striking woman with a comically expressive face, a dramatic way of operating the piano and a wardrobe of reds, blacks and whites that would upstage Miles Davis any night.

She plays the piano with dazzling speed, startling acceleration and what may be the most exquisite sense of touch in jazz. When, that is, she chooses to exercise it; her speed gets her further, faster, and to much showier effect. And show is all. Here and there, though, among all the fun, the games, her pounding pumps and — once — a sing-along, she would turn a phrase with breathtaking clarity and lightness. The moment passed quickly of course; everything in a Donegan solo performance passes quickly.

In another era, she'd be called a novelty pianist, or perhaps a piano shark, on the basis of the solo portion of this concert. She played blatantly to the house, setting the piano bench at an angle away from the keyboard so that she could lean back from time to time, vamp-like and exultant, using her right hand for support and her left to keep a bass roll going.

She played such familiar tunes as *Round Midnight* and *Tea for Two* and did unfamiliar things to them, turning them into rags or classical pieces and then spinning off in three or four directions at once. Digging into a boogie-woogie, she had the piano bench tilted up on two legs; digging further, she was on her feet.

The riot had begun.

Enter Phil Woods, who could be seen tugging his leather cap down firmly on his head, as if bracing for a hurricane on the horizon. But no, at least not immediately. The two musicians had never worked together before, and Woods' presence brought about a remarkable transformation in Donegan; she eventually brought about a transformation in him.

First, they played it straight, save possibly for the rather loaded titles of the tunes that Woods undertook — a self effacing *Don't Get around much Anymore* for starters, and the more pointed *(You Came to Me from) Out of Nowhere* later on. He, too, is a man with a sense of humour, though one a little less obvious than that of his new partner, and he too is a vigorous personality with a coarse, bursting sound and a command of the alto comparable to Donegan's facility at the piano.

Her accompaniment for his solos was nearly telepathic, her sense of anticipation and resolution so close that various short Woods quotes and cascades turned into Woods-Donegan unisons before they were finished. Her own solos were precisely the sort of inventions that could force a critical re-evaluation of her jazz instincts.

In the long run, though, the Théâtre Port-Royal audience was more interested in The Entertaining Miss Donegan. That irrepressible streak wasn't going to be repressed for very long. The affable Woods went along with her swings of mood, from a bit of *Rhapsody in Blue*, through some *C-Jam Blues* to a final *As Time Goes By*.

Donegan sang this last with new lyrics ("the fundamental things of life... cost") and then said good night to Ronnie, Nancy and all the American presidential contenders and their wives in her best George and Gracie voices. She missed a note by forgetting Brian and Mila — this is Canada, Miss D. — but that's surely the only note she missed all night.

July 6, 1988

"Odds"
John Zorn (1988)

"I've got this really short attention span," John Zorn advised a gathering of the media Saturday afternoon, roughly the halfway mark of the sixth annual Festival International de Musique Actuelle de Victoriaville. "I'm amazed that I'm still here," the lately celebrated New York composer and alto saxophonist added, breaking off a quick gesture to the room for a quicker glance at his watch. "It's been 10 minutes."

Zorn's time is valuable. "We're running a little late," he had suggested to his reluctant inquisitors after their initial few seconds of silence 10 minutes earlier. "So is that it? Can we go?" Imagine a Woody Allen type in his mid-30s, but a Woody Allen type whose myriad insecurities have given way to a kind of petulant disdain.

But Zorn is indeed a busy man, as busy as any of the FIMAV musicians. "This year," he noted, "my phone is ringing off the *hook*." He's a project-oriented musician whose recent efforts have included *The Big Gundown* (of music by film composer Ennio Morricone) for Elektra-Nonesuch, *Voodoo* (of music by jazz pianist Sonny Clark, with keyboard player Wayne Horvitz and others) for Black Saint, *News for Lulu* (of music by beboppers Hank Mobley and Kenny Dorham, with guitarist Bill Frisell and trombonist George Lewis) for hatART and *Spillane* (of Zorn's own compositions, with bluesman Albert Collins and others) again for Elektra-Nonesuch.

As this year's special guest at the FIMAV, he performed a striking set of duet improvisations Saturday night with his seatmate at the press conference, guitarist Fred Frith, and gave a more formal presentation last night with his newest group, Naked City.

Moreover, Victoriaville has several other visitors with Zorn connections — Frith, Frisell, Lewis and Horvitz for four, not to mention the saxophonist's avowed "hero," Anthony Braxton, whose septet followed Zorn and Frith Saturday night at the FIMAV's Grand Café. So perhaps Zorn had every right to act the star, leather jacket draped provocatively off-the-shoulder, as he worked selectively through and around the questions directed his way.

The talk was in large part about music and film. "Movie music is what got me into music generally," he said helpfully, establishing some general parameters for his interests. "Stravinsky from *Fantasia*, organ music from *Phantom of the Opera*, Morricone from spaghetti westerns."

Asked whether Naked City represented a new compositional concept — Zorn has employed a variety of interesting organizational strategies over the dozen years of his career — he replied unhelpfully, "It's the same old concept; you write the music and then you play it."

The new quintet, with Frith, Frisell, Horowitz and drummer Joey Baron, grew out of Zorn's listening habits. He buys "hundreds of records, thousands of records" and then fits them to his span of attention.

"So I'm making cassettes of records that I buy, with one track [from each]. I might start with some thrash, then I'll put on a [Henry] Mancini, some [Steve] Reich, some jazz, a country record... They're the things I listen to while I'm on the road, or even at home. This is the way I listen to music. One thing, then another, and another... I like that. It makes sense to me."

Interrupted Frith: "This is one of the great pleasures of driving to a gig with John; you never know what you're going to hear."

Continued Zorn: "I put together Naked City to do 'live' what I listen to at home. We do a soundtrack piece, then we do one of my hardcore pieces, then we do a blues..."

He had less to say about the Frith-Zorn duo and the free improvisational approach it would be taking that night. Nothing to say, in fact. But the concert spoke most eloquently for itself. It was a highly charged affair, between Frith's methods and Zorn's madness, between Frith's careful manipulation of texture, and Zorn's impulsive extremes of tone. These are masters of this game, a far cry from some of this year's FIMAV musicians who are still struggling to learn all the ground rules.

Zorn and Frith created several, just-long-enough pieces together and offered one solo improvisation each. According to the conventions of musical language, they spoke almost exclusively in expletives — expletives gathered into complete statements, however, not simply left dangling in strings. Their first piece developed out of long, linear screams, Frith's guitar and Zorn's alto in remarkable unison; the second evolved from the initial, offhand notes of *C-Jam Blues*. And so on, intense and yet, yes, attentive.

Of course, these two have been over all of this before. They have their own trademarks and they know each other's moves well. It was the Belgian pianist, Fred Van Hove, facing many of the same questioners a day earlier, who had suggested of such familiarity, "In improvised music, you play [only] one tune. You try to do it better each time. You maybe succeed only one in 10 times."

This time, the odds were smiling.

October 10, 1988

"Shivers"
John Zorn's Naked City (1989)

In the lexicon of music in the 1980s, Zorn — as in alto saxophonist and composer John Zorn — is a four-letter word. Like most four-letter words these days, it has had at least some acceptance in polite circles. There it is, among the composer credits of the latest Kronos String Quartet recording, and there again, on the program of the last New Music America outing in Miami.

But it still holds a certain shock value, especially at high volume, as witness the vivid and occasionally confrontational performance in Toronto of the Zorn quintet Naked City Thursday night at the du Maurier Theatre Centre as part of Harbourfront's Quay Works series.

The Z-word has been in circulation for a dozen years or so years. It is of New York origin. The exact meaning still isn't clear, but Naked City's marginally overlong, 105-minute performance for a full but strangely unresponsive house raised a few possibilities.

1. To survey broadly. Specifically, to survey the literature of mid-to-late twentieth-century popular music. Naked City serves just this repertorial purpose, as Zorn, keyboard player Wayne Horvitz, guitarist Bill Frisell, bassist Fred Frith and drummer Bobby Previte worked from a program that included film themes by Ennio Morricone, Henry Mancini, Johnny Mandel, John Barry and Bernard Hermann, jazz tunes from Big John Patton and Ornette Coleman, an affectionate surfing medley circa 1964 and some blistering material from the repertoires, or in the styles of, current New York hardcore bands Live Skull and Blind Idiot God.

2. To dwell, in a good-natured way, on violence and death. Some titles from Thursday night: *Reanimator*, *The Sicilian Clan*, *A Shot in the Dark*, *Back in the Earth*, *I Want to Live*, *Cold Blood* and *Graveyard Shift*.

3. To confuse, if not to confound. This was, Zorn advised, the music that he loves. But he played it remarkably straight and with razored precision. Its humour, apparently, was purely unintentional. This was not satire, he said. These were not parodies. If anything, this was show and tell, a rather hipper-than-thou presentation of Zorn's personal favourites — of music that he obviously thinks the rest of us should know about. And never mind where this over-the-shoulder band fits in with all of his other, over-the-horizon ventures.

4. To scorn lightly. The Toronto audience evidently wasn't quite up to Zorn's expectations. It missed some of his musicological quips. It reserved its loudest response for his loudest pieces. It failed to appreciate sufficiently one particular Horvitz solo — or so Zorn scolded when he returned to play a couple of encores.

And he was right. This was a killing performance from all involved, although a performance so tightly scripted, even at its fiercest, as to make difficult any distinction between effective arrangements and effective improvisation. Ironically, the pieces that gave the musicians their greatest freedom were easily the least interesting. They lacked the sudden, if contrived, drama and the quick, clean thrust that sent shivers through much of the other material.

5. To mix things that don't traditionally match. The bass line of Roy Orbison's *Pretty Woman*, for example, running under an atypically fractious version of Ornette Coleman's usually serene *Lonely Woman*. Zorn dresses in that manner, too. His footwear comes in singles, not pairs. One white running shoe, one black. One red sock, one green.

6. To do things strictly for effect.

7. To take, or be taken, just a little too seriously.

February 25, 1989

"Quality work"
Red Rodney (1989)

As far as Hollywood is concerned, the movie *Bird* is last year's news. For jazz, though, and particularly for Red Rodney, Clint Eastwood's feature film about Charlie Parker is still the talk of the town.

Rodney, who opened a week-long engagement at the Toronto jazz club East 85th on Tuesday night, was immortalized in *Bird* as the eager, young trumpeter who came under Parker's sway, first taking up the saxophonist's music and then his drug-dependent lifestyle. Rodney, unlike Parker, has lived to tell the tale; theirs was the one, well-developed musical relationship in *Bird*, and Rodney, now 62, has benefited greatly from the film's success.

"It has done me a world of good," he agreed, soon after stepping down from Tuesday's first set. "It has got me so much more work — quality work." That means concerts rather than club work, and the opportunity to travel with his own, New York musicians, rather than picking up rhythm sections at each new stop. (The Toronto engagement is half and half: Rodney and his regular pianist, Gary Dial, are working with three Toronto musicians, tenorman Pat LaBarbera, bassist Don Thompson and drummer Jerry Fuller.)

The real question, however, is whether jazz has benefited from *Bird*. While Dizzy Gillespie, another surviving bebopper who was accorded a lesser place in *Bird*, has avoided the need to comment by not seeing the film, Rodney faces the issue head on.

"I think so," he began cautiously. "I know where you're coming from, and I feel the same way. I feel cheated. They didn't show Charlie Parker to the masses. We knew who he was. I thought it was too much Chan [Bird's wife], too much love story, too dark, too much drugs. All of that would have been okay, if it had shown the world who Charlie Parker was. I even told Clint that later. I said, 'You didn't show the general public why a man like you would make a picture about Charlie Parker.'"

Nevertheless, Rodney admitted, "The entire world of jazz owes [Eastwood] a great deal of gratitude for making the picture. Albeit, he could have done it a little better, I think, but he still made it."

Rodney returned to the subject later on — to that "We," the world of jazz. "We are disturbed by things in that film, because [Bird] was our hero. We wanted it perfect. We didn't get it perfect, but we got something good."

As one, perhaps predictable result of *Bird*, Rodney noted, "I get complaints now: 'Mr. Rodney, you're not playing enough bebop.' And I have to laugh. Years ago when you played it, you couldn't get a job. Now, you see a grey-haired couple sitting in the corner, and he's saying, 'Martha, they're playing our song.' It's wonderful..."

There is a further irony here — that Rodney, of all people, should be drawn back to the music of the 1940s. He is, he admitted, working up a Bird medley, but he has long maintained that a musician shouldn't be trapped in history.

Yes, his first set at East 85th included some brisk, classic bop (Parker's impossible *Little Willie Leaps*), but it also featured two colour co-ordinated originals (Gary

Dial's *No Turn on Red* and Bobby Shew's *The Red Snapper*), a doloroso ballad dedicated to Chet Baker and a couple of timeless classics, *Love Letters* and *The Night Has a Thousand Eyes.*

Rodney played them with a kittenish tone and coltish enthusiasm as appropriate, turning perfect, lariat-like figures overhead in the high register and spinning knottier lines below. Few of bop's surviving early figures — drummers Max Roach and Roy Haynes come to mind — can still match the trumpeter on sheer form.

"Bebop of the Nineties" Rodney calls his music. "We're still bebop soloists; our improvisational ideology stems from that. But I've delved a lot into the younger music and I'm influenced by it. I'm 62, going on 35. At least the mind feels that way; the body sometimes doesn't."

That sounds like Dizzy Gillespie's standard line — the one about being 71, "going on 22." But, Rodney objected, "Dizzy hasn't changed his music." He softened almost immediately. "Of course, why should he have to change? He's Dizzy. Look what he's done. Many of my contemporaries haven't [changed]. And God bless 'em — if they're in their comfort zone, what they've done is enough. I don't feel that way. I feel I have to continue growing. My greatest years — my main improvement — have been between the ages of 50 and 60. Most people start sliding at that age."

Indeed, Rodney's is an altogether remarkable story, one that he is putting into shape as an autobiography. It has already drawn some "very good nibbles" of interest from Hollywood — one in fact from Clint Eastwood. The story, which began in Philadelphia and continued through clubs in New York, prison in Lexington, Kentucky, and showbands in Las Vegas, has now brought him comfortably to New Milford, New Jersey.

The theme, clearly, is survival. Survival and growth. "I happen to think, and this is speculation, that if Bird had lived, and had been reasonably healthy, he would have grown also. He would have embraced many of the new reforms. He was a very serious artist. I really believe that. Max Roach has grown. Roy Haynes has. For as many that haven't, we have as many that have. And that's great."

April 13, 1989

"Spontaneous architecture"
Walsh/Underhill Duo (1989)

For the first time in the four years that the Festival International de Jazz de Montréal's Concours de Jazz Alcan has been held on a national basis, a Toronto in Toronto entry, the Walsh/Underhill Duo, would seem to have a better than outside chance of coming away the winner.

For one thing, it's a bravely original effort, comprising one trombone player (Tom Walsh, leader of NOMA), one saxophonist (Richard Underhill, mastermind of the Shuffle Demons), a handful of melodic ideas and a lot of imagination. For another, there's no clear-cut favourite this year, as Saskatoon's Jon Ballantyne was in 1986, Vancouver's Hugh Fraser in 1987 or Jeff Johnston from St. John's in 1988. For a third, there's always the element of surprise in these affairs. Johnston, for example, didn't win after all.

But let's not get too carried away about this. The competition's mandatory test piece is *Parker's Mood*, a 40-year-old bebop line. And the competition's jury is headed by the U.S. vibraphonist Gary Burton, who's as conservative as he is popular.

Enter Walsh and Underhill, a tall team of a year's standing. Just moments after their short opening set for Bill Grove's Not King Fudge at the BamBoo in Toronto on Monday night, they were acknowledging the influence of contemporary theorist Anthony Braxton on their creative thinking and coining the verb "comprovise" to describe their creative procedure.

"Somebody says free improvisation," noted Underhill, "and everybody immediately starts squeaking and honking as hard as they can. We're trying to think along more compositional lines, where we'll take a certain phrase — it may even include a squeak or a honk — and that becomes thematic material we can work with and explore..."

Walsh cut it: "... trying lots of space and stuff. Basically it's like architecture, spontaneous architecture. That's what we do."

Spontaneous architecture. The Alcan folks will love that. All this, of course, to say that Walsh/Underhill deals in free improvisation, yes, but also in form. Songs, in fact. Some, like the half-dozen in the BamBoo set, are of their own making — riffs and rhythms given bumptious, braying performances. Some, notably the Ellington-Bigard collaboration *Mood Indigo*, are jazz classics. So maybe this competition business isn't really all that far fetched.

Walsh admitted to being skeptical about entering the "Central" (Ontario) regional run-off back in February. Underhill, however, took a more practical view. It is, he noted, the first year that duos have been eligible and, moreover, the competition has been taking "a fairly standard direction... I felt that maybe they'd be interested in a change, that maybe the people in the higher-up bureaucracy would be interested in a change for the health of the..."

Walsh cut in again:"... to legitimize it, really.You can't avoid Ornette Coleman and Cecil Taylor and Anthony Braxton — not in modern [jazz] anyway."

On va voir, as they say in Montreal. We'll see.★

June 7, 1989

"Sidelong"
Sarah Vaughan (1989)

First, it was send out the Kleenex. Later on, it was *Send in the Clowns*. Singer Sarah Vaughan covered all the bases, from impetuosity to high drama, during a routinely smashing performance Monday night before a full house at Roy Thomson Hall in Toronto.

One tune, maybe two, into her 90-minute set,Vaughan discovered that her tissue box was not in its proper place on George Gaffney's piano.

"I don't have my Kleenex!" she announced in mock horror. Sarah without her Kleenex, she said, was like Linus ("Who's that little guy in *Peanuts*?") without his blanket. "I'll go crazy!" she warned.

A box of Kleenex was delivered from the wings, and Vaughan marked its arrival with a short tantrum of tissue pulling, leaving the stage littered with small, white squares. Behind the big voice, there's a little girl who slips free and runs wild for a few moments at a time.

Monday's performance was, in this and most other respects, typical. That little girl took quick advantage of whatever was at hand, or not at hand as the case may be, to have some fun with her audience, her musicians and even the poor guy up in the Gods aiming the spotlight. Everything and everyone, it seemed, was fair game for her sidelong glances, and this small degree of apparent unpredictability worked well against the otherwise set patterns of her program.

The big voice, meanwhile, made short work of the fast tunes and lingered longer over her ballads. Contrary to common practice, the former served as breathers between the latter; the ballads represent Vaughan's toughest tasks and highest achievements. Her tonal control and her four-octave range were not merely put on display, they were invariably put to good use, integral elements of her interpretative approach rather than simply highlights of her technical skill.

★ The 1989 Concours de Jazz Alcan was won by the Vancouver quintet Fifth Avenue.

For much of the evening, though, Vaughan remained emotionally evasive. Her impetuosity was never far from the most dramatic of her songs except, finally, the most dramatic of all, *Send in the Clowns*. She even generated a few laughs in the poignant *Someone to Watch over Me*, apparently "forgetting" the Gershwin lyrics at one point and improvising her way out of trouble. The ballad nevertheless sparked the evening's first ovation.

Her version of Stephen Sondheim's *Clowns*, meanwhile, is now definitive. Although she has presented it more effectively on other occasions, a singer who reaches magnificence as often as Vaughan has with this particular song must be allowed, on occasion, merely to achieve greatness.

June 28, 1989

"Ladies first"
Michel Petrucciani (1989)

It was back in 1984 when Michel Petrucciani first made his mark on the Festival International de Jazz de Montréal. The tiny French pianist found, and quickly stole, the very heart of this huge event.

Five years later, he has returned with kind words for a festival that now, on the occasion of its 10th anniversary, hails him as one of its discoveries. "It's bigger and bigger," he said on Wednesday, suitably impressed.

Indeed, the festival has become so big that Petrucciani's latest visit went largely unnoticed: Montreal and, to a degree, jazz have turned their attention elsewhere in the interim, leaving him to face a small, uninterested gathering of the press during the afternoon and something less than a full house for his trio's concert with vibraphonist Gary Burton as its guest at the Théâtre St-Denis in the evening.

He has not, however, lost his dark-eyed charm. "Ladies first," he advised, peering up at the press conference microphones, when the first question was slow to come. And he certainly has not lost his physical domination of the piano, improbable though it may seem from someone a scant three feet tall; if anything, he has regained some of his early, explosive form.

Gone, though, is the degree of surprise that greeted his first performances in Europe during the late 1970s and the early 1980s in the United States with the quartet of reedman Charles Lloyd and, by 1984, on his own. It made Petrucciani a major story in jazz at mid-decade, after Wynton Marsalis and before Stanley Jordan. Five years further on, though, he's simply another remarkably good jazz pianist, which is very likely how he would have wanted it all along.

He lives in New York now — he was travelling out of California in 1984 — and he talks the American line on jazz, getting the words "art" and "products" into the same thought without apparent strain. To wit, on the effect of his nine years in the United States: "The music is definitely an American art form. I've met so many great musicians, I've learned a lot, and it's easier to put products together. I believe that if you want to be creative and on top of what's happening today, you have to be in the United States."

His performance at the Théâtre St-Denis echoed, in its sheer exuberance, his impressive FIJM debut five years ago. He has taken a more introspective line on piano jazz in the years between — and there was a little of it again in his *In a Sentimental Mood* here — but the old fire has returned.

There were several excited, mid-solo outbursts from the St-Denis audience as he developed the tension of his solos to a peak, sidestepped the breaking point and began the process anew at yet another level. He is a master at the repeated pattern — a rhythm or a melody, short in either case but worked over exhaustively and often reduced to single note or two, jack-hammered home at length.

With any given solo complete, and the tune in the hands of his bassist, Andy McKee, or his drummer, Victor Jones, Petrucciani would slip off the piano bench, stand at the far end and look on, leaning over the black leather padding just as anyone else might lean over the back-yard fence.

Enter Gary Burton. Or rather — in the oddest of sights — enter his vibraphone, emerging lengthwise, pipe by pipe, from the wings, Burton pushing from behind. Initially, his cool, methodical mallet work tended to slow Petrucciani down, but the natural urgency in the pianist's playing was infectious and both musicians were digging in enthusiastically before their third tune together was complete.

It was, in total, a triumphant performance for Petrucciani, no matter how little or much attention Montreal was paying this time around. Or why. At least one reporter, earlier that day, was still apparently not quite sure what to make of the man. "Would you mind telling us how old you are?" she asked finally, making a last effort to put him in *some* sort of context.

Petrucciani, already about a dozen years in the business, replied, "I'm 26, going on 27," and a degree of surprise registered in the room. Not quite to the degree that was once the case, but surprise nonetheless.

July 7, 1989

"Copacetic"
Steve Lacy (1990)

Had Steve Lacy left jazz in the late 1960s, he would be remembered as one of the early champions of Thelonious Monk's wonderful compositions and, perhaps secondarily, as the soprano saxophonist whose example inspired John Coltrane to take up the then-neglected straight horn for himself.

Of course Lacy, now 55, didn't leave jazz in the late 1960s at all. He left New York — first for Italy and then France, settling in Paris by 1970 and continuing to add to the list of quietly provocative things for which he will be remembered.

"Monk was my model — my model composer, bandleader and soloist," Lacy was saying last week from Los Angeles during a layover on the North American tour that will bring his quintet to Toronto for two shows at the Clinton Tavern. "I used his work as a model before I could do my own. So his work is behind mine... underneath it."

Even now, Lacy's study of Monk's music is not exactly complete. "I still mess with it," he admitted, adding that he recently recorded a follow-up★ to 1985's marvellous *Only Monk* (Soul Note), an album exclusively of solo soprano distillations of nine Monk tunes. His first all-Monk album, *Reflections* (New Jazz), dates back to 1958. Lacy would work briefly with the pianist himself two years later.

Of course, there's nothing unique about Monk-only sessions, especially in the years since the composer's death in 1982. But Lacy remembers another time. "In '55, when I really started getting into his music, it was an esoteric thing. Only musicians knew about it, and then only a few musicians... Now, I can hear his music in my supermarket."

With both Monk and the United States behind him, if only in a manner of speaking, Lacy's own work began. "In America," he remembered, "first of all, I wasn't able to have a band that stayed together; second of all, I wasn't able to get enough work for it; third of all, I couldn't develop my own music — it was too crowded in New York, too crowded with other musics."

In France, on the other hand, he has been encouraged to be himself. He recently received a commission from the government, for example, to write a piece about the French Revolution. "And there have been other situations like that," he noted. "Working with dancers, painters, poets... these things seem more possible there than they are [in America] — more usual."

The commissioned piece, *Prelude and Anthem*, has been released on the album *Anthem*, Lacy's third and latest for the RCA Novus label that has finally brought back

★ Issued as *More Monk* (Soul Note).

to North America on a reliable basis the fruits of his European labours. And the French government certainly got a good bang for its buck. *Prelude and Anthem* is a tribute to three revolutions at once: to the French Revolution, naturally, to the Russian Revolution (from which Lacy has drawn his text in the form of a poem written in 1918 by Ossip Mandelstam) and to the so-called October Revolution in modern jazz of 1964, whose freedoms Lacy and his musicians re-explore 25 years later.

"Revolution is a process," Lacy commented of the connection, "and there are certain similarities between all revolutions. When things get stifling, and when the desire for change becomes irresistible, it explodes..."

Lacy himself was there back in 1964, standing a little to the rear and the right of the Archie Shepps and Cecil Taylors, then as now bringing a dry intelligence, and a preference for fine detail over sweeping emotion, to contemporary jazz.

One revolution in a career, however, is apparently enough. "I'm not about to undertake another one," Lacy advised, "because we're not at that stage. We're not at all stifled. The exact opposite: we're coming in very well, we're realizing what we want to do, and the people are digging it. Everything is copacetic, so there's no reason for revolution right now in our case. There may be another camp of grumbly people ready to make a revolution, but I don't know about it."

Prelude and Anthem, unfortunately, is too complex a work for Lacy and his four musicians — vocalist and violinist Irene Aebi, saxophonist Steve Potts, bassist Jean-Jacques Avenel and drummer John Betsch — to play on tour. (The band's sixth member, pianist Bobby Few, is sidelined with a pinched nerve in his left hand.) Nor is there any Monk in the current repertoire, although Lacy acknowledged, "I always have that with me."

Instead he will draw on other material from the Novus releases, including his tunes *Number One* (dedicated to James Brown), *The Mantel* (with text by Irish-Canadian poet Mary Frazee), *The Bath* and *Blinks*. As well, a few earlier pieces have been reworked for the group. Altogether, it's a "mixture of old, middle and new" from Lacy's European period.

Incidentally, those concise titles — a single word, sometimes two, rarely three — may also follow Lacy into history. They're no accident. Indeed they reflect the feeling for essentials, for getting to the point, that dominates all the saxophonist's work. "There's so much verbiage in the world and personally I have no patience with long titles."

Charles Mingus, it was suggested, must have had him shaking his head. "Yeah," he agreed, citing Mingus' *The Shoes of the Fisherman's Wife Are Some Jive Ass Slippers* as an example. "I like poetry and all that, but I like very brief, succinct poetry best. I'm really more into boiling things down."

April 28, 1990

"Begat"
Ray Anderson (1990)

The names came slowly. "Vic Dickenson... Trummy Young... Frank Rosolino... Jack Teagarden..."

Ray Anderson, the brash New York trombonist who played the du Maurier Ltd. International Jazz Festival in Vancouver on Thursday, was tracing his musical forebears. A little reluctantly, it seemed.

"'Tricky Sam' [Nanton] and Lawrence Brown and Quentin Jackson and Jimmy Knepper... to *start*. That's only my 'slip horn' parentage. Then there's Louis [Armstrong], Coleman Hawkins, Roy Eldridge, Sonny Rollins..."

Anderson, 38, had raised the issue himself in a roundabout way. The trombonist of the hour, and quite possibly of the decade — either the '80s or the '90s, perhaps both — was challenging the prevailing view of jazz history as a linear concept.

"It's also very important to see the history in a more, say, circular way — as styles in space. Because what you really have in jazz is a history of people who succeed in being very much themselves. And when they do that, they become timeless. If you put on the Louis Armstrong and Fatha Hines [1928] *Weather Bird* duet, it doesn't sound dated. So it can be tricky to get too much into this linearity thing — 'he begat him, who begat him, who begat...' It's true in one sense, but what you really have are stylists."

It would be safe to say at this point that Ray Anderson himself has reached this same status of 'stylist,' and that he is now 'begetting' younger trombonists. It would be no less lacking in risk to suggest that he is one of the true characters of his generation in jazz, although this would prove more apparent in his gregarious performance with pianist Fumio Itabashi, bassist Mark Dresser and drummer Dion Parson at the Vancouver East Cultural Centre than it was in a quick chat over a late, take-out lunch a few hours earlier.

Anderson held the small stage at the "Cultch" with a patrolling sort of swagger, as though it were a street corner to be staked out against all comers. There was both boldness and self-deprecation to his manner, and a little of Louis Armstrong, which may seem odd coming from a white kid born in Chicago and first drawn to the jazz avant-garde in California. He's a hyper chap, and his extravagant trombone playing can be ridiculously good or just ridiculous.

There's also the small matter of his singing. On his most recent album, *What Because*, the song is *I'm Just a Lucky So and So*. On Thursday, the song was *Comes Love*, sung with great panache, as well as a touch of Louis Armstrong on the "Yeah... yeah..." and some startling, siren-like multiphonics — these are Anderson's alone — at just the right dramatic moments.

And who begat Ray Anderson the singer?

"Now that's a good question. I don't know where *that* mother came from."

Perhaps Ray Anderson the trombonist begat Ray Anderson the singer? "Yeah, that's right. I just started doing it without the horn. It's definitely the same thing. In fact it was when I had Bell's Palsy in 1983 and couldn't play the trombone that I started doing a lot of singing. I had sung before, in funk bands and with [the early 1980s band] Slickaphonics, but in '83, when the horn was *down*, I said, 'Well, what've we got left?'"

One way or another — the trombone playing, the singing, the four disparately original compositions that he contributed to his Vancouver set — Anderson is moving on a broad front. He takes exception to the idea that jazz musicians in the vanguard these days seem to be more concerned with reworking the known than with seeking the unknown.

"It sounds insulting to say, 'Well, all they're doing is mixing up elements, and there's nothing new happening...Jazz is no longer monolithic in the sense that one guy can come along — let's say, Bird or Ornette — and do one thing, and then everybody instantly follows that direction... or doesn't. It's no longer pointed that way. It's much more diffuse, and I think that's positive. To me that's healthy. I mean, I never heard anything exactly like the music I'm playing. You can call it a combination of different elements, but it's new."

And it does seem to make quite an impression.

As Anderson paused in the middle of his spirited performance at the "Cultch" for a swig from a plastic water bottle, a voice in the hall called out, "What have you *got* in there?"

This time the response came quickly.

"Jet fuel."

June 30, 1990

"Larger and smaller"
Paul Motian (1990)

Nearly 30 years have passed since Paul Motian participated in an important moment in jazz history as the drummer on the celebrated Bill Evans recordings from the Village Vanguard in New York. He has played in many other settings during the years since — the Paul Bley, Charlie Haden and Keith Jarrett bands, for three — but jazz history has a way of freezing musicians in place. For his work in the Evans trio, Motian, now 59, will be forever known as a drummer of subtlety and intuition, a masterful brushman with a colourist's instinct to match — a group player.

So there was Motian, sticks in hand from time to time Saturday night at the Euclid Theatre in Toronto, drumming away like a kid who has just found his first set of traps under the Christmas tree. So much for subtlety. So much for intuition. So much for history.

This, too, was a trio performance. Guitarist Bill Frisell and tenor saxophonist Joe Lovano complete a band that has been scaled down from a Motian quintet dating to the early '80s. If less hasn't exactly become more in this case, it still proves to be enough.

There is an openness to the instrumentation, and to Motian's use of it, that leaves sufficient room for his occasional boyish enthusiasms. The drummer controls the scale — the size — of the music closely, expanding and contracting the working space available to his sidemen from one piece to the next. To this extent, at least, Motian set the evening's agenda. The music was otherwise a co-operative effort.

The "smaller" of his pieces generally worked best. (The program, which passed entirely without comment from the drummer, included several Motian originals — some with their worried, Ornette Coleman-like melodies — as well as Thelonious Monk's *Reflections* and *Misterioso*, and a closing standard, *It Might as well Be Spring*.)

Invariably, Motian had his brushes out: they have a degree of pliability that complimented well the lyricism that Frisell and Lovano summoned up in such subdued situations. The drummer's rustlings and scurryings outlined a tune's dimensions softly, and in a manner that would give way slightly under the others' melodic probings.

This, in marked contrast to the rigidity of Motian's stick work, which chopped out large spaces for Frisell and Lovano and, at the same time, cut them off rather summarily — in effect offering them more room in which to move but finally giving them less. Motian alternated between sticks and brushes — between larger and smaller — before settling on the latter for most of the concert's second, and markedly stronger half.

Frisell and Lovano were responsive to both the freedoms and limitations that Motian established. Frisell, in the course of his trademark sonic warps and careful timbral manipulations, replayed the modern history of the guitar in jazz and popular music. It was a discontinuous replay, perhaps, but ultimately a complete one, and evidence once again of Frisell's pre-eminence among the guitarists of his generation.

Lovano, in turn, was more systematic in his improvisations, but drew just as resourcefully on the tenor tradition of the past 40 years. Both men seemed to keep somewhat under wraps in this setting and placed themselves second to the good of the group as a whole — rather the way Paul Motian did with Bill Evans 30 years ago. In this respect, at least, a tradition continues.

September 11, 1990

"Careering"
Jabbo Smith (1991)

Jabbo Smith died recently. His was not one of the great names of jazz history, but it was certainly one of the better ones. His mother called him Cladys, which is probably why everyone else preferred Jabbo, and he played the trumpet. In his prime, 60-odd years ago, the Georgia-born Smith was as spectacularly showy as Louis Armstrong and as boldly unpredictable as Henry "Red" Allen, if not quite as fundamentally melodic as either of his rivals from New Orleans. Just turned 82 at the time of his death last month in Manhattan, Smith was the last surviving virtuoso trumpet soloist from the earliest years of recorded jazz.

It may be, though, that the *example* of Smith's career has clearer echoes in 1991 than does the brilliance of his trumpeting. Not for the first time, jazz history seems to be repeating itself: what happened to Smith, whose later years found him renting cars for Avis in Milwaukee, could happen to any of today's young musicians who dare to be different.

Smith was ahead of his time when he played in New York with Duke Ellington on a single recording date in 1927, and when he made a handful of marvellous sides in Chicago with his own Rhythm Aces in 1929. That's very early in the history of jazz to be in the avant-garde. To that point, the line of development in jazz ran straight and it ran narrow; any deviation, however modest it may seem 60 years later, would not have gone unremarked and Smith played the trumpet in a particularly careering way.

It was in fact a point of honour with Smith that he played the trumpet like no one else. That made him one of those paradoxical figures in jazz history, a non-conformist in a music that has raised non-conformity to a high art. There are, of course, acceptable limits to non-conformity in jazz, as Thelonious Monk and Ornette Coleman, for two, would find — and fight — in later years.

It didn't help Smith's cause that the Depression hit just as Brunswick Records began to groom him as an Armstrong rival. After he cut the prophetic *Till Times Get Better* with his Aces in April of 1929, he did not record again as a leader until

1938. By then, Armstrong had moved beyond challengeable reach and jazz had simply moved elsewhere.

And it didn't help that Smith was known as a "difficult" personality, inclined to do everything, not just music, his own way. Typically, at a time when the usual route of professional migration in jazz ran south to north — via St. Louis or Kansas City to Chicago and New York — Smith went more or less east to west, from Philadelphia in 1925 through Atlantic City, New York and Chicago, and on to Milwaukee as early as 1930. So began his slow slide into obscurity: Smith would eventually spend 13 years with Avis.

The drift of Jabbo Smith's career should be a caution to a young musician in 1991, when the development of jazz is moving again on the straight and narrow. Just as the influence of Louis Armstrong was central to the late 1920s, the influence of a younger New Orleans trumpeter, Wynton Marsalis, dominates these early '90s. Arguably Marsalis' influence is even broader: his active support for the music's traditional values and his expressed disdain for the avant-garde have left little room for those of his contemporaries who would differ with this new conservatism.

There is, as a result, a growing number of young conformists whose particular point of honour is their very emulation of other musicians. Some, notably the New Orleans trumpeter Marlon Jordan, have gone as far as to emulate Marsalis. If, in 1991, no one yet has emerged to play Jabbo to Wynton's Louis, it may simply be too much to expect that he, or she, would be given much of a hearing in this reactionary climate — not, in any event, at the competitive, major-label level of recording necessary to present a real challenge to the status quo. Indeed it remains to be seen whether this new generation will make any breakthroughs of its own or whether its neo-traditionalism will simply stand as the barrier for a still younger generation to storm.

The Jabbo Smith story, meanwhile, does have a happy ending. He was rediscovered in Milwaukee during the 1970s and fêted as only surviving jazz veterans are. There were honours at home, tours abroad and three years in the Broadway musical *One Mo' Time*. After putting his horn down for good in 1983, Smith sang on occasion with another one-time avant-gardist, the trumpeter Don Cherry — the same Don Cherry who had been at Ornette Coleman's side during the tumultuous late 1950s. Smith and Cherry were, by all accounts, a most sympathetic pairing. Of course.

February 20, 1991

"Illusions"
Bobby Hutcherson (1991)

By and large, jazz musicians are all audio and no visual. The late Dexter Gordon was a notable exception, a man with a magnetic presence on stage. Bobby Hutcherson, the vibraphonist at the Top O' The Senator in Toronto this week, is another — in fact a kind of Dexter Gordon on fast-forward.

The two were label mates with Blue Note in its golden age 25 years ago and Hutcherson more recently appeared with Gordon in Bertrand Tavernier's film *Round Midnight* and on what proved to be the tenorman's farewell tour that followed. He is, as Gordon was, a joy to watch, and no less a joy to watch.

Consider the mechanics of playing the vibraphone: mallet head hits metal bar. That's about it, apart from a little footwork on the sustain pedal. Hutcherson, however, suggests a whole range of tones and colours through the liberal application of Body English — lazy sideswipes and vicious slashes, great flourishes, exaggerated forearm loops, a sag at the knees, a slow down-stroke and quick uptake, and furious tattoos that sustain a single pitch or note cluster for a full chorus.

The entire performance is accompanied by ever-changing facial expressions that are given unnatural, though highly effective illumination as the stage lights overhead reflect up off those metal bars below. Suddenly, the vibraphone seems like the most responsive musical instrument in jazz.

If some part of this is just an illusion, it's a good one. And even without it, Hutcherson would be an intense, exciting improviser. His preferred tempo during Tuesday night's opening set was "up," and he employed it in a variety of rhythmic and structural settings, including Cedar Walton's *Bolivia*, Miles Davis' *No Blues* and his own *Little B's Poem*, all handled with great ease by his trio of Ed Simon (piano), David Williams (bass) and Victor Lewis (drums). But he, and they, also proved no less capable of the poignancy required of a song once associated with Billie Holiday, *For Heaven's Sake*, which by comparison had scarcely any tempo at all.

The more common illusion in this performance, though, was one of great hurry — of balance lost and of balance regained. The vibraphonist seemed to be forever running back up onstage and catching the downbeat on the fly just as Simon wound up another fine solo. Hutcherson never missed his cue: his timing was precise and his flare for the dramatic quite brilliant.

June 6, 1991

"Sensible"
Rosemary Clooney (1991)

Now Rosemary Clooney is a sensible gal. "The glasses?" she asked rhetorically, and perhaps a little self-consciously, Monday night at Roy Thomson Hall, almost as soon as she had sung her way to centre stage and started talking with the audience. Clooney is a good talker, a very good talker, with an endearing line of self-deprecation. "It's a question," she declared, "of vanity or of walking off the front of the stage." Clooney has made her choice. It comes with attractive red frames.

Sensible gal that she is, Clooney took it as a point of order to set right the first wrong of the evening — and the only wrong, as it turned out — as quickly as possible. The five musicians already onstage — the Concord Jazz All Stars, and Clooney's co-stars — had gone without anything more than a collective introduction.

From the first newspaper ads for Clooney's appearance as a headliner in this week's du Maurier Ltd. Downtown Jazz festival to the entrance of the All Stars themselves at Roy Thomson Hall, not a musician's name had been mentioned. Only from the smallest print in the festival program could the curious learn that on this occasion they would be cornetist Warren Vaché, tenor saxophonist Scott Hamilton, pianist John Oddo, bassist Steve Wallace and drummer Joe Cocuzzo. Their presence, had it been more widely known, might have filled out an audience that came up several hundred shy of a full house.

Eyewear duly noted, Clooney made the introductions immediately. And well she might. The All Stars, with Vaché and Hamilton in pivotal solo and obbligato roles, would contribute substantially to the evening, playing a brief warmup set on their own and providing the singer with stellar accompaniment. But there's more to the All Stars' role here than met the ear: without them, and without the many other jazz musicians who have backed Clooney on her Concord Jazz recordings in recent years, there very likely wouldn't have even been an evening in the first place. Clooney's unpretentious performance should be welcome on most any stage, but it's the Concord connection that makes her particularly welcome these days on a jazz festival stage.

Until recently hers has been the career of the pop singer. She had several hits during the early 1950s and sang two of them more or less in passing on Monday, *Hey There* and *Come on-a My House*. Latterly, however, she has moved to the classics of the American pop song repertoire, and the pairing of her forthright vocal manner with the straightforward mainstream jazz of Vaché, Hamilton *et al.* has revitalized her career. The common element in this match seems to be rhythm. It's certainly not risk: both parties swing but only the musicians improvise.

Clooney's program on Monday was divided roughly between the songs of Irving Berlin — rather, Mister Berlin — and the Second World War-era material from her latest Concord album, *For the Duration*. Cole Porter — rather, Mister Porter — was also represented, once with *Don't Fence Me In* (written, she noted, for Roy Rogers and given a little whinny by Vaché as he set off on yet another near-perfect cornet solo) from *For the Duration*, and once with *Miss Otis Regrets*.

Her use of the formal "Mister" is a measure of the respect she brings to this music. She's careful not to overdo her material, preferring interpretations that tend to be unfussy over those with ambitions or implications that some listener somewhere might find inappropriate. She takes few liberties with a song, at least until her voice tires and she begins to level off the contours of a melody just a little. No, Clooney has her fun between songs, skillfully drawing the audience onside by working and reworking the airs and conventions of showbiz.

There's no business like it, she sang, quoting Mister Berlin to bring her first set to a rousing close. Came time to finish the second, though, she turned those conventions on their head. First she discouraged a standing ovation. "That's all right guys," she said, shooing the folks rising on the ground floor back into their seats. Then she declined to make the traditional walk into the wings and back before singing an encore. "It would be," she advised, "a waste of my time and yours."

Sensible, right?

June 26, 1991

"Hand in hand"
Carla Bley and Steve Swallow (1991)

If you were to ask the readers of *Down Beat* what they thought about this, that and the other, something that the respected Chicago magazine in fact does around this time of year, you would find that in their advised opinion Carla Bley is the premier composer and arranger in jazz. Moreover, according to the current *Down Beat* readers' poll, Steve Swallow, who is partnered with Bley both in real life and at the Bermuda Onion in Toronto until tomorrow night, is the top bass guitarist.

Down Beat, apparently, doesn't reach Toronto. Or no one here reads it. For all of their documented fan support, Bley and Swallow surveyed only a small audience as they began their first set of a rare, four-night club engagement on Thursday.

Now, Bley's honours have come in connection with her big band and her writing for Charlie Haden's Liberation Music Orchestra, and for Gary Burton, the Jazz Composers' Orchestra and Paul Bley before it. At the Onion, however, she is playing piano, a skill about which *Down Beat* readers have expressed no opinion at all, save possibly by omission.

To hear her playing her own compositions — *Sing Me Softly of the Blues*, *Copyright Royalties* and *Fleur Carnivore*, to name three in a set that also included Swallow's *Masquerade* — is not unlike hearing a famous author reading from her best-known works. Finally it's less important how well she does it than simply the fact that she's the one who's doing it.

In truth, this is one of the Bley-Swallow duo's charms. The compositions themselves are another — Swallow's no less than Bley's, for that matter. They have lovely, attenuated melodies that move gracefully over shifting harmonic and/or rhythmic ground. Their sudden drops and gradual swells create just a hint of tension, neatly dissolved with the mere jog of a phrase.

The Swallow bass guitar is the third of the duo's attractions, a warm, understated voice to go with the skeleton-like framework established by Bley at the piano. All that's missing — it's a lot actually — is some flesh for the bones, a body for the voice. This is where the Bley big band usually comes in, and where Bley's stiff elaborations-as-solos weren't a quite sufficient replacement.

Bley and Swallow were nevertheless very much in tune as a duo. Even the things that seemed contrary — her hard piano, his elastic bass, her clunky chords, his undulating lines — were an effective rather than negating match. The playing had its limitations, particularly in terms of tempos and expressivity, but these in turn gave it a degree of intimacy that matched perfectly the image of Bley and Swallow leaving the stage and walking all the way back to the far corner of the club hand in hand.

November 30, 1991

"Rules"
Betty Carter (1991)

In jazz, there are rules for singers, just as there are rules for everyone else. There have to be rules. There has to be something to break, right? Singers, who may have more rules than most, seem least inclined to break them, which may be one reason why the notion of the "jazz singer" sits in doubt with some jazz fans. After all, one of the rules in jazz is expressly this: break the rules.

Enter Betty Carter with a sardonic smile. The tempo is up. Her musicians already have established themselves as a superior trio, well up to the reputation that Carter trios long have held. Her first utterance onstage is an explosion of scatted syllables. The explosion passes, but the scatting continues for a good 10 minutes, interrupted only briefly on three occasions for the passing introduction of her side-men — "Clarence Penn, drums," and later "Ariel Roland, bass," and finally, "Cyrus Chestnut, piano."

Carter, the Detroit-born singer who was given the nickname "Betty Bebop" by Lionel Hampton more than 40 years ago, started her first set at the Bermuda Onion on Tuesday night in just this manner. The Onion is a new room for Carter, who last appeared in Toronto at the Top O' The Senator, and, who knows, this could have been in some part a new audience. Her reputation as a singer does continue to grow.

Play it safe, then? Get a sense of the audience's expectations, or lack of same? Break it to them gently? Not on your life, or hers. Carter was into the deep end from the downbeat. She took everyone in the place with her.

"I guess you think I can't sing any songs with words," she asked, 10 minutes later, still in her singing voice. "It's not true. I just get carried away." As proof, she sang *The Good Life*. "I recorded it a long time ago," she explained, singing her intro-duction. "So did Tony Bennett." Pause. "Guess who made the money?"

Well, yes, but guess who followed the rules? Or at least the melody. Carter invariably has other ideas, and often better ones; were royalties handed out after a typical Carter performance, the songwriters involved would be entitled to at best half, so substantial is her contribution to the songs in their final form.

Consider the word "goodbye," as in *Every Time We Say Goodbye*, which she sang after *The Good Life*. Just two syllables — one hard, and one softer — and two notes. Carter at one point managed seven or eight notes and three or four shades of sor-row between the "good" and the "bye." Of course it helped that her chosen tempo for the Cole Porter ballad was luxuriously slow and allowed for such minutely detailed revisionism — such *stylized* revisionism.

Carter is as stylized as singers come in jazz. But it's a good and influential sort of stylization, one that slides off her voice in the most evocative of ways, accompa-nied by an awkwardly graceful and always expressive form of body language that alternately underlines and offsets in visual terms the forever shifting balances that she maintains in her singing.

Her arrangements make much of the element of suddenness, in particular the sharp stroke to the snare drum, in tandem with a chord change at the piano, that simply electrifies the moment. Inevitably, the most customary of the songs in her repertoire — *You Go to My Head* and *What a Little Moonlight Can Do*, for two, in Tuesday's 90-minute set — receive the most uncustomary of treatments. *Moonlight* especially has always been associated with Billie Holiday, an early model for Carter, no less than for any other singer coming up in jazz during the 1940s. It's not a song to be trifled with lightly, if at all. For Carter in her prime, though, that simply becomes another rule to break.

December 13, 1991

"Heroes"
Dave Frishberg (1992)

Tsongas. What rhymes with Tsongas? If anyone knows — if anyone *cares* at this stage of events in the race to head the Democratic ticket in the U.S. November elections — it's probably Dave Frishberg, the erudite songwriter, satirist, singer and jazz pianist who is in town from Portland, Ore., for a week at the Top O' The Senator.

Frishberg, 59, has made an art out of reducing — or, in some cases, elevating — America's concerns to rhyming couplets. Clinton and Brown are easy, but Tsongas, now *that's* a challenge. Frishberg could be working on it right now at the hotel, with his tapes of Ivie Anderson and the Duke Ellington Orchestra playing in the background. Just in case the former Massachusetts senator changes his mind again about running for president.

Frishberg, after all, is the fellow who wrote the nostalgic *Van Lingle Mungo*, whose lyrics consist of the names, and only the names, of early 20th-century baseball players. It's one of his classics, to be set alongside things like *Peel Me a Grape* and *My Attorney Bernie*, each a small masterpiece of word play.

Van Lingle Mungo wasn't among the 14 songs of Frishberg's first set Wednesday night at the Senator, but he did sing an equally nostalgic item about Christy Mathewson, who played for the New York Giants between 1900 and 1916. "Matty" was one of four "heroes" to whom Frishberg paid his respects early in the set. The aforementioned Bernie was another. Marilyn Monroe and Zoot Sims rounded out the quartet. A ball player, a lawyer, a Hollywood goddess and a tenor saxophonist; what could be more American than that?

Some of Frishberg's material wasn't quite so culturally specific. *You'd Rather Have the Blues, I Can't Take You Nowhere, Quality Time* and *Blizzard of Lies* are more generically pop psychology or pop sociology, as the case may be. But Frishberg also reviewed world events of the past four years in a song commissioned for the recent Winter Olympics; it may or may not be called *Report from the Planet Earth,** but typically it reflected a perspective as seen only from below the 49th Parallel.

* Indeed it is.

Frishberg even indulged in a little fashionably liberal America-bashing with a ditty based on a variant pledge of allegiance set to *Yankee Doodle*. (The fact that he wasn't in the United States doesn't seem to have entered into his performance at all. And, again, what could be more American than that? America's concerns are everybody's concerns, right?)

Frishberg's lyrics range from the literate through the witty and the clever to the merely cute. Their craftsmanship, in any event, makes a stronger impression than their message. He sings them in a direct, conversational manner that rarely gets in their way, and he supports them expertly at the piano.

Ah yes, the piano. Frishberg began his performing career as an accompanist in the 1960s to such substantial figures as Bud Freeman, Pee Wee Russell, Rex Stewart, Ben Webster, Al Cohn and Zoot Sims. Jazz still figures to some degree in his performances: there was a nifty solo Wednesday in his Sims tribute (based on the tenorman's unofficial theme, *Red Door*) and a loving instrumental medley of "music I listen to in my hotel room" — those songs that Ivie Anderson sang with Duke Ellington. These are more or less set-pieces now, though, like everything else in a Frishberg show; satire's gain, it seems, is increasingly jazz piano's loss.

April 10, 1992

"Firstness"
Original Dixieland Jazz Band:
The 75th Anniversary [CD] (1992)

It all started right here. Well, it had to start somewhere. Not jazz, but the commercialization of jazz. In late February of 1917 the Original Dixieland Jass (later Jazz) Band from New Orleans recorded *Livery Stable Blues* and *Dixieland Jass Band One-Step* for the Victor company in New York. By spring, the tunes were national hits. To the dismay of future historians, they were also the first examples of jazz on record to be marketed as such.

The historians' problem is twofold: the ODJB comprised five white musicians playing a music of recent, African-American origin and, moreover, playing it in a sensationalized manner that, for example, populated their "livery stable" with all manner of whinnying and mooing animals. Other, and presumably better, black musicians and bands would go unrecorded for several years more, while cornetist Nick LaRocca, trombonist Eddie Edwards, clarinetist Larry Shields, pianist Henry Ragas and drummer Tony Sbarbaro of the ODJB became rich and famous. Sound familiar?

History's solution has been to grant the ODJB recordings their "firstness" while denying them almost everything else. It might be argued, though, that the band's bright tempos, vigorous spirit, exaggerated effects and *lack* of improvisation were just what jazz needed to jump start the public's interest.

Esthetically, the 23 tunes from 1917 to 1921 reissued here on CD by RCA/Bluebird are neither curios nor classics. Originally released at intervals of up to a year, they suffer from the proverbial too much of a muchness when packaged together and spaced a few seconds apart. If the band had a limited interpretive range, though, it was still a tight, musicianly outfit, whatever its members' protestations were to the contrary. (LaRocca, knowing a good story when he told it, reportedly lamented the number of pianists the band had to audition before it finally found one who *couldn't* read music.) By 1925 it had broken up, effectively a victim of its own success. Better, in this case, a victim of success than of failure. Think about it: what if that first jazz record had been a flop?

May 4, 1992

"Five figures"
Red Richards (1993)

There was a certain irony, intended or not, to Charles (Red) Richards' rendition of the old Louis Armstrong hit *What A Wonderful World,* sung to a loudly uninterested crowd Tuesday night at the Montreal Bistro in Toronto. Richards followed, pointedly or not, with a minor item from the Billie Holiday repertoire, *I'm Fooling Myself.*

Who knows whether the New York pianist was putting an inside joke across to those few folks who were paying him any mind. Jazz musicians have been known to send out just such sly signals from the bandstand. Then again, these are precisely the sorts of songs that the amiable octogenarian has performed night after night for years. So let's call Richards' programming fortuitous. At the very least.

Actually, song titles are as good a place as any to look for real meaning in his performances. Richards' music is generally deeper in historical roots — Harlem piano jazz of the 1930s, to be specific — than it is in emotional implications. He plays engagingly across the surface of his classic American pop songs, keeping everything upbeat and chipper. The heaviest thing going is invariably his right foot, pounding solidly into the Bistro's carpeted floor.

His piano playing ripples lightly for the most part; the odd chord generates a little splash, but only the brightest of tempos develop a real rhythmic chop. His

Stéphane Grappelli, Toronto, 1981. Photograph by Mark Miller.

Benny Carter, Montreal, 1986. Photograph by Mark Miller.

Carla Bley, Montreal, 1983. Photograph by Mark Miller.

Ray Anderson, Toronto, 1996. Photography by Mark Miller.

Michel Petrucciani, Toronto, 1984. Photograph by Mark Miller.

Cassandra Wilson, Toronto, 1995. Photograph by Mark Miller.

Phil Minton, Montreal, 1990. Photograph by Mark Miller.

Enrico Rava, Toronto, 1997. Photograph by Mark Miller.

Han Bennink, Toronto, 1993. Photograph by Mark Miller.

singing voice, meanwhile, is almost beyond description, a high, spirited and moistly sibilant tenor with an unusually androgynous interpretive range — as well-suited, with its warm, lived-in rasp, to the songs of the great women in jazz as to those of the men.

Richards, of course, was on speaking terms with most of those women and men over the years, which is another way of saying that the man is living history, though you'd never guess by looking. Or listening. After countless versions of Fats Waller's *Honeysuckle Rose* — it must be into five figures — he's still not only interested but demonstrably enthused. And after almost as many versions of Waller's *Keepin' out of Mischief Now*, he still has a twinkle in his eye.

March 4, 1993

"Circus show"
Rabih Abou-Khalil (1993)

It is revealing of both Rabih Abou-Khalil and the Festival International de Jazz de Montréal that the Lebanese oud virtuoso should have made his North American debut here, of all possible places. World Music accounts for about 25 of the festival's nearly 400 concerts this year, a small portion of the total but still a large number as jazz festivals go. Abou-Khalil, for his part, claims greater comfort at jazz festivals than at World Music events.

"My audience is more a jazz audience," he was saying earlier this week, with the first of his sextet's two concerts at the Salle du Gesù behind him. He's an engaging, humorous man in his mid-30s — fluent, it seems, in several languages, English very impressively among them. "It's not the usual World Music audience," he continued. "That, on one hand, surprises me. But, on the other hand, I feel more flattered."

The jazz audience may well be attracted at first blush to Abou-Khalil's choice of frontline musicians — saxophonists Sonny Fortune and Charlie Mariano and trumpeter Kenny Wheeler on the recent CDs *Al-Jadida* and *Blue Camel* (both for Enja), tuba player Bob Stewart and harmonica player Howard Levy at the festival — as much as to the music itself, which is very much in the Arabic tradition.

The flattery involved is part of what Abou-Khalil described as the "higher quality standard" at jazz festivals. "I have some problems with what's called World Music in general," he noted, somewhat contentiously. "I find, especially where the quality of the musicians or the music is concerned, anything that is foreign and that can be called ethnic is okay, no matter how good it is."

Or — as Abou-Khalil's point surely is — how bad. His perspective on the matter is unique. As a boy in Lebanon he was exposed to his mother's Frank Sinatra records and his father's love of Arabic music. He studied both the oud and the flute in Beirut and, following the outbreak of the Lebanese civil war in 1978, the flute alone at the Munich Academy of Music. He continues to reside in Germany.

"I hate to admit it, but I'm actually a product of the West," he confessed. "My consciousness toward my own culture was actually shaped in the West. I came here and I studied classical music."

Eventually, however, he returned to the *oud* and to the Arabic traditions. "It's the thing I feel most comfortable with. It's like speaking a foreign language and then going up onstage, speaking your own language and finding out that the people understand *that* even better."

Abou-Khalil likes the analogy to language. It served him again to illustrate the manner in which he uses the jazz musicians in his employ. It's not, he said, "really what you call a 'fusion.' I ask them only to play Arabic music. It's like asking a Frenchman to speak English; he'd have an accent that would give it a texture and colour... I don't want [jazz musicians] to play jazz, I want them to play my music but the way *they* would interpret it."

There are two components to Abou-Khalil's music, as there are to all Arabic music — rhythm and melody, the latter based on as many as 300 different modes or scales, each with its own emotional weighting. "There is one for sad," he explained, now in French, at the Salle du Gesù. "There is one for very sad and one for *unbelievably* sad." The saddest of them all, he added, was the one he used to compose *Dream of a Dying City*, dedicated to Beirut.

Most of Abou-Khalil's concert was rather more upbeat, chugging along lightly — at times very lightly — atop the drumming of Ramesh Shotham (traps and pots), Nabil Khaiat (frame drum) and the Milton Cardona (congas). It took the heavier churn of Abou-Khalil's oud, however, to pull the formation together and really get it moving in these, the sextet's first public performances. (Next stop Amsterdam, and then on to Taiwan. This, travelling on a Lebanese passport...)

"It looks like a circus show," Abou-Khalil mused. "I was worried that people would wonder where the acrobats were. Tuba, harmonica, oud and the drums — this is a very strange thing. You might think it wouldn't come together."

Abou-Khalil, of course, was sure it would, right?

"I was *hoping*..."

No acrobats, but with Stewart's tuba and Levy's harmonica, the equivalent of an elephant and a mouse. Levy's cupped, bluesy style, heard in recent years with Bela Fleck and the Flecktones, was particularly effective in capturing the subtleties of a melodic tradition filled with little twists and small graces — a tradition in fact developed by a centuries-long succession of singers. Jazz instrumentalists, of course, have always shown a striking vocal quality in their playing; moreover, jazz musicians generally share Abou-Khalil's cosmopolitan view of the world.

"I find that jazz musicians never have problems listening to Arabic music," he noted. "I haven't met one who would say 'Turn that off.' You will hear that from classical musicians, but not from jazz musicians." Nor — judging by the warmth of his reception at the Salle du Gesù — from jazz audiences.

July 10, 1993

"A few tunes to play"
Bill Mays and Ed Bickert (1994)

Come Monday, pianist Bill Mays and guitarist Ed Bickert will be in Berkeley, California, to record for the Concord Jazz label's Maybeck Recital Hall series.★ For the moment, they're warming up at the Montreal Bistro in Toronto, trying — as Bickert mused before Tuesday's first set — "to find a few tunes to play."

It shouldn't be a problem. Not for two musicians capable of smart, bantering duets that come with plenty of quiet interludes but rarely the proverbial dull moment. And in fact Mays, who's up from New York, and Bickert, who's down from Scarborough, found seven tunes without as much as breaking a sweat in this, their opening set of the week.

Initially, they seemed to be freely associating song titles as they worked up something of a "foreplay" suite — Duke Ellington's *Prelude to a Kiss*, the Gershwins' *Embraceable You* and a second Ellington item, *Just Squeeze Me* — before Mays salvaged a PG rating for the performance with an off-topic ballad/waltz of his own. (Tune five? *Dancing in the Dark...*)

Actually, just about everything in a Mays-Bickert duet seems to be the product of free association. The level of improvisation involved is remarkably sophisticated, far above mundane concerns of style, roles, right notes and wrong notes. That's cerebral territory, to be sure, but between Bickert's bluesy streak and tidy swing, and Mays' crisp touch and quick sense of humour, the two musicians repeatedly bring the music down to earth.

They're a study both in co-operation and in contrasts as they trade responsibilities easily, playing bass lines, harmony and straight rhythm for one another's solos. Equally, they set each other up, and off. Bickert's soft chords cushion Mays' hard fingering; Mays' occasional irreverence (a jolly quote from *Sailor's Hornpipe*, for

★ Released as *Bill Mays/Ed Bickert*.

example, in the set's last tune, *Taking a Chance on Love*) plays off Bickert's air of solemnity. One way and the other, a Mays–Bickert duet usually stands complete. Whatever they leave out is not missed. Whatever they include seems exactly right.

March 3, 1994

"Textures"
Festival International de Jazz de Montréal (1994)

To appreciate the achievement of the Festival International de Jazz de Montréal, which concluded its 15th season on Sunday, is to stand at the top end of the *rue* Ste-Catherine strip that runs through the heart of the event's downtown site. There, as Ste-Catherine rises sharply between Jeanne-Mance and Bleury, is as good a vantage point as any to take in the grand *tableau* of Canada's largest and most successful jazz festival.

A half-block away, a FIJM sponsor's hot-air balloon hovers portentously. Flying overheard, a small airplane flashes "J-A-Z-Z" across the electronic sign under its wings. Down Ste-Catherine, a crowd in the tens of thousands, framed against the theatres of Place des Arts, has gathered before a large, temporary stage, perhaps 40 feet by 60, set at the corner of Jeanne-Mance. The band onstage might be the catholics, the Mighty Clouds of Joy, the Heavy Metal Horns or the Montreal orchestras of Denny Christianson and Vic Vogel. Actually, it might be *anybody* and it may or may not be playing jazz. As a former local club owner commented in the Montreal weekly, *Mirror*, before the festival began, "You have a band playing in front of 100,000 people and most of the crowd doesn't know who the hell is on stage."

Whether this is good, or bad, it's certainly an impressive marketing triumph in a city whose year-round jazz scene is relatively quiet. But consider this: the FIJM's promotional budget for 1994 was something on the order of $1.2-million, which is more than most — if not all — other Canadian jazz festivals spend for their entire operations. Indeed, the FIJM's revenues, which will exceed $8-million, would buy and pay for the next half-dozen largest events in the country.

Jazz has lent itself well to such elaborate enterprise. It's upscale enough to attract corporate sponsorship and enjoy civic forbearance, yet funky enough to draw the public in great numbers — a record 1.5 million this year, according to the festival's early tally. And it defines itself — or allows itself to *be* defined — so generally that there's room for a lot of other types of music that aren't strictly or even loosely speaking, jazz.

This last issue was raised at the festival's closing press conference on Sunday afternoon. How much of the music at the festival was actually jazz? "It's a question that comes year after year," vice-president André Ménard admitted. He harked back to the example of Irish rocker Van Morrison, whose presence in 1986 brought the festival such criticism. Morrison, he suggested, is closer in creative spirit to John Coltrane than to Paul McCartney; the popular saxophonist Kenny G, on the other hand, is the opposite, closer to Paul McCartney than to 'Trane. (Does this mean G doesn't have a future with the festival? *Damn.*)

Ménard spoke not in terms of traditions but of textures; a texture from jazz was enough for the festival to justify a music's or musician's inclusion among its more than 400 concerts. As to the actual proportion of jazz versus non-jazz, he concluded, "I would have a very hard time defining that squarely and precisely. Music is not square."

FIJM president Alain Simard, however, seemed to have something quite precise in mind when he noted, "The quantity of tickets we sell to real jazz concerts is phenomenal during the jazz festival. It's not normal, so people are taking chances."

It may in fact be that the people, and only the people, were taking chances in 1994. When pianists Paul Bley and Michele Rosewoman were as close as the festival got to a cutting edge on Saturday — apologies to Montreal singer Tena Palmer, whose daring vocalese vied for an early-evening crowd's attention on Ste-Catherine with a fellow juggling torches from a 10-foot unicycle — then it's clear that the festival has become a safe, mainstream event, at least on the "real" jazz side. (Other relative visionaries over its 11 nights included Americans Bill Frisell, David Murray, and Pharoah Sanders and Montreal's Justine.) Even the Canadian Bley caught some of this prevailing conservatism in his brief, nostalgic solo concert at the Théâtre Maisonneuve; Oakland's Rosewoman was as intense and unsettled as usual with a trio at the Salle du Gesù.

Like anything else, the festival looks a little different from the bottom than from the top — from the stage down at the corner of Ste-Catherine and St-Urbain, for example, where the festival plays out at a more personal level.

It was here that guitarist Nelson Symonds, who as much as any single musician kept jazz alive in Montreal during the pre-FIJM 1960s and 1970s, appeared last Friday. The festival may have altered everything else about jazz in the city, but it hasn't changed Symonds. He might still have been playing in one of his old haunts, The Black Bottom or Rockhead's Paradise, for all of his self-absorption, no matter that several thousand people were now listening in. His solos on *Milestones* and *Bemsha Swing* were wild and furious, drawing the audience in closer and closer to the edge of the low stage. A surprised Symonds found himself with outstretched hands to shake when his hour was up.

And it was here, in a moment of spontaneity rare at this always orderly event, that Montreal's Charles Papasoff unpacked his baritone saxophone and blew a mighty, roaring *Au Privave* with the trio of the Swiss pianist Moncef Genoud to close a concert late Saturday night. Great cheers followed on cue, but the crowd melted away almost immediately, leaving Papasoff alone with just a few well-wishers, an instant preview of the next 50 weeks to come.

July 12, 1994

"Commitment"
CCMC (1995)

The remarkable thing about the Toronto improvisational ensemble known simply as CCMC is not just that it has lasted now 21 years but that it has done so with very little public encouragement. There were about 30 listeners on hand for its free (as in no admission charge) concert at the Music Gallery earlier this week; that's a larger crowd than CCMC usually draws to its Tuesday night performances, but once the evening's intermission was complete, the audience had dwindled by half.

One of the C's in CCMC must stand for "commitment." The musicians' loyalty to free (as in wholly spontaneous) improvisation is unswerving in the face of such a lack of interest. No one is more committed to the cause than pianist and synthesizer player Michael Snow, the lone remaining original from 1974. Public or no public, Snow, alto saxophonist John Oswald, sound poet Paul Dutton and drummer Jack Vorvis get together anyway, like four guys meeting for a weekly poker game, albeit a poker game in which all of the cards are wild.

On its last CD, *Decisive Moments* (Track & Light), CCMC referred to its efforts as "Hot Real-Time Electro-Acoustic Collective Composition." With the departure in the interim of electro-acousticians Al Mattes and John Kamevaar, the band has become less "electro" and more acoustic. But Oswald and Dutton, each with his own self-devised vocabulary of gibbers and glisses, still make sport of matching noises with Snow's archaic CAT synthesizer, which sounds like an old tube radio tuned between stations late at night, when the interference is strongest.

Working without Vorvis on this occasion, and missing the textural variety that his drumming might have provided, Snow, Oswald and Dutton developed three pieces on the spot with the proverbial mixed results. "Development" is a relative concept here, the by-product of a responsive improvisational process that sees the players bouncing sounds, melodic details and rhythmic effects back and forth freely; the music edges forward slowly even as it moves quickly from side to side.

Of the three participants, Snow seems most inclined to pre-empt this gradual flow and impose some sort of larger structure. In Tuesday's second and least effective improvisation, he introduced a walking-bass figure at the piano and then broke into several choruses of 12-bar blues. Now there's nothing in the rule book on free improvisation that disallows the use of such a standard convention, but the result of Snow's impetuous desire for a little order was, ironically, a lot of chaos. In turn, and no less ironically, the cacophony revealed how carefully — how intelligently — the music that preceded it had been fashioned.

January 19, 1995

"The academy"
D.D. Jackson (1995)

"Ah, no."

A long "ah." A concise "no."

D. D. Jackson is talking about the neo-traditional movement in jazz. Has he — one of Canada's rising stars in New York City, capital of the neo-traditionalists' world — ever felt its temptations? Not a few of his peers have succumbed, only to see their careers soar.

Ah, no. He laughs a soft laugh, barely audible over the Muzak playing in the concourse of the Holiday Inn on King Street in downtown Toronto.

It's a dangerous admission to make in these times of high ideological dudgeon in jazz. But Jackson, 28, has stood up to the academy before. He was at Indiana University on that occasion, not long out of high school in Ottawa and continuing his studies as a classical pianist. The teenager, product of an African-American/Asian family, was obviously gifted. His teacher, the renowned Menahem Pressler, generally took only graduate students; Jackson was a mere freshman. But...

"It wasn't the ideal situation for me," he remembers, looking back not very fondly. "He was a very rigid classical guy. He had very little tolerance for people who were creative in different ways. And maybe he didn't have to: he was used to having students who would come to him to study so that they would not only learn from him but sound like him. His ideal student was [someone] who looked exactly like him, had short, rounded fingers, played Mozart like him, and so on. I didn't fit into that mould at all."

And so Jackson changed teachers, apparently something that's just not *done* in classical circles, in order to finish off his degree. And then, in 1989, he moved on altogether — to the Manhattan School of Music in New York and to jazz. "I was always more of an improviser anyway, growing up. That was another reason why classical music wasn't the right fit... Even my classical interpretations were often very improvised."

Jazz, clearly, is a much better fit. A looser fit, really, one that Jackson wears comfortably as he kicks off his first Canadian tour this week with an engagement at the Holiday Inn nightspot known quaintly as Judy Jazz. He's travelling with two musicians from the Ottawa band Chelsea Bridge, bassist John Geggie and drummer Jean Martin; they appeared on Jackson's debut CD for the Montreal label Justin Time, *Peace-Song*, which also featured the volatile American tenor saxophonist David Murray.

The Jackson-Murray connection dates to the summer of 1992, when both musicians toured Europe in the ensemble of composer Kip Hanrahan. Jackson has since played in several of Murray's bands of various sizes and was recently at the saxophonist's side in Philadelphia as the rehearsal accompanist for developmental work on a new musical about baseball great Satchel Paige.

Jackson's early credits also include appearances with violinist Billy Bang and saxophonists Jane Bunnett, Dewey Redman and Carlos Ward, no mean achievement for someone who has been playing jazz for all of six years. That speaks well of the direction offered Jackson at the Manhattan School of Music by his next two teachers, Jaki Byard and Don Pullen.

Byard, "a walking encyclopedia of jazz piano," took Jackson through the history of the tradition, while Pullen put music into a larger context. "When I think of Don's influence, I think of the whole picture, not just his style, but his whole 'life' approach to music and to jazz."

Byard, he suggests, "could tell that I had talent, but he couldn't quite figure me out... He really didn't know what I was trying to do, and perhaps I didn't know either, until I hooked up with Don."

The iconoclastic Pullen, who died this year, encouraged Jackson's adventurous spirit — "Don't be afraid to take chances" — and provided some early employment opportunities by sending the young Canadian out on engagements that he couldn't make himself. The Hanrahan tour was just one.

Pullen's direct influence on the more explosive aspects of Jackson's piano style is apparent but not burdensome. Iconoclasm, after all, *should* breed iconoclasm. Which brings Jackson back to the prevailing neo-traditionalist mindset in jazz.

"It's a very similar mentality to what I left at Indiana. It's alarming at times, this close-minded mentality I've seen in New York. I hate to sound negative, but it gets to a point where it's very frustrating. The whole Wynton Marsalis school and so on: It's not so much that they're *pro* what they do — this is a generalization — but they're so unnecessarily outspoken against people who are doing other stuff that's perfectly legitimate."

And so Jackson, who seems *necessarily* outspoken, stands up to the academy again.

November 2, 1995

"Relentless"
Chick Corea (1995)

Chick Corea, personable chap that he is, was chatting with folks in the first few rows of the sold-out George Weston Recital Hall in Toronto on Saturday night. Just back from intermission, the pianist seated himself at the edge of the stage — legs dangling, microphone in hand — and began talking casually about one thing and another. Nothing of particular consequence, just his son's birthday that day, his son's age, his own age...

Suddenly, Corea — who's 54 — looked up and out into the hall. "Any requests?"

Requests? You bet. Tune titles began to rain down on the stage. *Spain, La Fiesta, The Yellow Nimbus, 500 Miles High* — a veritable inventory of Corea's most popular compositions from his time — more than 25 years — in the limelight of contemporary jazz as the leader of the influential fusion band Return to Forever and of a variety of other worthy acoustic and electric formations.

Now you'd think Corea might have acted on a few of those suggestions. After all, he had just given the first half of his solo concert over to a review of the music that he "grew up with" — specifically, to pieces played in honour of his father (*Armando's Rhumba*), Duke Ellington (*Sophisticated Lady*), Bud Powell (*How Deep Is the Ocean*) and Thelonious Monk (*Pannonica, Round Midnight* and *Trinkle Tinkle*). What better way to put his own *oeuvre* in context?

But no. Corea had other ideas. Instead of moving ahead, he reached even further back, retrieving the score for Alexander Scriabin's *Prelude No. 2*, written in 1893, and giving it a rather choppy, brittle reading with little of the fluidity and cleanly chiseled sculpting that characterizes his own keyboard work at its improvised best.

Corea continued with a dozen of his own *Children's Songs (1971-84)*, coy and clever miniatures again played from their scores, although with rather more vivacity. And that was the sum of the evening, save for an encore of *Someday My Prince*

Will Come and a final interlude that saw a volunteer from the audience, identified only as "Dave," join Corea in a round of "piano four-hands" with the audience soon invited to sing along.

For all that — and it was certainly a lot — the concert seemed incomplete. Corea had raised an expectation only to ignore it and, with it, the repertoire by which he is most closely identified. It wasn't as though he was in a hurry to get to his latest music. This program was entirely retrospective, as far as it went, which is no less odd coming from a musician who has always had something new on the go.

What Corea did play, the Scriabin prelude aside, he played very well, intermittently accompanying himself with the emphatic application of heel and/or toe to the stage floor. He is an exemplary pianist and a relentless sort of performer — relentlessly inventive, relentlessly melodic, relentlessly cheerful. He's also prone to silliness, prefacing his encore by easing the lectern off the piano and asking the audience to pass the black, oblong slab of wood over its collective head, row by row, toward the back of the hall — the last, if not the least, of this evening's several curious turns.

November 14, 1995

"The chase"
Ralph Sutton (1996)

It says something about the wonderfully odd logic of jazz that the septuagenarian stride pianist Ralph Sutton could show up at the Montreal Bistro with two more musicians than usual and end up working harder than ever.

Solo Sutton — which is the way Toronto has heard the Missouri-born musician most frequently in recent years at the Bistro, and at the Café des Copains before it — is measured Sutton. Always in control. Sutton in a band setting, however, gets adrenalized. Suddenly he finds things in need of doing — melodies to counterpoint, harmonies to enrich and rhythms to bolster. *Especially* rhythms to bolster. Needless to say, a hardworking Sutton can be an exciting Sutton.

He has two Toronto musicians to keep him busy this week, soprano saxophonist Jim Galloway and drummer Don Vickery, Bistro stalwarts both. They, of course, are simply doing their usual thing, Galloway blowing brightly with heart on sleeve, and Vickery brushing the time away — *whisk, whisk* — discreetly. It's enough, though, to get Sutton involved.

He was particularly responsive to Galloway during Wednesday night's first set, orchestrating a red-carpet sort of accompaniment that seemed to roll out just a step ahead of the saxophonist's next idea. Galloway solos effectively became Galloway-Sutton duets, so imaginative were the pianist's interventions.

As befits a master of the old Harlem style of jazz piano known as stride, Sutton's left-hand work — not to mention his rhythmic authority in general — was a marvel, constantly changing the momentum and texture of the music with a mere shift of the wrist. *Honeysuckle Rose*, from Sutton's favoured repertoire of Fats Waller songs, underwent the greatest overall transformation, building from a gentle, introductory musing to a rocking crescendo that had Vickery, for perhaps only the second time of the set, reaching for his drumsticks.

For old time's sake, or maybe just for variety, Sutton included one unaccompanied improvisation among his half-dozen trio performances, lingering over an obscure Waller melody with a lovely word image as its title, *Clothes Line Ballet*. For the rest of the set, though, Sutton happily cut to the chase, still very much in control but now promising something new and surprising at almost every turn.

February 9, 1996

"Imperative case"
Blossom Dearie (1996)

The word "unique" was being bandied about freely on Thursday night at the Top O'The Senator as a couple of long-time Blossom Dearie fans attempted to explain the American singer-pianist's appeal. It's as good a word as any.

There's nothing else in jazz, or anywhere nearby, quite like the girlish whisper of Dearie's voice, a small, high sound — shading toward whiny at its highest — cushioned by the sparing accompaniment that she gives herself at the piano and by the equally restrained assistance of her bassist, Ray Kilday, and percussionist, Luiz Peralta. When she scats, she summons up the image of Betty Boop. Needless to say, she doesn't scat often.

This, from a woman of 70 who has been associated with enough hip characters around New York and in Europe over the years — Woody Herman, Annie Ross and Bobby Jaspar, for three — to pick up a taste for the style of jazz without giving herself over entirely to the substance. And so she was able on Thursday to transform a jazz club like the Senator neatly into a cabaret, with a pat and efficient performance that drew a full house for her opening set and had the rapt attention of all concerned.

When Dearie's voice begins to lose some of its intrigue, as it did by about the fifth of the eight songs in that set, she has a strong fallback position: the songs themselves. She's a lyricist's dream. If there's a story to tell, it gets told; if there's an image to evoke, consider it evoked. Some singers don't miss a beat. Dearie doesn't miss a word.

The word in this instance might belong to a lyricist on the literate order of Stephen Sondheim (*The Ladies Who Lunch*), Johnny Mercer (*I'm Shadowing You*, to music by Dearie herself), Dave Frishberg *(Peel Me a Grape)* and others less well-known but just as gifted with a sharp turn of phrase or a telling observation. Her own *I Like You, You're Nice* is cut from similarly candid, if softer, verbal cloth.

Frishberg's *Peel Me a Grape*, with thanks to Mae West, is one of the staples in Dearie's repertoire. It's the sort of song that she'll use to close off a set with a flourish, playing up Frishberg's creative use of nouns as verbs in the imperative case: "mink me," "champagne me," "cashmere me," and so on.

You might expect a sultry, West-like performance here, but where West would have beckoned, Dearie makes demands, turning the song into something of a high-priced shopping list. Dearie's just not the Mae West type — or any other type, for that matter. The lady's one of a kind.

August 31, 1996

"Why now?"
Joe Henderson (1997)

There are several ways of measuring Joe Henderson's surprising success in recent years. Record sales are surely one. *Double Rainbow*, for example, the U.S. tenor saxophonist's tribute to Antonio Carlos Jobim, has topped the 300,000 mark since its release in 1995, an impressive figure indeed for a jazz record.

Grammy awards are another. Henderson has three: one for 1992's *Lush Life: The Music of Billy Strayhorn* and two for 1993's *So Near, so Far (Musings for Miles)*.

More routinely, interviews are a third. He did a European promotion tour in 1995 — "like an author or a movie star" — spending four days each in London, Paris, Milan and Hamburg. "Four days," he remembers, "*nine* interviews a day." He still sounds daunted by the idea.

The rise of Henderson's star coincides directly with his affiliation with Verve Records, a company that has had a tremendous impact on jazz in the 1990s with its imaginative packaging and aggressive promotion. Its current Verve JazzFest tour is typical, putting Henderson's trio with bassist George Mraz and drummer Al Foster on a bill with bassist Charlie Haden's Quartet West and a big band drawn from musicians who appeared in the Robert Altman film *Kansas City*.

Until he signed with Verve, Henderson's career was bolstered only by his standing among the cognoscenti as a master improviser, his reputation based on a handful of early and influential post-bop recordings for Blue Note, from *Page One* in 1963 through *Mode for Joe* three years later. Now 59, he has remained a remarkably consistent performer throughout his career, one who could release two LPs (now CDs) in the late 1980s bearing the title *The State of the Tenor* without fear of argument.

"Whatever it is that I'm about, I think I've been it for a long time," he noted in a telephone interview from his home in San Francisco. "That's why, when all of this press started, this high level of visibility, I wondered, 'Why now? What am I doing different?' I see myself as being essentially the same person as I've been all along. So what's all this stuff about? You change as time goes by, but I don't see it as being like midnight one moment and high noon the next."

His weariness with interviews notwithstanding, Henderson is generous with his thoughts. "He's a talker," warned his California publicist. Yes, he is, and the conversation, like one of his solos, goes pretty much where he chooses to take it.

His topic of choice on this occasion was his latest CD, *Big Band*, a project that he described as "an opportunity to revisit my past." It's Henderson history that few of his fans would likely know about, a period beginning in the summer of 1966 when he and trumpeter Kenny Dorham formed a rehearsal orchestra in New York to explore their interests as arrangers.

There would be a few public appearances in the course of the next four or five years, but the musicians basically played for themselves — and for their peers who slipped unseen into the afternoon gloom of the East Village night club where the orchestra rehearsed. "In some cases they told me this 10, 15 years later," the saxophonist recalled of his hidden listeners. "I had no idea they were even back there."

By the time Henderson moved to San Francisco in 1972, he had a small library of original arrangements to show for his labours. (He also had some rehearsal tapes as a keepsake. His assessment? "The band didn't sound bad at all.") The charts served him well whenever he conducted clinics with music students, but otherwise they "sat on a shelf, collecting dust."

Not until a concert in March of 1992 at Alice Tully Hall in New York did *Big Band* begin to take shape. Three of its nine tracks were recorded at that time; the success of *Lush Life*, followed closely by that of *So Near, So Far* and *Double Rainbow*, pushed the rest back to last June.

Even after 30 years in the making, *Big Band* is a timely response to concerns that the saxophonist was becoming typecast by the tribute "concept" of his Billy

Strayhorn, Miles Davis and Antonio Carlos Jobim recordings. "People would come up to me and say, 'Joe — *man* — when are we going to get a chance to hear Joe Henderson playing *Joe Henderson*?' And I'm thinking, 'Hey, pretty good idea.' It never occurred to me that I was viewed in a favourable light as a composer."

That seems like a rather modest admission from a man who's responsible for several classic lines of the 1960s, among them *Isotope, Inner Urge, Black Narcissus, A Shade of Jade* and *Recordame*, five of the pieces that appear in big-band settings on the new CD. Then again, Henderson — for all of his critical and popular accolades — seems like a modest man, further blessed with a charitable view of the music business and his fortunes in it.

Consider his quite earnest suggestion that perhaps the jazz media have just been "asleep at the wheel," and the intensity of their current interest may be "their way of apologizing for having overlooked something that's been in their faces — in this case, their ears — all these years."

The jazz media should be so polite. But the point is, thanks to Verve, they are paying attention now. "I just had no idea," Henderson admitted, "how that factors into the overall equation of whether one may or may not become successful."

But now, in his way, he understands. "People need to know about you. If they don't, well... it's like gold... gold's not worth anything if it hasn't been found."

January 25, 1997

"Happy melodies"
Doc Cheatham (1997)

There are 87 pages of text to Adolphus (Doc) Cheatham's modest autobiography, *I Guess I'll Get the Papers and Go Home* — just under a page for every year of the venerable jazz trumpeter's long life to date. The book was published in 1995, at which point he signed off at the age of 89 with this wish: "I just hope the chops hold out a little longer."

Two years later, the chops — the combined skills required to play the horn — are holding up just fine, thank you. "In fact," he confides, "the more I play, the better my lip."

And Cheatham continues to play a great deal. He's not quite the world traveller he once was with the bands of Sam Wooding, Cab Calloway, Machito and Benny Goodman, but he still gets around. He's in Toronto this week for five nights at the Montreal Bistro, and there are trips in the offing to Sarasota, New Orleans and, for the umpteenth time since 1928, various cities in Europe. Back home in New York, he has had a regular Sunday matinée at Sweet Basil for almost 20 years.

There will undoubtedly be even more calls for his services after the release next month of a new CD from Verve Records★ that pairs Cheatham with fellow trumpeter Nicholas Payton, who's 67 years his junior and one of the rising stars in jazz, for a variety of old favourites played in a dixie-swing setting. There has been talk of a tour, but Cheatham's not so sure. While he clearly admires Payton, calling him "one of the best trumpet players we have today," there are other considerations. Practical considerations.

"I realize that I have to slow down to a certain degree," he admits, with mild understatement. "I'm accepting what [work] I want; what I don't want, I don't accept. When I was very young I'd go anywhere, play anything. Now I'm watching my health. My health has been very good, but I still watch it carefully — what I do, where I go, what I eat."

In truth, there is a fragility about the man as he sits in the lobby of his Toronto hotel, shifting uncomfortably to ease the pain of the arthritis in his legs. He's still every inch the sport, though, what with his checked cap, his string tie and his high-hitched pants held up by red Christmas suspenders emblazoned with tiny Santa Claus faces.

In the spirit of "slowing down," he arrived in town a day early in order to relax before the Bistro engagement started, only to find that he couldn't smoke cigars in his hotel room — or almost anywhere else in Toronto for that matter. Cheatham has been a lifelong teetotaller, but he developed a liking for the taste — and only the taste — of cigars at the age of 15.

"My father smoked a cigar," he explains. "He'd smoke half of it; the other half he'd leave on the fence in the back yard, and walk away. I'd pick up the butts. I never inhaled, though. I tried to inhale once, choked me near to death."

The back yard was in a racially mixed neighbourhood of Nashville. Cheatham pointed to the photograph of his teenaged self on the front cover of *I Guess I'll Get the Papers and Go Home*. That's young Adolphus, looking spiffy in a tux, with a soprano saxophone on a strap around his neck and a cornet on a table by his side.

"My father gave me those horns," he recalls. "Because I was in Nashville, I had to teach myself how to play them. I couldn't get a teacher to teach me, because of the segregation around there in those days." His self-instruction was nevertheless thorough enough to bring him work in circus bands and in vaudeville. "The older musicians liked me," he says now. "I was young and I was loud."

★ *Doc Cheatham & Nicholas Payton.*

By the age of 20, he had dismissed his father's notion that he might become a pharmacist — the soubriquet "Doc" dates to his short stay at medical school — and found his way instead to Chicago. There, in 1926, he made his first recordings with the legendary blues singer Ma Rainey and took jobs that no less a figure than the great Louis Armstrong inexplicably directed his way. (Years later, Cheatham understood: when Armstrong's success generated resentment among his fellow New Orleans jazzmen in Chicago, he responded by hiring musicians who originated in other parts of the country.) And so the parade of bands began: Sam Wooding's orchestra in Berlin and other European cities, McKinney's Cotton Pickers out of Detroit, Cab Calloway's Cotton Club Revue in New York...

"I think McKinney's was the best musical, entertaining band I ever played in," he enthuses, looking back to an orchestra that, in its day, was one of the three leading black bands in jazz, rivalling those of Duke Ellington and Fletcher Henderson. But its day was almost over when Cheatham hired on briefly in 1931. "I loved playing with the Cotton Pickers. Cab's band was all right; Cab paid well. But the Cotton Pickers, they scuffled. They never made any money."

Cheatham spent a total of nine years with Calloway and then freelanced through the 1940s before starting a 20-year association with New York's Latin bands. In each case, he played lead trumpet, a position that offered him a lot of responsibility but few, if any solos. That would change around 1970; at a point when most working folks would be thinking of retirement, Cheatham simply retooled, emerging as an eloquent soloist and sweet singer with the gentle and unhurried graces of another era.

As far as eras go, of course, he has seen them all. He's a rather reluctant witness to jazz history, though. His autobiography, which has been edited down by Alyn Shipton from taped reminiscences, is chatty but discreet: Cheatham settles a couple of scores, yes, but moves through the first 75 years of his career quite blithely. Talk to him now about the history of jazz, and he tends to hedge. "I don't know much about it, because I was in Europe quite a number of times, so I missed things."

And jazz itself? "Anyone asks what jazz is, I don't know what to say. It's just happy melodies, that's all."

March 19, 1997

"Jumble"
Myra Melford (1997)

Myra Melford positions herself at the piano just below middle C. That puts her a little left of centre, so to speak, which is as good a place as any in these conservative times to find a different perspective on the jazz piano tradition. Sure enough, Melford's fine New York trio, completed by bassist Lindsay Horner and drummer Reggie Nicholson, takes a new line on some old ideas — old avant-garde ideas, that is — and whips them into a light but fresh fury.

Everything is grist for Melford's mill, actually, from funk figures to forearm smashes. Her first tune on Tuesday night at the Arts and Letters Club in Toronto, *Evening Might Still*, had the funk figures, and her second, *Crush*, the forearms. It sounds a lot like a pastiche over the duration of a concert — Bobby Timmons at one point, Cecil Taylor at another, Don Pullen at yet a third — but the very jumble of her music becomes its defining quality, further enhanced by the engaging awkwardness of several of her themes.

Originally — think of Taylor — those same avant-garde ideas and techniques served purely expressive purposes. As Melford presses, pounds and pummels them into service again, though, they take on a lesser, merely dramatic function. They quicken the pulse, yes, and generate a degree of tension, to be sure, but they give way to one structural convention or another before things get entirely out of hand. The music's quite deceptive that way; however spontaneous it may sound — however "free" — it's really quite carefully controlled.

To that end, the three musicians work extremely well together as a fully integrated unit, not simply as a leader and her two follow-me sidemen. Even playing without amplification in the natural acoustic setting of the Arts and Letters Club hall, with its high, vaulted wood ceiling, they settled quickly and comfortably on a level of interaction that favoured Nicholson's brisk drumming over Horner's impeccable bass work only slightly.

The trio bounced and bumped along cheerfully for the most part. Now and then — Melford's *Changes One*, for example — it would swing unreservedly. Or at least Horner and Nicholson were swinging unreservedly; Melford simply lit out on a wild, exhilarating and multidirectional solo that compressed into a single improvisation the ambitious stylistic length and breadth of the entire evening.

May 2, 1997

"Latin soul"
Charles Papasoff (1997)

It's lunch time at De Ville, a comfortably hip bistro on the *boulevard* St-Laurent, the street that historically has separated the English from the French in Montreal. De Ville, which has a narrow *terrace* with room enough for only a single row of small, round tables serviced by a slim waitress, is on the east side of the street. Not very long ago, that would have meant the French side. But nothing in this city is quite so simple any more.

Take, for example, that waitress. She's an anglophone — no doubt about it. And take, for another example, one of her customers on this sunny spring afternoon, jazz musician Charles Papasoff, one of the Canadian scene's true originals.

The explosive baritone saxophonist was born 40 years ago in Montreal of Bulgarian stock and now divides his time between Quebec and the west of France. "I speak both languages fluently and sometimes without an accent," he explained very convincingly in English. "But my upbringing was French, so I have a Latin soul in that respect. I like to play music with energy. I like it to swing very hard. When it hurts, I want it to hurt *bad*. When it's soft, it has got to be nice and..." His voice trailed off, lost to the sounds on the street.

The Papasoff Trio, a rough-and-ready unit with bassist George Mitchell and drummer Martin Auguste, is one of several Montreal bands touring Canada during the jazz festival season just now getting under way. Montreal is particularly well represented on the circuit this year, between Papasoff, pianist Jean Beaudet's trio, bassist Sylvain Gagnon's quartet, the *musique actuelle* trio Île Bizarre and the eight-piece Swing Dynamique with legendary drummer Guy Nadon.

"It's an exciting time for Montreal," Papasoff observed, speaking in general terms. "We've almost come to terms with the linguistic thing — well, maybe — and we're reaping the benefits. Because the linguistic thing does have its up side: it creates two cultures, and there's a lot of movement in between."

The city's jazz musicians are a case in point, no longer quite as split by all that the *boulevard* St-Laurent symbolizes. "The jazz community is starting to mesh," Papasoff noted. "It comes from the quality of players. You get a sax player like André Leroux; everybody wants to play with him, including the English. And you get a sax player like Kelly Jefferson, who's English, and the French want to play with him. The music will prevail."

Papasoff himself, sweetly gregarious fellow that he is, has always worked both sides of the street, so to speak. And down all the alleys; he is no more limited by musical style than he is by language. His credits in recent years range from an informal association with a heavy-metal band, The Thrill of It All (known now as Spackle), to a collaboration with Les Ballets Jazz de Montréal on the production of *Tristan Iseult* that was seen at last summer's Festival International de Jazz de Montréal.

Virtually all of Papasoff's ventures revolve around the baritone saxophone, although he has also been known to play soprano saxophone, flute and bass clarinet in jazz settings, and can handle guitar and keyboards as his studio projects — film scores mostly — require.

The baritone, for all its bluster, has had a rather modest place in jazz history, usually in a functional rather than featured role. Its acknowledged masters have been few: Harry Carney with the Duke Ellington Orchestra, Leo Parker, Serge Chaloff, Gerry Mulligan and Pepper Adams in the bop era, John Surman and Hamiet Bluiett in more recent times, and not many more. Papasoff, surely, is one, albeit as yet unrecognized as such outside Quebec and parts of Europe.

"It's a great instrument that hasn't really been exploited to its maximum potential by the players who've lived before us," he suggested, having certainly done his fair share for the cause. Not only has he pushed the instrument to the very limits of its range, both high notes and low, with tremendous assurance, he is the driving force behind the rip-roaring International Baritone Conspiracy, which comprises two Canadians (Jean Derome and David Mott), two Europeans (Christian Gavillet and Bo Van Der Werf) and an American (Hamiet Bluiett). The ensemble has performed in concert only once, at the *musique actuelle* festival in Victoriaville, Quebec, in 1995, but has a terrific CD, *International Baritone Conspiracy* (Victo) to show for the occasion.

"It warrants another record," he insisted. "The music warrants that we get another crack at it, to see how far we can take it this time."

Still, in Papasoff's estimation, it will be up to the next generation, and the one after, to break the baritone's place in jazz wide open. And to hear him talk, it won't be an easy task. "A guy coming up now who listens to John Surman — or to Charles Papasoff — has to be able to play four octaves at least. If he listens to Gerry Mulligan, he has to be able to play round, and sweet, and within the chord changes. If he listens to Hamiet Bluiett, he has to have a rocking bottom end, man, *rocking*. Take all of those things, and a kid who's just starting, he has his work cut out for him. But it's there. It has been done. It *can* be done, so he'll do it, and he's going to stretch from there and show *us* what to do."

In the meantime, Papasoff shows the world what he can do on his new trio CD, *Painless* (Nisapa Productions), released just in time to capitalize on the Canadian festivals and on the short tour of Italy that will follow in mid-July. The trio's music, which is coarse, bullish and angular, might be called "free-bop" for its mix of older and newer traditions. But what, then, to make of its funk influences? Or of the asymmetrical rhythms that echo Papasoff's Bulgarian heritage?

In truth, Papasoff can no more easily be categorized than the French and English of Montreal can be divided by a single downtown street. He evokes the memory of the late Pepper Adams, with whom he studied briefly in New York before the American's death in 1986.

"Pepper never described himself as a bebop player. His thing was always 'Make your voice, do your own thing. You've got to sound the way *you* sound.' He had his own sound on baritone sax, and even though he did play a lot of bebop, he had his own way of doing it. But he didn't describe himself as a player of that school.

"It took me a while to understand why, but it was exactly *because* he had his own voice. And that's what has stayed with me: You've got to sound the way you sound, because at the end of the line, if you don't, you sound like somebody else."

June 19, 1997

"A kind of arrow"
Christopher Cauley (1998)

So far, Christopher Cauley can claim only a modest career in jazz — if indeed the Canadian alto saxophonist wishes to call it a career at all. He is not, on any count save perhaps one, typical of this country's jazz musicians, which is precisely what makes him so intriguing.

Consider just one Cauley assertion: "The Holy Trinity of the alto saxophone, for me, is Ornette, Dolphy and Jimmy Lyons. That's the way it is." Ornette Coleman, Eric Dolphy and Jimmy Lyons, visionaries all. The last — and least-known — was pianist Cecil Taylor's right-hand man for 25 years.

These are not points of reference often heard in any discussion of jazz as it is played in Canada, where a musician strays from the mainstream strictly at his or her own peril. But these are the improvisers, Lyons especially, from whom Cauley springs. He has coined the expression "style as DNA" in part to explain just such connections.

Cauley's style — at times terse, at times searing — can be heard on four CDs to date, his own *FINland*, issued last summer by the small Massachusetts company Eremite, as well as bassist Lisle Ellis' *Elevations* (Victo), the Glenn Spearman/John Heward Group's *th* (CIMP) and the Montreal *musique actuelle* trio Kl'axon Gueul'e's *Bavard* (Ambiances Magnétiques).

But four CDs, three of them — *FINland, th* and *Bavard* — released in one year, do not necessarily a career make. If they did, perhaps Cauley at 37 would be living somewhere other than Peterborough, in the Kawartha Lakes district northeast of Toronto. And then again, perhaps not. His — he says over a Louisiana lunch downtown at Hot Belly Mama's — is "an old-fashioned, romantic approach to life with a good measure of existential underpinning and a little bit of mystical longing thrown in."

In other words, this is one of those artist-in-a-garret stories. For 14 years, until last June, Cauley's garret was an apartment on *rue* St-Urbain in Montreal. He spent most of the 1980s in literary pursuits, with published poems to show for his efforts. In 1990, he returned to music, taking up where he had left off as a teenaged saxophonist in Cornwall, Ontario, and working at Montreal's Bar G-Sharp with two bands led by Lisle Ellis, Free Force and Line of Descent.

He counts his association with Ellis, as well as with the Montreal drummer John Heward, among his formative experiences in freely improvised music; he also spent time visiting in New York on several occasions with saxophonist David S. Ware and once — for a memorable 14-hour stretch — with Cecil Taylor. He's careful not to describe either Ware or Taylor as teachers, but it's clear that his contact with each man was profound.

New York, you'd think, is really where Cauley should be. On that count, and that count alone, he sounds like any other Canadian jazz musician: "I'd love to be in New York." Instead of the singular figure that he is in Peterborough, and the marginal figure he was in Montreal, he would belong to a creative community of some size. It's no accident that the three other musicians on *FINland* are stalwarts of the New York scene, trombonist Steve Swell, bassist William Parker and drummer Gregg Bendian.

San Francisco, where Lisle Ellis now makes his home, might also be a possibility — a possibility that Cauley resists. "It's not that interesting to be a poor, illegal saxophone player at 37," he counters, reviewing his prospects *anywhere* stateside. "If I was 23 or 24, and a bit more hardcore," he adds, voice trailing off, "If I was in a fever about it..."

A romantic he may be, but impractical he's not. "It's hard to be in America." As opposed to being in Canada? "As opposed to being in Canada — as opposed to being any place where you have some kind of history and some way of supporting yourself. You know David Ware was driving taxi cabs up till recently? That's serious. I've seen saxophonist Charles Gayle perform at the Knitting Factory [in New York] with two people in the audience. I played there last year with Marco Eneidi's Jungle Orchestra; there were 14 people in the band and nine people in the audience."

That's a reality as cold as a gray January afternoon in the Kawarthas. Instead, Cauley measures his progress in other ways. Returning to this curious notion of a "career," he will go as far as to admit that, yes, perhaps he has one.

"But it's not a commercial career," he cautions. "Putting out those records is like putting out books of poetry. You know that the people who buy them generally are on side to begin with. Typically, they're tilted at as different an angle to the world as you are, they're kind of left field, they're into the struggle and they probably have similar views of class analysis and of life as a religious experience."

And they, like Cauley, would probably see art as a process, not a product — a source of revelation rather than revenue. "There might be four or five people who hear *FINland* — people who haven't been exposed to this kind of music before. And now they are, just because the record is there. So maybe those four or five people will begin to wend their way — maybe they'll pick up a William Parker record, or a Steve Swell record or a Gregg Bendian record. Or maybe they'll like the AR Ammons poem that appears on the CD insert and will chase down AR Ammons. It's really about being a kind of arrow. Everything points to something else."

February 21, 1998

"Syntax"
Steve Lacy and Danilo Pérez (1998)

It could be argued that the music of Thelonious Monk (1917-82) is a dialect unique in the language of jazz. Aside from the pianist himself, few musicians have truly mastered its rhythmic, melodic and harmonic intricacy. Some can come up with a couple of words, figuratively speaking. ("Round" is usually one, and "Midnight" the other.) And some can even put together a sentence or two, all the while grasping for syntax and proper tense.

Not so the American soprano saxophonist Steve Lacy and the Panamanian pianist Danilo Pérez, who were clearly enjoying each other's company on Wednesday night at the du Maurier Theatre Centre as part of Toronto's du Maurier Downtown jazz festival.

These men know their Monk. Lacy especially. He made his first all-Monk LP, *Reflections* (New Jazz), in 1958 at the age of 24 and worked with Monk himself in the early 1960s. Pérez, a younger man by 32 years, has also been a quick study. He recorded *his* first Monk CD, *PanaMonk* (Impulse!), in 1996 and may ultimately benefit as much from working alongside Lacy as did Lacy from playing with Monk.

Lacy and Pérez naturally took Monk as their concert's point of reference, starting and ending the 70-minute performance with Monk's compositions and using his *Trinkle Tinkle* and possibly other pieces more obscure as beacons along the way. In time, everything on the program seemed to acquire a Monk-ish accent, Monk tune or not.

Lacy was Lacy — that pursed, purple tone and that nervous, whistling-by-the-graveyard sense of melody, with its stops, starts and furtive over-the-shoulder glances. His solos were consistently thoughtful and occasionally electrifying, their focus intense and unshakable.

Pérez, meanwhile, is not by nature a very Monk-like pianist. (Less so, for example, than another Lacy partner, Mal Waldron.) He is, however, an extremely smart improviser, as quick of mind as of hand. That can lead to a certain glibness, but it can also take the music in some surprising directions. His hypnotic vamp on the evening's encore, *Evidence*, for example, was simply — and uncharacteristically — *bravura* Monk. No more, no less.

June 26, 1998

"What Mahler doesn't know..."
Uri Caine (1998)

Uri Caine played Gustav Mahler on Thursday night at the Festival International de Jazz de Montréal. That's right, jazz musician tackles classical composer. Ho-hum. But this is not just any jazz musician, nor just any classical composer.

Caine is a youngish American pianist of some vision and great curiosity; like the other six musicians in his New York ensemble, he has been known back home to frequent the Knitting Factory, a wayside inn for postmodernists, deconstructionists and musical malcontents alike. Mahler, of course, was the Austrian composer who died in 1911, leaving behind a body of widely sourced and remarkably expressive music, from songs to symphonies, that for all of its Olde World charm and haunting melodic dignity anticipated postmodernism by the better part of a century.

So Caine isn't simply playing Jacques Loussier to Mahler's J. S. Bach — swinging the classics lightly and politely, giving offence to no one. That alone would not have brought Caine's marvellous Mahler Project, as it was billed in its Canadian premiere, a place in the FIJM's Jazz dans la Nuit series at the intimate Salle du Gesù. To the extent that the festival has a forum for new directions in jazz, this is it.

Caine has in fact suggested that Mahler would be less than pleased to learn of the fate that has befallen his music. But what Mahler doesn't know won't hurt him.

Still, he'd recognize some of his most evocative melodies, either whole or in fragmented form. And how could he not be moved by the vivacious fiddling of Caine's violinist, Mark Feldman? But try to explain to a 19th-century mind, even a progressive 19th-century mind, the concept of a "turntable artist" — in this case DJ Olive — who extracts a miscellany of discreet background voices and effects from old LPs. Where even to start?

Feldman and Olive aside, the Caine septet was recognizably a jazz band, with trumpeter Ralph Alessi, alto saxophonist Dave Binney, bassist Michael Formanek and drummer Jim Black filling out the ranks. (A 1996 recording of this music, *Urlicht/Primal Light* for the German Winter & Winter label, also includes a cantor and two other singers.) Caine likes his Mahler busy, at times clamorous, with a degree of exaggeration where it's appropriate and occasionally where it's not. Melodramatics can be such a mixed blessing.

Feldman and the peppery Black were the ensemble's key members on Thursday night, playing as if men possessed. Indeed, it might be said they stole the show twice over — once from Caine and once more from Mahler. Of course the composer is an entirely unwitting participant in these proceedings and should not be held accountable for whatever might transpire, good or bad. Credit or blame — credit in this case, certainly — belongs to Caine and to Caine alone.

July 4, 1998

"Integrity"
Peter Leitch and Gary Bartz (1998)

It was an impressive sight: several stretch limousines lined up outside of the Top O'The Senator on Tuesday night, just a few minutes before the New York duo of guitarist Peter Leitch and saxophonist Gary Bartz was set to start its first set of the week.

Could this be? Limos for jazz?

No, as it turned out, not for a moment. A Toronto International Film Festival function was underway in the Senator's third-floor lounge.

Well, it did seem rather improbable, didn't it? Leitch and Bartz have nothing to do with glitz and glamour. They're purists of a sort — men in their 50s who've seen it all as far as jazz is concerned, done most of it, and understand what's important and — especially — what's not.

What's important, for example, is spontaneity. Leitch and Bartz like to keep things informal, the better to respond immediately to the inspiration of the moment. Not that they're unpredictable; they're too loyal to the integrity of the tradition of modern jazz to really startle an audience. (But what was that quote from Miles Davis's *Jean-Pierre* doing in the middle of Thelonious Monk's *Rhythm-a-ning?*)

As is so often the case, their success as a team has as much to do with their differences as with their common qualities. They obviously share similar interests when it comes to repertoire: Monk tunes, Billy Strayhorn melodies and semi-obscure items from the classic American songbook — all of which were represented in their first, 75-minute set.

But Bartz plays on emotion, Leitch on logic. Bartz is singleminded in the way he develops a solo, while Leitch constantly juggles his options, making split-second decisions with each passing bar. Bartz's horns are vivid; his soprano is bright and metallic in tone and his alto is rich, occasionally to the point of harshness. Leitch's guitar, on the other hand, is rather dry, understating his extraordinary facility for moving harmony, rhythm and bass lines around on the instrument.

Bartz provides the music's intensity and Leitch takes care of everything else. Their duets become impromptu mini-concertos for saxophone and orchestra. And never mind those stretch limos, this orchestra can go home in a cab.

Previously unpublished; September 1998

"Impeccable"
Dick Hyman (1998)

Dick Hyman made a quick return to Toronto on Friday night, appearing at the George Weston Recital Hall just six months after his most recent engagement at the Montreal Bistro. His move "uptown" — figuratively from a small club to a medium-sized concert hall, geographically from Sherbourne Street to Yonge and Sheppard — should not be misinterpreted. This is no sudden, Diana-like Krall to stardom. Hyman at 71 has already done just about everything a jazz musician can do in New York, up to and including the scores for several Woody Allen films.

Moreover, the two halves of Hyman's recital on Friday could have been any two sets back at the Bistro, including the portion of the evening that he turned over to requests from the audience. True, the concert came with a 22-page program, a theme — "Hot Piano, Sweet Piano, Stride Piano" — and a corporate sponsor, Investors Group.

But *plus ça change...* Hyman was his usual mild-mannered and erudite self; his pianism, so typically, was impeccable.

That program promised music by George Gershwin, Duke Ellington, James P. Johnson, Fats Waller, Jelly Roll Morton, Irving Berlin, Cole Porter and Harold

Arlen. Hyman, however, had other ideas. He started with a boppish version of *Blue Skies* — the first of several Berlin songs — then moved on to piano rags by Scott Joplin, Edward B. Claypoole and Roy Bargy, and concluded the first half of the evening with three Waller tunes.

Ellington and Gershwin were the featured composers in the second half, followed by three requested pieces, Zez Confrey's *Kitten on the Keys*, Con Conrad's *The Continental* and Gene DePaul's *I'll Remember April*.

Hyman played them all without effort. In fact, a little more apparent strain — *any* apparent strain — might have given his playing even greater dazzle. As it was, his extraordinary facility made his solos look and sound almost too easy, a curious example of a skill level so high that it begins to diminish its own impact.

It also had the effect of homogenizing his material a little, so smoothly did he play it. But just a little. Hyman distinguished neatly between the formality of the classic Joplin rag *Heliotrope Bouquet* and the more fanciful nature of Claypoole's *Ragging the Scale* and Bargy's *Pianoflage*. His Waller tunes alternated between frolic and rollick, while his medley from Gershwin's *Porgy and Bess* was expansive. And although he skimmed the depths of his chosen Ellingtonia rather lightly at times, his version of Ellington's *Come Sunday* may have been the sweetest piece of the night — complete with church bells — and his dash through Duke's *Jubilee Stomp* the hottest.

November 2, 1998

"Revisionism"
Don Thompson (1999)

There are two ways to look at Don Thompson's bold and timely tribute to the music of Duke Ellington, recorded in concert Saturday night for broadcast on CBC Radio Two's Onstage next May 2, three days after the 100th anniversary of the U.S. composer's birth.

On one hand, Thompson's performance at the Glenn Gould Studio with seven of Toronto's finest jazz musicians didn't sound particularly Duke-ish. Alternating between piano and vibraphone, Thompson led the band through several standard Ellington tunes (*Take the "A" Train, In a Sentimental Mood, Cotton Tail*) as well as some very rare items (*I'm Gonna Go Fishin', Le Sucrier Velour, Blue Rose*). But Thompson's extraordinarily adroit arrangements, adjustments and amendments cast everything in a new and modern light — one so bright in its audacity and erudition that it often obscured the defining characteristics of the original compositions.

On the other hand, Thompson's head-turning take on Ellington is very much in the same creative spirit that sustained the composer himself throughout his long and distinguished career. Whenever asked, Ellington always said his favourite composition was "the next one." Thompson was similarly looking at least as far forward as back.

Like Ellington before him, he has shown great respect for his musicians, asking that they simply be themselves — that the free-thinking alto saxophonist Roy Styffe, for example, be Roy Styffe, not a facsimile of the old Ellington orchestra's Johnny Hodges. Of course, Styffe, tenor saxophonist Phil Dwyer, baritone saxophonist Alex Dean, cornet and flugelhorn player John MacLeod, trombonist Terry Promane, bassist Pat Collins and drummer Jerry Fuller all start stylistically from bop or postbop beginnings, throwing Thompson's Ellingtonia yet another contemporary curve.

The problem, if it was a problem, had nothing to do with the music or the musicians, and everything to do with what listeners to an Ellington tribute tend to expect — the familiar and the sentimental, not the new and challenging. By that measure, Thompson's revisionism could have seemed impersonal, even impertinent. By any other measure, it was exceeedingly impressive.

February 8, 1999

"Cats is swinging"
Jay McShann (1999)

They call him Hootie, a sobriquet derived from "hooted," which in jazz parlance has something to do with the state of grace achieved after copious intake of unspecified alcoholic refreshment.

The nickname dates back to Jay McShann's earliest days around Kansas City — back to about 1937, when the Oklahoma-born pianist and singer arrived in town after touring in the southwestern states with a couple of obscure territory bands. Remind him now, on his latest trip to Toronto, that he has been travelling as a musician for more than 60 years — and that he has been reprising his first hit, *Hootie Blues*, for almost as long — and he feigns good-natured surprise.

"That's right!," he exclaims, shifting himself on the couch in his Toronto hotel suite. "*My* goodness."

His arthritis has him sitting a little uncomfortably. A cane is within easy reach. A copy of the Kansas City *Star* lies nearby, partially read. He has been away from home for just a few hours; his airline ticket peeks out from the inside right pocket of his light blue suit jacket.

So then, Hootie must have been enjoying himself all those years? Apparently yes. He led a popular, blues-based swing band out of Kansas City from 1939 to 1942 — a still-unknown Charlie Parker was one of its alto saxophonists — and then worked with a variety of smaller groups on both coasts of the country. After a lull of sorts in Kansas City during the 1950s and 1960s, he made a comeback that has kept him on the international stage for the better part of the next 30 years.

"I did have a good time," he agrees, in the high, nasal tenor that serves as both his speaking and singing voice. "Sometimes you get out there when you're not feeling no pain, you know, and you lose track of, like, four, five, 10 years. Don't let nobody kid you. Ten years can pass and someone says, 'Well, what have you done in 10 years?' And you don't know because you was having a ball."

But that was then, and this is now. "Well, I'm 83, and I feel 83," he admits, fielding a query about his health. He has been lucky, he notes, "but sooner or later, the arthritis hits, maybe a little heart trouble, and you start feeling pains that you haven't felt before."

He's not travelling very much any more — "I knew I had to shut that down" — but he still appears annually at the Montreal Bistro in Toronto, health permitting. This latest visit precedes by a week the release of a new and remarkably vital CD, *Still Jumpin' the Blues*, his second collaboration with guitarist Duke Robillard for the Edmonton label Stony Plain.

McShann has in fact done very well by Canadian record companies. He has made at least 10 LPs and CDs for the Sackville label in Toronto since 1972. The first, *The Man from Muskogee*, coincided with his re-emergence from Kansas City. Several of the others find him playing with the Toronto saxophonist Jim Galloway, who is again his bandmate for this current visit to the Bistro.

And how are things on the Kansas City scene that McShann has momentarily left behind? "Well, let's see," he replies cautiously, "cats is swinging."

Of course cats always was, but clearly times have changed. Used to be, during the 1930s, that the city was home to a couple of dozen clubs, most of them between 12th Street and 18th.

McShann has been back to visit the old district within recent memory. "You go around, look at the old places. I remember the first place I played in Kansas City, the Monroe Inn. It's still there. I was so surprised! It was just a kick to go by, stand outside. And you go by other places you remember, and you sort of visualize all the things that was happening in those days."

He paints a vivid picture of the Swing era in Kansas City, when Count Basie, Lester Young, Big Joe Turner, Pete Johnson, Hot Lips Page, Mary Lou Williams and, of course, Bird — the young Charlie Parker — were all on the scene. "Before you'd even get to 18th Street, or 12th Street, you'd hear all the music blaring out from the clubs. They'd have speakers right at the door; you'd hear old Joe Turner hollering those blues."

McShann discovered Parker in just this way. "First time I heard Parker," he remembers, "I was coming down 12th Street, past a club called the Bar Le Duc, another fellow and myself — the two of us together. We heard this music piped out. Said, 'Hey man, who's that?' Said, 'I don't know. Let's go see.' We went in listening to this cat blow. It was Bird. We went up to talk to him. Said, 'Hey man, where you been? We ain't heard *no*body around here blowing like *that*.'"

Sixty years on, McShann hasn't seen Robert Altman's recent film, *Kansas City*, which attempted to recreate the city's golden age of jazz. He is, however, aware of the "swing revival" that has momentarily caught the U.S. recording industry's fancy. He's not quite sure what the Cherry Poppin' Daddies, the Royal Crown Revue and Big Bad Voodoo Daddy sound like, but he admits that he's curious.

"They say swing is back again. I haven't been listening too much, to tell you the truth, but I'm going to have to get out — start cocking my ear."

March 3, 1999

"Big Finish"
Tony Bennett (1999)

Tony Bennett would have us believe that he was the "Madonna of his day." He said so himself Tuesday night, to general laughter at Roy Thomson Hall. However tongue-in-cheek the comment may have been — however self-congratulatory — there's at least one thing wrong with the 72-year-old American singer's analogy. It suggests that his day is past.

The evidence points to another conclusion altogether: that Tony Bennett is the Tony Bennett of his day, a performer to whom others will be compared — perhaps even the Material Girl, if her career lasts into its 50th year, as his now has.

Bennett's fans span a full three generations, judging by the folks who filled Roy Thomson Hall to all four corners. His records continue to win Grammys. He himself remains in good voice, one part ache and two parts optimism. His singing is inevitably a little tauter and a shade less resonant than it once was, but it's powerful enough that he still can put down his microphone relatively late in a concert and handle *Fly Me to the Moon, au naturel*. (Okay, it's a gimmick — always has been — but it works.)

Bennett began his latest Toronto performance by making promises. He sang *The Best is Yet to Come* for starters, casting a surely unintended (and certainly unwarranted) aspersion on the evening's brief and cheerfully cryptic opening set by his fellow singer Nnenna Freelon. Bennett continued with *If I Could Be with You One Hour Tonight* and actually stayed on stage with pianist Ralph Sharon's quartet a half-hour longer than that.

At 90 minutes, though, the show was a rather curious piece of work. Bennett flitted through the first 60 and dawdled over the last 30, covering nearly two dozen songs along the way. Most were truncated: a verse and chorus or two and then the Big Finish — either a long, held note or a belted-out final few words. In the process, he came uncomfortably close to caricaturing himself.

He seemed to relax a little, however, as the evening neared its conclusion. By the time he had sung tributes to everyone from Ethel Merman and Judy Garland to Fred Astaire and Billie Holiday, interspersed with a sampling of his own hits, he'd caught his second wind. He then added another half-dozen songs, any one of which would have served him well as a finale. But he just kept on going.

This is a new element in Bennett performances of late: a certain sentimentality. Sure, he's the guy who sang *I Left My Heart in San Francisco*. (He sang it again Tuesday: verse, chorus, Big Finish.) What could be more sentimental than that? But this is something else — this is a veteran artist basking in his fans' adulation and not wanting it to end. And who can blame him? It can't go on forever. Then again, maybe it can. After all, we're talking about Tony Bennett here, not... well... Madonna.

March 11, 1999

"Sheer persistence"
Paul Plimley (1999)

Paul Plimley doesn't want to do just another interview. Not for him the same old questions. Can we, he wonders, take the conversation somewhere else? Can he — the Vancouver jazz pianist seems to be suggesting on this rainy afternoon over red wine and pizza slivers in a bar on Toronto's College Street — call the shots?

Well, no, he can't. Not completely

That's fine: Plimley isn't really the controlling type. He's just naturally gregarious, a high-adrenaline, take-charge kind of guy who seems to know precisely how far to push and exactly when to draw back.

So ask him anything. Ask him, for example, about his latest CD, *Safe-Crackers*, released this past weekend at the Festival International de Musique Actuelle de Victoriaville on the Quebec festival's own Victo label. Plimley, bassist L.S. (Lisle) Ellis and drummer Scott Amendola appeared there in concert on Saturday to celebrate the occasion.

It's Plimley's 10th CD in as many years, and the seventh with Ellis in either a collaborative or accompanying role. Among Canadian pianists who have followed Oscar Peterson and Paul Bley onto the international stage, only Oliver Jones has recorded more often. Jones, of course, is a mainstreamer through and through. Plimley, on the other hand, works in what is still called — for want of a better term — the avant-garde.

But avant-garde is a relative concept, and Plimley, now 46, is a restless musician. He seems to have been repositioning himself of late. "Lisle and I, in the '90s," he suggests, "have been moving away from some of the — let's say — more 'standardized' free-form elements and areas that Cecil Taylor has worked in and, at the same time, we're incorporating the forward momentum that's inherently a part of the swing and funk traditions."

Cecil Taylor's name often comes up in discussions of Plimley's music; the visionary American pianist shadows any pianist who has challenged the orthodoxies of modern jazz. "I would say it's still a reference point," Plimley agrees, having just used Taylor's name himself, "but things that I've been developing on my own are coming more to the fore and there are certain times when I sound absolutely nothing like Cecil."

Back, then, to *Safe-Crackers*. This new interest in "forward momentum" has led Plimley and Ellis to Scott Amendola, who gave guitarist Charlie Hunter's funky San Francisco quartet such an in-the-pocket "groove" a couple of years ago. The trio is now developing its own rhythmic concept based on "a multiplicity of different tempos." And if that's not enough of a shift in direction, Plimley also describes *Safe-Crackers* as the most lyrical and melodic of his recordings.

"So we're working in a number of different areas and we're still, of course, using some of those other completely open, post-Taylor methodologies."

In truth, Plimley seems quite happy to play it any way it lays, pre-Taylor or post-Taylor. There he is on *Yo Miles!*, a recent CD tribute to trumpeter Miles Davis. And here he is in Toronto, readying himself for a solo concert at the Music Gallery, where he might just play a few Frank Zappa pieces in anticipation of the Zappa tribute that he plans to record later this year for the Swiss label hatOLOGY.★

And there's Plimley again, scheduled for no less than six concerts next month at the du Maurier International Jazz Festival back home in Vancouver. Five will be

★ This project was in fact not realized.

completely spontaneous encounters, matching Plimley with several of his peers in the international avant-garde — bassist William Parker and drummers Han Bennink, Gerry Hemingway and Susie Ibarra among them.

Unlike his work over the years with Ellis, which he describes as "accumulative" and "evolving," these one-offs — a Plimley tradition at the Vancouver festival during the 1990s — have the "jolt of the moment" to recommend them. "It is," he says of each new encounter, "sort of a do-or-die situation."

Of course, if Plimley's willingness to mount and invariably meet such a variety of creative challenges makes him the most important Canadian jazz pianist of the 1990s, it will never make him the most popular.

"I'll always be out of the mass mainstream," he concurs, while arguing that his "sheer persistence" and his growing body of work can't be denied forever. And there's something else, too. "I think I'm paying more and more attention to the melodic capacity of music — which I've always loved anyway."

Folks, in other words, may yet come around.

Plimley returns to *Safe-Crackers*. "If you heard the music," he speculates, "you'd say, 'Okay, this is not essentially wild music. It is a little outside the mainstream, but there is a knowledge of the tradition here and there is a pronounced lyrical sensibility.'"

He has been talking for nearly an hour. The wine and pizza are finished. He's starting to fidget. There remains a question or two to be asked, but all this talk of jolts and do-or-die situations seems to have his adrenaline going again.

"Are we done, do you think, pretty well?" he asks cheerfully but firmly, calling the last shot.

Pretty well, yes.

May 28, 1999

"Calling card"
Ian Bargh (2000)

Ian Bargh is giving up his day job. Retiring, actually. He turns 65 on Saturday and is leaving a long career as an engineer at the end of the month. His night job, as it were, awaits. He's one of Toronto's finest jazz pianists; had he so chosen, he might well have made music his life all along.

Bargh is getting a jump on retirement this week at the Montreal Bistro, where he's working in the company of another T.O. veteran, vibraphonist Frank Wright.

To mark the occasion, three of Bargh's well-placed friends and admirers — Ted O'Reilly of Toronto's CJRT-FM, John Norris of Sackville Records and Jim Galloway of Toronto's Downtown Jazz festival — conspired on Tuesday evening to present him with the "calling card" that every career-bent musician needs these days, his own CD.

Bargh, it should be noted, wasn't in on the idea. The disc, titled *Only Trust Your Heart*, came as "a complete surprise." (The music was originally recorded by O'Reilly in a CJRT studio six years ago when Bargh stopped by to put a new piano through its paces.) But if the CD is unauthorized, it can hardly be unwelcome; Bargh has recorded only twice before in jazz settings, once with Jim Galloway and trumpeter Doc Cheatham 15 years ago and once with drummer Larry Dubin's Big Muddies another 20 years earlier.

Both albums are in a dixie-swing style, which is scarcely the half of Bargh's interests as a pianist. His first set with Frank Wright at the Bistro, no less than his 11 unaccompanied performances on *Only Trust Your Heart*, was rather more revealing. More modern, for one thing — in a vigorous swing-to-bop manner.

In truth, Bargh doesn't pay much mind to the purity of any particular style. His knowledge of piano jazz from the 1930s through the 1950s is encyclopedic, but his erudition is largely untutored, which allows him to make his own, fresh sense of the jazz tradition with each new improvisation as he moves quickly, impulsively and often forcefully around the keyboard.

He was giving Wright a band's worth of support on Tuesday — bass lines, harmonies and filigree, all jockeying for position behind the vibraphonist's melodies. Wright in turn is a fairly earnest and uncomplicated soloist whose only real eccentricity is his taste in mallets and their corresponding timbral qualities. One pair, quite long in the stick and heavily padded, generated more of a sharp slap than any discernible pitch on *Sweet Sue*; another, shorter set rang hard and true on *I Remember April*.

The novelty of *Sweet Sue* and the linear whirl of *I Remember April* represented the extremes of the duo's efforts stylistically — from near-vaudeville to near-Lennie Tristano on the historical continuum of jazz. It's still old music, really, but Bargh has exactly the sort of imagination and energy needed to keep it alive and swinging in the 21st century. Soon enough, he'll have the time as well.

January 6, 2000

"Muscle and bone"
JoAnne Brackeen (2000)

JoAnne Brackeen is something of a contrary thinker. How else to describe a pianist who plays *Yesterdays* with a purposeful sort of immediacy that puts it very much in the present tense? Who dresses the pretty melody of *Emily* not in a frilly frock but a pair of coveralls? Whose *Body and Soul* is mostly muscle and bone? Whose *Days of Wine and Roses* is tart and thorny?

Brackeen did and played all of these things in her vigorous and sometimes exhilarating opening set with bassist Neil Swainson at the Montreal Bistro on Tuesday night. Not for this New York musician mere sentimentality. She's an improviser first and an interpreter distantly second; it's the musical challenge of her material, not the emotional core, that draws her attention as she breaks down and rebuilds each piece on her set list into something new and far more elaborate than the original.

Those contrary ideas may really just be accidental by-products of this process. Indeed, every tune she plays proves to be purposeful and immediate, every solo all muscle and bone. And yet — again contrarily — Brackeen's not without a sense of whimsy. Take the title of her latest CD, the Grammy-nominated *Pink Elephant Magic*. Or the inspiration for one of her other tunes on that disc, *Ghost Butter*, a yogurt-like confection that apparently blends the taste of peanut butter and German chocolate cake. Or the rather fanciful way in which she slipped out of several tunes the other night, putting a bluesy tag on *Body and Soul*, for example, and letting *Wine and Roses* just drift away note by note to... nothing.

She's a difficult pianist to pin down stylistically at this point, more than 40 years into a career that has seen her playing alongside Dexter Gordon, Woody Shaw, Art Blakey and Stan Getz. They were all boppers of one sort or another in their day; Brackeen now seems to be once-removed from bop of any sort and instead works her way around the piano in a jostling, percussive manner fuelled by an assertive and often abstract imagination that will not be hindered by idiomatic niceties.

She has in Neil Swainson a highly effective foil. The Toronto bassist relaxed her precipitous angle of attack in each of his own solos on Tuesday and balanced her sometimes brittle touch with his own, more supple fingerwork. Whenever she was in flight, he kept his accompaniment simple. He wasn't being contrary himself, mind you, just practical.

February 4, 2000

"Excitement is one thing"
Cyrus Chestnut (2000)

Among the jazz pianists of his generation — he's 37 — Cyrus Chestnut is the guy with all the personality. Even his hands have personality, what with their extravagant flips and flourishes of the wrist and their high, swooping dives to the keyboard, landing not with the expected crash of a chord or a cluster but with the sweet chirp of a single, struck note.

The American's reputation apparently precedes him. He took to the stage of the George Weston Recital Hall on Saturday night with a genial "How's everybody?" and almost immediately had someone in the hall calling out a question about his daughter. ("She's two going on 10," Chestnut replied smoothly.) And just in case anyone hadn't caught the among-friends spirit of the evening, he followed his first two rousing tunes, *Hot Tamales* and *Country Time Blues*, with the announcement that his "mission" was "to send [us] away feeling good."

Well, mission accomplished. (Some of us, however, might have gone away feeling even better had his bassist been suppler than Kengo Nakamura and his drummer subtler than Neil Smith.) Chestnut covered a great deal of the jazz piano tradition in the course of a dozen tunes, stopping safely short of the avant-garde but heartily embracing just about everything else, from the music's gospel roots, through its stride rhythms, to its blues derivatives and its hard-bop overtones.

Along the way, the trio moved between two clear, historical points of reference, from the classic trio of Ahmad Jamal on one hand to the equally classic trio of Oscar Peterson on the other. From reserve to exuberance, tension to release — occasionally within a chorus or two of each other. Such was particularly the case with Chestnut's arrangement of *It Don't Mean a Thing (If It Ain't Got That Swing)*, which got an audible rise out of the normally circumspect Weston Hall audience.

Chestnut showed Jamal's delicate touch and timing, but boasted Peterson's power and acceleration; he worked these qualities into his solos almost interchangeably. His purest piano playing, however, was to be found in his two unaccompanied pieces, the quirky *Nutman's Invention* and the hymn *Sweet Hour of Prayer*, and in his ballad for that precocious two-year-old back home, *Elegant Flower*. Excitement is one thing — Chestnut generated plenty of that — but music of this beauty is quite another.

March 6, 2000

"Beyond prediction"
Cassandra Wilson (2000)

Cassandra Wilson, it seems, has the perfect audience. Not that the Mississippi-born, Manhattan-based singer is clear as to exactly who's going to show up on any given night — tomorrow night, for example, at Massey Hall in Toronto. "I don't know whether they're jazzheads, purists, pop followers or whatever," she admitted in a recent telephone interview. "I just know that they're there."

They're there and there are plenty of them, enough to account for sales of more than a million between her first two CDs for Blue Note, *Blue Light 'til Dawn* (1993) and *New Moon Daughter* (1996). Better yet, Wilson's fans are prepared to take her on faith. Wherever she wants to go and whatever she wants to do is fine by them. And Wilson, who is "early 40-something" and a good 15 years into her recording career, has long since proven herself to be beyond prediction.

"Generally," she noted, "I find that the audiences that come to see me expect something old and something new." And surely something borrowed and something blue — hers is, after all, a marriage of rural and urban musical Americana, combining classic Robert Johnson and Son House songs, direct from the Mississippi Delta, with jazz standards and more recent hits from the Joni Mitchell, Monkees and Neil Young catalogues.

"Yeah, borrowed and blue," she agreed with a light laugh. "My fans tend to expect that of me, really. They want to see some sort of evolution. They don't want to see the same show as they saw last year."

Last year's show was in fact built around her third Blue Note CD, *Traveling Miles* (1999), with which she paid tribute to the legacy of the late jazz trumpeter Miles Davis. This year's program still includes some of that same material, along with songs drawn from as far back as *Jumpworld*, a 1989 recording for the German JMT label, and new pieces that are still taking shape for her next Blue Note CD.

If there's a clue as to what that CD might sound like, it could lie in Wilson's own listening pleasures these days, the Cuban band Synthesis foremost among them. Everybody, but everybody, is going Cuban these days; Wilson's naturally cagey about the extent to which she might be jumping on that particular bandwagon.

"I don't know if you can hear [the influence] directly. What do they say, good composers borrow, great composers steal? You don't want to really be obvious with what you're experiencing at the moment, you want to blend it in with your own personal style."

Speaking of listening pleasures, how about Joni Mitchell's recent foray into jazz, *Both Sides Now*? Wilson has freely acknowledged the influence of Mitchell's earlier work as a folk singer and songwriter on her own music; she must have some thoughts on Mitchell's latest transformation. Indeed, she offers it a ringing endorsement.

"I think it's wonderful and I think it's about time. I think she can flourish in this music. She has always been a jazz artist to my ears, and it's just now that people are beginning to allow her that context."

Both Sides Now finds Mitchell singing jazz and pop standards to full orchestral accompaniment, strings soaring. That's something that Wilson herself has not yet done, but she admits that she's interested. "I think every singer at some point wants to be inside of an orchestra, to have that kind of lush context to relax in. There's a certain energy you can always rely on when you have that many musicians around you. So yeah, every singer would love to be in that situation — maybe not all the time, but once in a while."

To date, of course, Wilson has pursued a very different musical esthetic. Her bands have been fairly small, somewhat eclectic and very loose; spontaneity is key and textures are important. "I tend not to like to be in situations where the music is rigid, where there are parts that you know are going to be played the same way every night. I prefer being in the moment and being able to access all kinds of weird energies on the stage."

Some of the weirdest energies in recent years have been supplied by the Toronto guitarist Kevin Breit, whose other commitments — including a Blue Note CD of his own — have kept him from touring with Wilson again this year. Marvin Sewell is handling her guitar work these days; bassist Lonnie Plaxico and percussionist Jeff Haynes continue as before, while pianist George Colligan and drummer Lionel Cordew are new since Wilson's last Toronto appearance at Harbourfront in June, 1999.

Those among her fans who continue to look for "some sort of evolution," as she puts it, will no doubt have also remarked on her growing confidence and looming personality onstage. She's a much bolder and more expansive performer than the fragile figure who seemed swept along by the music of *Blue Light 'til Dawn* just a few years ago.

Wilson doesn't disagree. "This time around," she promised, "I'm even bolder. I find I'm moving more on stage, dancing more. I think I'm a late bloomer in a lot of respects. I have so concentrated on the music — on honing my skills inside the music — that performance has come to me gradually. I used to really love to hide inside the music and be a part of the fabric of it. I didn't feel that it was important to stand out front and take the role of leader so obviously. But the older I get, I realize, 'Yeah, I can do that.' For my benefit — and for the audience."

June 13, 2000

"Niche"
Phil Minton (2001)

His mother was a soprano, his father a baritone. An uncle had "a very nice high tenor." As a young English lad growing up in Torquay, Devon, Phil Minton "would want to try to sound like all of them." And so began the vocal adventures of an extraordinary singer and improviser who defies description, let alone category or tradition.

"I was intrigued by voices," Minton, now 60, continues, "and it was something I could do quite well as a child. I liked rough voices as well. Jimmy Durante — I used to love his sound. Of course I had a boy-soprano voice and I'd try to impersonate him."

Minton laughs at the memory of such an improbable match, offering an adult impression of Durante that breaks up as it crosses the Atlantic Ocean by cellphone from Munich — one stop on the tour that brings him to Canada presently for performances in Montreal with the Swiss dancer Katharina Vogel and in Toronto with a fellow vocal experimentalist, the Canadian Paul Dutton.

In truth, Minton doesn't really do impressions any more. Hasn't for many years. Not since his days with dance bands around Devon. "My natural voice is a very high baritone; I can sing quite high and I have ways of singing low, so I could get right the way through the whole range. I'd be sounding like Paul Simon on one song and Wilson Pickett the next."

But Minton's is no mere André-Philippe Gagnon act, no crazed, avant-garde *We Are the World.* "I've found my own little niche," he suggests now rather modestly. "I sort of invent things." All manner of odd and impolite things, in fact. Natters, yips, wheezes, snorts and sputters, which have become his vocabulary for an improvisational and highly theatrical train of thought that runs from the delirious to the damn-near demented.

Of course Minton can sing straight when he wants to, whether he's recording the texts of Federico Garcia Lorca, Hermann Hesse and Arthur Rimbaud with British jazz composer Mike Westbrook on *The Cortège* (Enja), the poems of Ho Chi Minh with pianist Veryan Weston on *Songs from a Prison Diary* (Leo) or passages from James Joyce on his own quartet's CD *Mouthfull of Ecstasy* (Victo).

If Minton has any vocal counterpart at all, it would be the American Bobby McFerrin. But even that seems a real stretch. Minton's far more subversive; it's a long way from *Don't Worry, Be Happy* to *Finnegans Wake.*

He remembers being moved as a teenager by Jackson Pollock's "action painting" to indulge in bouts of what he calls "action music." And if the noted American abstract expressionist, and the visual arts more generally, aren't quite the inspiration that they once were on his music, he still appreciates "some of the naughty, conceptual things that go on; I have quite a lot of respect for people who break the rules."

On that count, it comes as no surprise that he would call Louis Armstrong "a great inspiration." And coincidentally like Armstrong — who revolutionized popular singing in the 1930s — Minton has been known to play trumpet, albeit in a style shaped by the more modern jazzers Miles Davis, Booker Little and Don Cherry.

This might be enough to get him a seat at the table of the jazz tradition, if only below the salt. "That's up to people who say what jazz is," he observes, quite realistically. "I'm sure Wynton Marsalis wouldn't say I was part of the jazz tradition. There are others who might think so. I'd be proud to be part of it if somebody said I was."

And what of his mother and father, whose voices first inspired him? How have they reacted to his singing? Both of his parents are now deceased, he notes, but each came to terms with his various vocal ways and wiles. "My mother was quite interested. My father — well, he didn't like dissonance so much. It used to grind on him a little bit. But I think he was quite surprised that I managed to make some sort of living at this."

January 18, 2001

"Ephemeral"
Tristan Honsinger and
Misha Mengelberg (2001)

Some things you don't usually see or hear at the Top O' The Senator, one of Toronto's premier jazz rooms:

(1) The club as a concert hall, its black drapes drawn to block the lights outside on Victoria Street, and its table service suspended during the performance.

(2) A cellist — in this case, Tristan Honsinger.

Concert hall? Cellist? Sounds serious, classical even. But look again: there's (3) a grey windbreaker, hung indecorously — as if an item of laundry — over the raised lid of the Senator's piano, throwing a shadow back onto Misha Mengelberg, Honsinger's partner on Sunday evening and a fellow stalwart of (4) European avant-garde jazz.

Mengelberg and Honsinger play in the avant-garde's Dutch division, the pianist since the late 1960s, and the cellist since 1974. That's an important qualification inasmuch as it anticipates their fondness for the whimsical, which was evident in this performance's lapses into (5) a little theatre of the absurd.

Even without acting, Mengelberg and Honsinger presented themselves as Beckett-like creations. But Honsinger took appearances a step further in the evening's first set when he broke into an oblique dialogue with himself, one voice male and English, the other female and French. (Something about a lost hat.) He revived the two characters near the end of the second set, with Mengelberg joining in the general nonsense.

It was all quite diverting, and equally rather ephemeral. Mengelberg and Honsinger are past masters at this sort of thing, both theatrically and musically speaking. Performance art comes easily to them: Mengelberg plays his role as straight man at the piano with devious intelligence, hemming, hawing and hunting around the keyboard, while Honsinger is all impulse and inspiration with the cello, gleeful to the very point of madness.

Their mutual sense of timing is innate, although it's not as though they're up to anything especially difficult. They can improvise together in agreement or in opposition, knowing after all these years that either approach will work on its own terms. Free improvisation is very forgiving that way.

And so they nattered along on Sunday until some modest idea or small gesture suddenly took on a life of its own and the music momentarily soared. Then it was back to the mundane; very Beckett-like indeed.

But will the Senator ever be the same again? Yes, of course it will. In fact, a bastion of the jazz mainstream, Toronto's Brass Connection, opens there tonight for the week.

March 20, 2001

"Protected"
Wayne Shorter (2003)

There's an air of vulnerability about Wayne Shorter these days, a suggestion of slight uncertainty and mild self-absorption that belies his 67 years in a way that his soft, unlined face does not.

The *tableau* onstage at the Théâtre Maisonneuve, where the American tenor and soprano saxophonist gave the Festival International de Jazz de Montréal such an exquisite performance on Sunday, was revealing. There stood Shorter, not front and centre as would befit a musician of his importance, but off to one side, backed into the curve of the theatre's Steinway grand piano, with a small table to his right, music stands to his left and two microphones in front of him. Anyone else would have looked caged; Shorter seemed protected.

His three younger musicians were extremely attentive. Pianist Danilo Pérez, bassist John Patitucci and drummer Brian Blade behaved as though they could hardly believe their luck to be working with such a legend and were still reconciling their former role as his fans — whether of his work as a member of trumpeter Miles Davis's illustrious quintet of the mid-1960s or of Weather Report in the 1970s — with their new status as his accompanists.

More than once Pérez turned to the audience and shook his head in amazement at something that Shorter had just played; on one occasion, Blade, caught up by the vehemence of Shorter's declamations, jumped straight to his feet with a crash of cymbals and an electrifying yell of of his own.

It is a marvellous band — as much to hear as to watch. Shorter has selected musicians who know how to play softly and when not to play at all, gifts of intuition that serve his purposeful vagueness very well. He finds great freedom in ambiguity; a direction that is at best merely implicit can be changed easily, and Shorter was changing direction sharply and often on Sunday, thriving on the oblique and the unpredictable. Pérez, Patitucci and Blade were quick to follow and indeed at times took the lead, which was apparently fine with Shorter, who looked on distantly from the centre of the swirl generated by their initiatives.

If there's a precedent for this level of collective interaction it is that same Davis quintet of nearly 40 years ago, although Shorter and company are, it must be said, generally of a more benign temperament. The saxophonist, who was one of the fiercest personalities in the Davis band, has lost some of his old power. His plaintive soprano now carries more effectively than his dry, haunted tenor. But his sense of drama remains fully engaged; if anything, it has been heightened by his increasingly enigmatic persona.

There were eight pieces in the concert, Shorter's classic *Footprints* central among them, followed by the signature Davis tune *All Blues* as an encore. The evening unfolded like a dawning realization, with the audience a bit baffled at first, perhaps disoriented by the playfully amorphous nature of the music. But the response from the hall grew slowly and by concert's end — when it was clear that something quite extraordinary had taken place — was just shy of rapturous. Shorter, now rightly at centre stage in the embrace of his musicians, suddenly seemed vulnerable again in face of the tumult — vulnerable but very pleased.

July 3, 2001

"At the top"
Enrico Rava (2001)

How many jazz musicians have told a story just like this?

"When I was 10 years old, I was crazy about [cornetist] Bix Beiderbecke. I had all his records, which wasn't hard because he didn't make very many. In my room when I was 11, there were all kinds of pictures of Bix and Frankie Trumbauer. My day was [spent] listening to 78s. My mother was desperate: I was doing very bad in school, because I didn't care about anything else."

The jazz musician in this case is trumpeter Enrico Rava. But here's the twist: his story takes place in Turin, Italy. And so begins the musical life of one of the foremost figures on the European scene.

At 15 he discovered Chet Baker, by his description "the modern Bix." Even now, 46 years later, when Rava finds himself suffering jet lag after his transatlantic jump to the Festival International de Jazz de Montréal, he turns for comfort in his hotel room to a Baker recording from 1954.

Bix, Chet and, inevitably, Miles Davis: this is Rava's lineage — musicians "with a sense of melody" and, equally, romantics, "without being too sweet or milky." But there's much more to Rava than that. There is, for example, his work during the past 35 years with American avant-gardists — Steve Lacy, Roswell Rudd and the redoubtable Cecil Taylor among them. A mere romantic would be taking his life in his hands at Taylor's side.

Rava in fact spent 10 years in New York, beginning in 1967. The sojourn, one of the earliest undertaken by an Italian jazz musician, would leave its mark. "It gave me a sense that when you go onstage, it's something very special," he explains in soft, accented English. "You have to be there 100 per cent. It's something that's very American, this urgency."

The experience also changed the way in which Rava regarded himself and, no less, the way in which he would be viewed in Europe. On the one hand, he remembers, "it made me much more sure of myself. For 10 years I played with the very best and I was okay." On the other, he returned to the Italian scene as something of a star.

Ah, yes, the Italian scene. To ask Rava about jazz in Italy is to get a quick lesson in cultural history. "People say 'Italy' and they think it's one homogenous thing," he begins. "It absolutely is not. It is many countries together. For instance, if I speak my dialect in Sicily nobody understands me; they don't have an idea even vaguely of what I'm talking about. We are many people with many different traditions... The only thing we *all* have is the opera."

He is hesitant to call opera Italy's "national folklore," but admits, "Personally, I am a jazz musician rooted in a very melodic sense of playing probably because of the strong presence of opera — Puccini, Verdi...'"

Still, Rava and opera have had something of a love-hate relationship. "In Italy you cannot turn on the radio without hearing some opera singer. For years I couldn't stand it, then one day I found I liked it." Soon enough, he adapted the themes from Bizet's *Carmen* for jazz ensemble. "I don't know how a psychoanalyst would describe it, but it was my way of getting out of that conflict."

His relationship with American jazz is perhaps not quite so readily resolved. The underlying emotion is obviously love; there is no hate, but there is a pull and push between inspiration and independence.

For the first of his four concerts in Montreal this year, an evening of duets with pianist Stefano Bollani, Rava mixed classic jazz themes with original compositions. Bollani was inclined to turn the music encyclopedic, but Rava held his focus clearly, while distancing himself from the Baker-Davis aspects of his lineage only by virtue of his own personality and playfulness.

In conversation, however, he becomes comparatively bolder, suggesting that the European scene is now richer, more interesting and "much more fun" than its American counterpart. Nevertheless he's quick to add, "Nobody will ever reach the level that the Americans reached between, let's say, 1925 — Louis Armstrong and the Hot Five — and 1965. That is one of the richest periods in the whole history of art. The only thing similar I can think of is the Renaissance with all those amazing painters."

High praise indeed, and from an Italian no less. But note the time frame. It ends 35 years ago. "I would say to my friends in Italy — many of them who are successful internationally — that we are lucky, because if the American scene was today what it was when I was a teenager, we would be playing at the bottom of the bill. Now if we are at the top it's only because they are not at the top any more."

July 14, 2001

"The game continues"
Les Projectionnistes (2001)

Claude St-Jean has written a piece of music that he calls *Vacances* — in English, *Holidays*. St-Jean is the bright bulb that illuminates Montreal's Projectionnistes; *Vacances* was the first tune of their opening set at the NOW Lounge Thursday evening during a Toronto stopover en route to their U.S. debut at Edgefest in Ann Arbor, Michigan, last night.

Vacances started at a light swing, switched into cranked-up rock and wound up as a march. That's the sort of stylistic progression that Carla Bley might follow, or Frank Zappa, although St-Jean tends to be more direct in his writing than Bley, less complex than Zappa.

And so begins — yet again — the game of trying to put into words exactly what it is that les Projectionnistes do. It's a game played whenever anyone from Quebec's resourceful *musique actuelle* scene ventures beyond the province's borders, be it the multi-instrumentalist Jean Derome, the guitarist René Lussier or the band Justine.

St-Jean is a 20-plus-year veteran of that scene, his activities in fact predating the term *musique actuelle*. He has wielded his trombone in more conventional jazz settings as well, and he's by far the strongest player that les Projectionnistes — even expanded now to seven members from the original five — have to offer in any strict jazz sense. But there's more to the man, and thus to the band, which explains why everyone from the Lounge Lizards to Magma turns up as points of comparison in its press dossier.

Typically, that first Toronto set also drew on funk, reggae and tango rhythms in the course of eight St-Jean compositions delivered in a manner that ranged from the declamatory to the histrionic, the fractious to the frenetic. There is, in short, a lot of energy in the music. St-Jean, however, keeps it under tight control and, as the cinematic metaphor would have it, sharply in focus.

His writing for his own trombone, the saxophones of Pierre Labbé and Roberto Murray and the sousaphone of Jean Sabourin is clean in its simplicity, while his demands on guitarist Bernard Falaise, bassist Tommy Babin and Rémi Leclerc are quite reasonable, no matter how many different ways he can find to break up four beats in a bar of music. Falaise, an improviser with a particularly frisky imagination, gets to work a little closer to the edge than the others, though more in the role of wild card than loose cannon.

Indeed, it's St-Jean himself who's the bully in this band. But he's a bully with a sweet sense of humour, as well as a deft way with the plunger mute — a québécois Ray Anderson of sorts, if perhaps a little less technically astute. And so the game continues.

October 6, 2001

"A friend to chaos"
Misha Mengelberg (2001)

Misha Mengelberg remembers well the time that he met Thelonious Monk. The encounter, as he describes it nearly 40 years later, is revealing of both pianists — of Mengelberg, now 66 and the leader of Amsterdam's ICP (Instant Composers Pool) Orchestra, which is currently on a 14-city North American tour, and of Monk, one of the most important, if enigmatic figures in modern jazz.

"He was already on a very dark path," Mengelberg recalls of Monk's demeanour during his visit to the Netherlands. "There was a lot of booze involved. It was difficult for me to speak with him. Of course I had some things to discuss, but he was not very approachable — until I finally got up and played *Criss Cross* the way he had played it about 12 years before, in 1949 I think. And then he recognized something; it was almost a perfect imitation. Here was some idiotic little guy in Holland who could imitate him. He thought that was interesting enough to talk with me — finally, a little bit."

Monk was and remains one of Mengelberg's touchstones. The lesser-known Herbie Nichols, Monk's contemporary in New York, is another, and the redoubtable Duke Ellington a third. The compositions of all three have been staples of the ICP Orchestra in recent years. But this is no mere repertory jazz band — no transatlantic Lincoln Center Jazz Orchestra. Not with the rumpled Mengelberg, that character out of a Beckett play, at its helm; nor with the capricious Han Bennink — a character no writer could invent — at the drums.

Moreover, the nine-piece ICP Orchestra casts its net widely and well beyond jazz. Its allegiances and allusions to a variety of European perspectives — from classical avant-garde to beer-hall pop — strain against the American traditions that Monk, Nichols and Ellington represent.

Mengelberg and Bennink are the orchestra's two surviving originals — in both senses of the word — from its days as one of several informal groupings associated with the Instant Composers Pool, an Amsterdam musicians' collective established in 1967. The two men have had an on-and-off, and at times difficult, working relationship for still longer. Even now, Mengelberg suggests mildly in a telephone interview from Amsterdam, "We are eternal enemies, of course, but at the same time I have a very big respect for Han Bennink."

In the beginning, the ICP's members were centrally involved in the burgeoning continental avant-garde that simultaneously built on and broke away from the ideas of its American counterpart; for the first time — Django Reinhardt and Joe Harriott aside — jazz musicians in Europe had developed an improvisational language of their own. Mengelberg, Bennink and company described their particular vernacular as "instant composition" and gave the title *Groupcomposing* to an LP made in 1970 by a forerunner of the ICP Orchestra.

One of their number, the German saxophonist Peter Brötzmann, had already defined the emerging European aesthetic in 1968 with his LP *Machine Gun* (FMP), an octet recording of a tumult and ferocity previously unknown and since unsurpassed in improvised music. "I'm not opposed to chaos, I'm a friend to chaos," Mengelberg notes in retrospect, of the sound and fury that *Machine Gun* came to signify. "But at the time — speaking of the beginning of the '70s — there was a tendency towards not listening at all to each other and just making as much noise as possible."

He calls that period "a temporary goodbye to the American fundamentals of improvised music." The estrangement lasted for Mengelberg until the early 1980s when he returned with the ICP Orchestra in tow to the music that had so intrigued him as a younger man — to Monk, and to the compositions of Herbie Nichols that had been available in Holland during the late 1950s on two Blue Note LPs. "Twenty pieces or so, maybe two more or two less," he remembers now of his Nichols repertoire. "I never counted them."

He did, however, analyze them closely. "That was during my time at the conservatory in the Hague. Instead of analyzing for the 170th time some Beethoven sonatas, or some Brahms, or whatever they wanted me to do — I was studying music theory — I analyzed the music of Thelonious Monk and Herbie Nichols."

Drawing on this knowledge, Mengelberg worked up the music for the CD *Two Programs: The ICP Orchestra Performs Nichols-Monk* (ICP), recorded in 1984 and 1986. An Ellington project followed, as documented by *Bospaadje Konijnehol* (ICP) from 1990 and 1991. And so, with this re-infusion of American jazz, albeit skewed to fit Mengelberg's Dutch designs, the band was made new again, its personnel stabilizing by mid-decade at Mengelberg, Bennink, trumpeter Thomas Heberer, trombonist Wolter Wierbos, reed players Ab Baars and Michael Moore, cellist Tristan Honsinger and bassist Ernst Glerum, with violinist Mary Oliver a more recent addition still.

All of which might just give the band's current North American concerts — the 10 dates in the U.S. especially — a certain significance. Mengelberg, however, is unmoved by the suggestion; this is not the same young Netherlander who approached the great Thelonious Monk so tentatively 40 years ago. Instead, he sees the trip strictly in practical terms. "America is a market for our music. Somehow, there are consumers there that are interested in coming to our concerts. I think that's enough reason to go."

Nothing symbolic, then?

"Symbolic? Well... well... symbolic? That's far fetched." He's scoffing at the very idea. "I'm not into symbolism at all."

November 16, 2001

"Agenda"
Wynton Marsalis (2002)

The Wynton Marsalis Septet doesn't play "gigs" the way any other jazz band does. No, Marsalis and his fellow musicians from New York "convene on the bandstand." That's how the oft-honoured trumpeter put it at Massey Hall on Sunday, making his latest concert in Toronto sound as though it was a meeting of the board. (Make that a meeting of the executive, inasmuch as the septet is drawn from the larger Lincoln Center Jazz Orchestra that Marsalis has directed since 1988.)

So let the minutes show that Marsalis, alto and sopranino saxophonist Wess Anderson, tenor saxophonist and clarinetist Victor Goines, trombonist Ronald Westray, pianist Richard Johnson, bassist Reginald Veal and drummer Herlin Riley were all present. Judging by the empty seats out in the hall, a few hundred Torontonians sent regrets.

On the agenda — Marsalis, traditionalist that he is, always has an agenda — was a review of the first half, roughly speaking, of jazz history as we know it, from the field hollers of the trumpeter's own *Uptown Ruler* to the still-sleek modern jags of Thelonious Monk's *Four in One*.

Monk, in fact was the man of these two hours. Marsalis programmed new and sonorous arrangements of no less than four Monk compositions — *Green Chimneys, Hackensack* and *Reflections* were the other three — but offset this modest burst of revisionism in the evening's first half with the hoariest of revivalist routines, a mock New Orleans funeral procession, in the second.

Of course Monk's idiosyncrasies, at least, do not readily avail themselves to a board-meeting mentality. Save for the deliberately Monkish piano solo that Johnson plunked down in the middle of *Hackensack*, the septet fairly breezed past all the things that make Monk's music unique, surely leaving the Massey Hall audience to wonder what all the fuss was about.

The band had a predictably stronger impact with its funeral numbers — first the solemn dirge to the graveyard and then the high-stepping strut home. Both Marsalis and Goines, the later playing clarinet, generated a Pavlovian sort of response from the crowd when they ran their respective solos on *Just a Close Walk with Thee* up to long, held high notes.

It must be said that Marsalis' long, held high notes are always a wonder, as is his trumpeting more generally. His command of the instrument and its effects, both rhythmic and tonal, is effortless, and his improvisations — unlike the flailing efforts on Sunday of Anderson and Goines — have a marvellous sense of authority. While a lesser trumpeter with the same historical pre-occupations might simply sound corny, Marsalis brings to them a certain dignity. That's enough to carry his agenda forward, but still not sufficient to make it completely convincing.

Previously unpublished; March 2002

"The bones ache"
Peter Brötzmann (2002)

How long can the avant-garde go on being the avant-garde? In jazz, apparently, 40 years and counting. Four decades on, and the avant-garde's liberating innovations and extremes have yet to be either absorbed or eclipsed. The German saxophonist Peter Brötzmann, 61, who has been in the very thick of things for just as long, can see the oddity now of his position in the music's history — his position and that of his fellow veterans, Europeans and Americans alike, of those revolutionary 1960s.

"It's a funny thing," he observes in a telephone conversation from Chicago, the jump-off point of his so-called Chicago Tentet's current tour of a dozen U.S. and Canadian cities. "If I look around at what the younger players are doing in Europe, and maybe here too, I must say that people like [saxophonist] Evan Parker, [drummer] Han Bennink, [pianist] Misha Mengelberg — and maybe including myself — we are in a way still avant-garde. It's very funny, because we are old men!"

Well, 61 is not really that old. And at least some younger players have been keeping the faith. In fact, Brötzmann has several in the Chicago Tentet. But his point still stands. "I wish it would be different, but I think at the moment it's not the time to develop really new stuff or go in new directions. It's the way history goes; it always has its ups and downs. At the moment, it's the time for looking around, searching, and maybe the young people don't have the will, or the energy, to fight for something."

Certainly Brötzmann has never lacked for these qualities. He is as bellicose an improviser as any in jazz; it may be no coincidence at all that his most celebrated recording, an octet session from 1968 with Dutch, English, Swedish and German musicians, bears the title *Machine Gun* (FMP), establishing a metaphor that carries over to the unrelenting attack of the music itself.

Brötzmann's was the first generation of European jazz musicians to turn consciously away from the U.S. model, in part as a response to that country's domestic and foreign policies of the 1960s — not least in the matters of civil rights and the war in Vietnam. Whatever Brötzmann himself may have thought about those issues, though, he was not quite so anti-American when it came to music.

"That, I must say, was never the thing with me. I have to give a big 'Thank you' to some of my American friends, like [trumpeter] Don Cherry and [saxophonist] Steve Lacy. At that time, when no one took me seriously, they said, 'Okay, Brötzmann, go and do your thing.' They invited me to play with them, which helped me a lot. And anyway, there is something in American jazz music that Europeans don't have, and you know I'm always interested in things I don't have."

Brötzmann nevertheless still asserts his early independence from U.S. influences — especially from that of the New York saxophonist Albert Ayler, with whom he has been widely compared over the years and to whom he has paid tribute with the band Die like a Dog. (The quartet's name is a blunt allusion to the ignominy of the American's death in 1970; Ayler's body was found in the East Hudson River.)

"If you listen a bit carefully," Brötzmann suggests of their respective styles, "I think it's very obvious that — at the same time, on different continents, not knowing each other — we tried to do a similar thing. We had our handling of the saxophone in common — the harmonics, the scales. When I got the very first Albert Ayler records at that time, the ones he produced in Denmark and Sweden, I of course felt very close to him, ja. Here was a man on the other side of the world doing similar things."

Of course the world seems much smaller now. Brötzmann, who has lived since the late 1950s in Wuppertal, is no stranger to America (or, further afield, to Japan). He was a member of the quartet Last Exit with three New Yorkers (notably guitarist Sonny Sharrock) during the late 1980s and early 1990s, overlapping his continuing association with drummer Hamid Drake, a mainstay of Die like a Dog and the Chicago Tentet.

The latter band, which dates to 1997, also boasts among its members the saxophonists Mats Gustaffson, Ken Vandermark and Mars Williams, multi-instrumentalist Joe McPhee, trombonist Jeb Bishop, cellist Fred Lonberg-Holm, bassist Kent Kessler and a second drummer, Michael Zerang.

They'd give Brötzmann a run for his money — if there were any money in the avant-garde. It's not sometimes called "free jazz" for nothing. But seriously folks, Brötzmann has been more than holding his own against all comers for a long time. And it's not getting any easier — "Being 61, I tell you, the bones ache every morning" — but he remains a legend for the harrowing intensity of his saxophone solos.

"People are making that up," he scoffs, of the suggestion, before going on more or less to confirm it. "I mean, I like to use the horn in a powerful way. Playing is, for me, a body thing, a physical thing. Where the energy comes from, I don't know. Maybe I just believe in what I'm doing; you give, every time, everything you have."

June 4, 2002

"Firm"
Fred Hersch (2002)

Fred Hersch is not one to pretend that things aren't what they are. After all, the New York pianist has made no secret of the fact that he's gay and HIV-positive. This, in a sphere of music — jazz — that has never been particularly enlightened when it comes to matters of sexuality.

So when — at an admittedly far more trivial level — the Markham International Jazz Festival advertises Hersch's concert tomorrow night with the Toronto Sinfonietta as "A Tribute to Bill Evans," he doesn't hesitate to set things straight. It's not.

Originally, he was asked by the festival to participate in a performance of the orchestral arrangements that Claus Ogerman wrote for a recording by the late pianist in 1965.

"I said 'No,'" Hersch explains in a telephone interview from New York. "But I do have a whole program that I've arranged for jazz trio and chamber orchestra. It's the same flavour, but it's mine, and that's what we went with. What will it have to do with Bill Evans specifically? Not much, except both of us like classical music and both of us have done stuff with orchestra."

Indeed, instead of performing music directly associated with Evans, Hersch will be presenting pieces by Bach, Debussy, Fauré, Scriabin and Ravel from the classical world, and by Thelonious Monk and Billy Strayhorn from jazz. "It's certainly not 'pops,'" he says, "but it's a crossover-y sort of program."

Truth to tell, Hersch seems a bit rankled by comparisons to Evans, who died in 1980. "It's funny, being thrown in the Bill Evans 'bin.' That's been happening to me for so many years. I mean, I'd rather be compared to Bill Evans than to some hack — it's not an insult by any stretch — but it's so inaccurate. Just stylistically, I owe as much to Thelonious Monk as I do to Bill Evans. But people say, 'Oh, white guy, plays ballads — Bill Evans...' Or 'sensitive and lyrical,' which can be a subtext for 'gay.' I get that too.' "

It's not as though Hersch at 46 isn't all of those things. But he's also a composer whose latest effort is a virtuoso classical piece, comprising 24 variations on a Bach chorale. And he's a teacher, both privately in New York and, until this past May, on staff at the New England Conservatory of Music in Boston.

Meanwhile, his credits as a pianist include more than 30 CDs and LPs as a leader or co-leader since his move to New York from Cincinnati in 1977. Songbook sets (Monk, Strayhorn, Rodgers & Hammerstein, Russian and French classics). Collaborations with singers (Janis Siegel, Jay Clayton, Jeri Brown) and instrumentalists (Jane Ira Bloom, Bill Frisell, Toots Thielemans). Solo recordings. Even a 1990 tribute to, yes, Bill Evans — *Evanessence* (Evidence).

But Hersch remains firm on the Evans issue.

"There are so many pianists," he suggests, "whether it's Keith Jarrett or Paul Bley, who owe a debt to Bill Evans, and we all sound different. Just like a lot of painters owe a debt to Cézanne or Picasso, or composers to Stravinsky or Schoenberg, but that doesn't mean they don't have their own identity.

"And, of course, that's the idea of jazz. That's what I'm constantly emphasizing to the pianists I work with, trying to get them to be personal, to really hear the tradition, to respect it and to build on it in their own way."

As Thelonious Monk did, for example. But to ask Hersch about Monk in particular is to get an insightful digression about jazz more generally. "Most of the pianists I listen to and revere are pure improvisers," he begins. Implicitly Monk is one of them. "I revere Earl Hines — he was just out of his *mind*; his solo work is about as far out as anybody goes. So I would always rather hear Earl Hines than Art Tatum, much as I love Art Tatum. And I'd rather hear Tommy Flanagan than Hank Jones, or Oscar Peterson, because I think Tommy in his way took more chances."

Hersch turns to saxophonists, then guitarists. "Much as I adore John Coltrane, I'd rather hear Sonny Rollins. I'd rather hear Jim Hall than Joe Pass. That's not to put down any of these players, but what I listen for in jazz and what excites me in jazz — playing it, and listening to it — is that sense of danger, or of taking risks."

Speaking of which, his next compositional project, *Leaves of Grass,*★ for two voices and eight instruments, represents a risk of a different sort. It draws on the words and thoughts of the mid-19th-century American poet Walt Whitman, whose ideas about democracy and the freedom of man, shaped in the years around the Civil War, have acquired new relevance in the aftermath of the events of September 11th.

"I've been fascinated by Walt Whitman for a long time," Hersch notes, "and not just because of the gay thing, but because he's a quintessentially American artist. I just love what he had to say. He sputtered a lot as he said it, but I think [what he said] is important now that — in the name of security — some of our personal freedoms are being eroded."

The risk here is simply the fact that Hersch, always the activist, will be taking yet another stand, this one counter to the prevailing mood of his country — again refusing to pretend that things aren't what they are.

"I find myself becoming more political," he admits. "I feel like I need to be. I've always been very political about gay issues, and HIV issues — I'm sort of the poster boy for that kind of stuff. It has been part of my life and an important one,

---

★ Issued on CD by Palmetto in 2005.

and I can look back at the money I've raised, the consciousness I've raised. I'm very proud of that. But there are a lot of things about this country now, and where the world is at now, that I'm not proud of."

And so he has turned to Walt Whitman. They have a lot in common, the pianist and the poet. "Whitman was such an idealist and embraced so much," says the one about the other. "Especially when you consider the times that he lived in."

Yes, especially.

August 15, 2002

"The finish line"
William Parker (2002)

If it's not one thing, it's another. William Parker has a bill collector on the line and an interviewer who's trying to get through. He puts one on hold and ends up losing both.

It's the interviewer who gets the return call. Parker offers a second, private number at his home on New York's Lower East Side with the promise that there'll be no interruptions. And indeed there aren't, as he talks about his 30 years as a bassist and bandleader in the jazz avant-garde and more specifically about the inter-disciplinary production of his poem *Music and the Shadow People* that is being mounted at the Guelph Jazz Festival this week.

Those 30 years haven't been especially easy. Careers on the margins of music rarely are, even careers as productive as Parker's has been — between his associations with pianist Cecil Taylor, trumpeters Bill Dixon and Don Cherry and saxophonists David S. Ware and Peter Brötzmann, among many others, and his work with his own bands, notably the Little Huey Creative Music Orchestra and a smaller unit that bears the pragmatic name In Order to Survive.

The saving grace, Parker explains, has been the music itself.

"Say you've got a bill collector calling," he begins, with a knowing laugh. "You've got this problem and that problem. And all these things are happening in the world; the world looks like it's about to fall apart. But when you get on the bandstand and the music starts, you really get into it and you don't think about any of those things, you just go to some place else. When the music's really working, you step into another world."

Parker has a name for it, The Tone World. That, admittedly, sounds rather nebulous coming from a musician who's known by the sheer brawn and trenchancy of his performances. And how about those Shadow People, to whom Parker, trumpeter Lewis Barnes, saxophonist Rob Brown, drummer Hamid Drake and dancers Patricia Nicholson, Jason Jordan, Miriam Parker and Maria Mitchell will be paying tribute in Guelph? Apparently the Shadow People live in The Tone World.

This, of course, is all allegorical. It's Parker's way of dealing with a much harder reality faced by artists — shadow people by another name — who are, in his words, "trying to do something creative in a world that is saying 'No.'"

Be advised that Parker himself has never taken "No" for an answer. He has simply forged on, however meagre the rewards of working in the avant-garde have sometimes been — the fees, the record sales, the attendance figures.

"You really have to have faith that the result of what you're doing will be miraculous," he says, speaking inspirationally.

"If something more happens," he continues, now talking in commercial terms, "that's wonderful, but you can't let that be your guideline. I learned that a long time ago, when we did concerts and nobody showed up. If we waited for someone to show up before we could play, we'd never take the first step. So you just continue, knowing that playing the music is in some way helping to keep the world balanced. If people come, that's wonderful, too."

As difficult as those early years may have been, Parker still admits that he was very lucky. "Once I decided that I was going to get involved in music, with every step I took, there was another path to go down."

Indeed his luck began the day he bought his first bass; he still seems amazed by the memory. "I got it at a music store on Webster Avenue in the Bronx and I was going back home to the Projects with it when someone stopped and offered me a gig."

Naturally, Parker took it. "That's basically how I learned to play music — on the bandstand."

He was welcomed into the avant-garde almost immediately, appearing as early as 1973 on tenor saxophonist Frank Lowe's *Black Beings* for the legendary New York label ESP. (Parker's website lists another 180 LPs and CDs as an accompanist or leader through 2001, most of them for small, independent labels. He must be closer to 200 by now? "Oh yeah, we're closer to 200," he agrees, suddenly sounding weary. "I've got to update that... been running around too much.")

Of course the skeptic — and there are many in jazz — would suggest that the avant-garde, with its reliance on "free" improvisation, avails itself to the newcomer in a way that the structural demands of bebop, for example, do not.

"I played [bop], too," Parker responds quickly. "See, at the same time I was playing with Frank Lowe, I was playing with [swing vocalist] Maxine Sullivan. And I was playing with Walter Bishop [senior], who was [bop pianist] Walter Bishop Jr.'s father; we used to do weddings in The Hamptons. Even though maybe I wanted to play hardcore avant-garde music, I knew at the same time that to be a good bass player, and to do what I wanted to do, I had to play as much music with as many people as I could."

In particular, he played a great deal of music throughout the 1980s with Cecil Taylor. His recollections of the pianist, a singular figure in jazz history, dispel another myth of the avant-garde — the one that concerns the relative values of freedom and discipline.

"When we would prepare for a concert," Parker remembers, "we would practise for about eight hours a day, going over the music. And when we would leave, he'd have his tea, put it by the piano, and continue to practise. A lot of people would criticize him, saying 'he's just playing free' and this and that. But he had a system he'd developed and he really worked on that system."

And there's more. Never mind that Parker is speaking in the past tense here; Taylor at 73 remains remarkably vital. "He wasn't at all concerned about what others said about him, or with the hardships of life. He didn't have it easy, but he was able to focus and concentrate."

So it is with Parker at 50. The next phone call might be for a gig or an interview. Or it might be from a bill collector. No matter. "You're used to that," he says, sounding resolute even in the second person. "If you've stuck around this long — 20, 30 years — I think you can make it to the finish line."

September 5, 2002

"Wares"
Willem Breuker Kollektief (2002)

Time marches on and the Willem Breuker Kollektief marches with it — marches, waltzes, swings, tangos and fox trots.

The Amsterdam ensemble, currently 10 musicians strong, is in its 28th year now. There has been some turnover in personnel — alto saxophonist Hermine Deurloo and trombonist Andy Bruce are quite new to Breuker's crew — but there's still more grey hair in the band than any other colour, where there's hair at all.

For its longevity, and for Breuker's sustained creative energy as a composer, arranger and saxophonist, the Kollektief is an institution in modern European jazz. That it's not an institution in jazz, period, says something about the guarded way in which North America, or at least the United States, views jazz from the Continent. The Kollektief, for its part, fuels suspicions with its tendency to play *at* playing jazz, and from a distance not strictly measured in kilometres or miles.

Indeed, to walk in and out of its Toronto concert at various points on Saturday night would be to think that there were several different bands on the evening's bill. They all looked the same, but one was a chamber ensemble of the classical sort, one a show band, one a swing orchestra, one a contemporary big band and one a rabble of free-jazz rousers.

To sit through the entirety of the 90-minute performance at St. George the Martyr Church was to marvel at the superior musicianship and remarkable discipline of the group, no matter what its momentary guise might be. And to what larger purpose, ultimately? Hard to say. Some of these incarnations came with a certain irony — indeed, some were outright satire, usually at the expense of one jazz convention or another — but just as many of them were serious.

Not deadly so, mind you: Breuker's writing for the band's three reeds, two trumpets and two trombones was melodically eventful and harmonically sonorous. There was always something very fine and often dazzling for the listening, even as the concert ceased to be a convincing presentation in favour of any one, identifiable Breukerian philosophy, school or style and turned instead into a random, though lively, sampling of the Kollektief's wares.

Random? How about some swing arrangements of Jimmie Lunceford-like precision, a sing-along, a cut-up version of *Yes! We Have No Bananas* complete with fruit plate and ukulele, and an architectural redesign of *I'll Remember April*?

Add a little mugging and some choreography. Throw in Breuker's now-standard parody of an avant-garde jazz saxophonist, and fill out the program with the requisite round of features for the other members of the band, notably trumpeters Boy Raaymakers and Andy Altenfelder, and this was good — no, great — fun. But perhaps not, on this night, a lot more.

September 30, 2002

"The inner detail"
Maria Schneider (2002)

It's a story that Maria Schneider has told before. How, within a couple of years of moving to New York in 1985, she had the opportunity to compose for the famed Mel Lewis Jazz Orchestra. Still in her 20s — she's 42 now — she was studying privately at the time with one of the great writers in modern jazz, Bob Brookmeyer, and working as an assistant to perhaps the greatest, Gil Evans.

So there was Schneider, the pride of Windom, Minnesota, arguing with Lewis, a drummer no less, about the appropriate tempo for one of her pieces. Her preference was quick. His, slow.

"I had my opinion about it," she remembers, "and he had another. And he was the leader, so his won. But I felt, 'Wait, it's *my* music,' and I wanted it played the way I wanted it to be played. He suggested that I start my own band — and he suggested it in a kind of sarcastic way. But he was absolutely right. Even though I was hurt when he said it, I realized later that it was the best thing he could have said."

And when Schneider, together with trombonist John Fedchock, followed the drummer's advice in 1989, Lewis — though ill with the cancer that would take his life early the following year — turned up at their first rehearsal to offer moral support.

Schneider has scarcely looked back since. Her own 17-piece orchestra, which dates to 1991, has been responsible for three of the most interesting big-band CDs of recent years, *Evanescence* (1992), *Coming About* (1995) and *Allégresse* (2000), all for the German company Enja. And Schneider herself is now in great demand internationally as a guest composer and conductor, roles that brought her to Toronto recently for a concert with the Humber College Faculty/Alumni Big Band.

For that performance, as for others as far afield as Europe and Australia, she sent the scores of her compositions along well in advance, allowing the host orchestra to familiarize itself with their intricacies. "I'll just come in," she explains, "and give the musicians the details that make the music work for me."

Indeed, there are themes to draw out, colours to lighten or darken and moods to deepen. All this, in perhaps just a single rehearsal. And of course no two orchestras are the same. "You encounter different strengths and weaknesses in each group, but I think by now I've encountered just about everything," she notes with a cheerful laugh.

"I know what I want, and I work very quickly," she adds. Quickly and precisely: her conducting style is almost schoolmarmish in its firmness and definition, rather at odds with the breezy sensuality of her writing.

Schneider's travels have come at the expense of work with her own orchestra, which had a weekly residency at the New York restaurant Visiones from 1993 to 1998 but has since performed less frequently. Whatever and wherever the ensemble involved, though, there's one constant — the music will be hers and hers alone.

In this, she's following the practical example of Bob Brookmeyer and Gil Evans. "I saw that the strength in their music was in their own personalities, which they developed by not working for other people as much as doing their own thing."

More directly, Brookmeyer, as a teacher, helped her with form and development, while Evans, as an employer, revealed to her little by little the importance of what she calls "the inner detail — the sense of line on the inside and how the lines in each part can create tension vertically." Inevitably, she has seen her music compared to that of both men; each has had a marked influence on modern jazz orchestration — Evans, who died in 1988, especially.

"Sometimes people compare my music to Gil's," she suggests, "because I use woodwinds and mutes, but I don't think my music sounds anything like his. Maybe there are touches here and there, but it's hard for anyone to avoid them, especially if you use mutes and you write something in a minor key!"

These, of course, are Evans trademarks. But Schneider knows better than to aspire to mere imitation. "The reason Gil's music was so powerful is that it was unique to him, and I saw that my only chance at true expression and uniqueness in art was to find my own voice. People can try to imitate Gil, but nobody's going to do it. Same thing with Thad [Jones]: I never heard anyone write an arrangement in Thad's style that had the exuberance and joy of Thad's music. Or even with bebop. Play a bebop alto solo with the same kind of lilt and spirit as Charlie Parker? It's never going to happen. Or imitate Monk? So I realized I had to find what's unique to me."

To that end, Schneider is not among those New York musicians of her generation who are notoriously hidebound by tradition — "not one of those people who sit around asking, 'What is jazz?'" Moreover, she sets her orchestra somewhat apart from the big band tradition by describing it as a "chamber group" that takes its jazz content from the improvisations of her soloists.

Turning philosophical, she puts her work in a still larger, and yet more personal context. "Music is nothing more than just an expression of life. The things that inspired me to do music when I was a child were the things I did in life — going out bird watching, sailing with my family, playing with my friends, enjoying the outdoors, brooding indoors on a winter day, or whatever. When you sit down and make music, it encompasses those feelings. You express them all; they just pour out through the music."

And never mind that *contretemps* with Mel Lewis over tempo in 1989. These days, Schneider leaves plenty of leeway for input and interpretation. She tells another story, this one about a recent concert with an Italian orchestra whose guitarist was enamoured of Miles Davis' music from the 1970s, all wa-wa pedals and other electronic effects.

"He put everything through that 'filter' and it was amazing," she recalls, of the guitarist's performance. "I loved it. It put a whole new spin on my music and made the soloists approach it in an entirely different way. I like when that happens. So there is room for my music to become different things with different people playing it. That's part of the reason I really love writing for improvisers. The music — everywhere I go — becomes a mix of me and them."

Coda Magazine, *September/October 2003*

"Neither Jekyll nor Hyde"
Kate Hammett-Vaughan (2002)

It is, by all accounts, a good time in jazz for singers. They're the ones who are garnering all the hype and selling all the records right now — Diana Krall, Norah Jones, Jane Monheit and the rest.

Kate Hammett-Vaughan is having her moments, too. Fresh from concerts in Europe with the American trombonist and conductor George Lewis and Vancouver's NOW Orchestra, she is kicking off a Canadian tour with her own musicians tonight at Edmonton's Yardbird Suite in support of her latest CD, *Devil May Care* (Maximum Jazz).

But Hammett-Vaughan isn't exactly one of "the rest." Or, as she observes in a telephone interview from her home in Vancouver, "I don't really have much sense of a trickle-down effect from the Diana Krall phenomenon."

At 45, she's a little older and a lot more experienced than the Krall crowd, boasting a career that predates by several years her move in 1979 to Vancouver from her native Nova Scotia. She's also cut from rather different cloth, as vocalists in jazz go these days. "I'm not particularly fascinated by the idea of being a clone of a 1950s jazz singer," she admits, "which is not to say I don't have great admiration for that, but for me, it doesn't seem to be relevant to where I want to be."

And where does Hammett-Vaughan want to be?

It's a simple question without a simple answer, unless it's this: "somewhere provocative." Consider her quintet, which is completed by tenor saxophonist Jim Pinchin, pianist Chris Gestrin, bassist André Lachance and drummer Tom Foster. That's a standard enough jazz configuration, and it does indeed find Hammett-Vaughan singing the songs that a 1950s jazz singer might. Cole Porter classics are a particular favourite.

But she also has been sorting carefully through the contemporary pop repertoire for new material; Tom Waits' *Strange Weather* appears on *Devil May Care* and two Joni Mitchell songs, *For the Roses* and *Cold Blue Steel and Sweet Fire*, are recent additions to her live shows.

"These are tunes that, for me, have open possibilities," she explains, of the Mitchell songs. "When I listen to some of her other tunes, they seem so much like *her* music. Stevie Wonder's tunes, too. Beautiful tunes, but how are you going to approach them so it just doesn't sound as though you're doing a lame cover version?"

She certainly has no worries on that count when she's singing with the NOW Orchestra. There she is, smack dab in the middle of a 15-piece band, doubling lines with the horns around her and improvising wordless solos brimming with odd sounds, syllables, utterances and ululations on her own.

"I've always had an interest in dissonant music," she notes, putting in a personal context her sympathy for the orchestra's avant-garde inclinations and for New Music more generally. "When I was a kid playing *Chopsticks* on the piano, that initial, tone-apart thing was so attractive to my ear; when you moved [the notes] further away to the more consonant sounds, it was like 'ho-hum.' When I finally heard [Thelonious] Monk's music when I was a teenager, I said, 'Oh, he's my guy.' So crunchy sounds have never been a scary thing for me."

Of course, it's a long way from Cole Porter and Joni Mitchell lyrics to wordless improvs. Lately, Hammett-Vaughan has been trying to shorten the distance by integrating elements of each approach into the other and finding a place that's entirely her own, neither Jekyll nor Hyde, somewhere on the continuum between them.

"I'm hoping that people would just hear *me*," she says of her desired result. "It's a tough goal that I've set for myself, and I don't know if I'll get there or not — if I'll ever get to a place where it feels as integrated to the people in the audience as it does to me."

So she'll go off into something "weird" — it's her word — with the quintet every now and then. And for good measure she was heard recently to break unexpectedly into *Body and Soul* with George Lewis and the NOW Orchestra, prompting Lewis — typically at least one step ahead of everybody at all times — to coach the rest of the orchestra into chanting the song's refrain "sad and lonely" behind her.

It was Lewis, in fact, who introduced Hammett-Vaughan to improvisation during a class at the Banff Jazz Workshop in 1986. And it is Lewis who continues to present her with new challenges, as he did during the NOW Orchestra's concert at the Chicago Jazz Festival this past September. "George gave me a lot of rope to hang myself with; he gave me this big solo space and he said, 'You go out there and show them what you can do.'"

Chicago, Lewis subsequently reported, was quite impressed by what Hammett-Vaughan did. His latest notion, apparently, is that she should make a move on the Windy City by herself. "George is telling me, 'Don't wait too long; those people in Chicago know who you are now.'"

Still, singing at the Chicago Jazz Festival with Lewis and the NOW Orchestra is one thing, and singing at Edmonton's Yardbird Suite or Toronto's Top O' The Senator with her own musicians is quite another. Hammett-Vaughan takes a practical view of the accommodations that are required.

"I'm not into shoving anything down anyone's throat. I think you have to play to the crowd to a degree. But I've always felt that it was part of my job to be in the business of audience education. Not in a pedantic sense, but just to say, 'This is what an artist's search is about.'"

In Hammett-Vaughan's case, the artist's search has been about giving compromise the cold shoulder — "I'm not wanting to make a painting to match anybody's couch," is the way she puts it — and simply persevering for more than 25 years. "I know of a few other singers who are exploring the improvised thing," she comments, "but I don't know of anybody else in Canada who has been as weird for as long as I have — if I can put it that way."

She can if she wants, and she does so with a throaty laugh that she quickly cuts short. "I don't know, is it weird? For me, it's not. I still maintain that it's all music. And I haven't really driven anybody out of the house yet."

November 15, 2002

"Blue-skying"
Bill Mays (2002)

There is still, it seems, a little mileage left on the piano trio in jazz. Bill Mays, Neil Swainson and Terry Clarke had it out for a spin on Tuesday at the Montreal Bistro. The ride was terrific.

In fact, the ride belied the casual circumstances of this engagement, circumstances familiar to Bistro patrons who've seen many a visiting star at work with a local rhythm section. Pianist Mays, the visiting star, is up from the New York scene for the week; bassist Swainson and drummer Clarke, the local rhythm section, are regulars among the club's rotation of accompanists.

The three musicians have played together here before, though, a fact that goes some way toward explaining their remarkable rapport. But there's something more involved, something particular to Mays alone. It can surely be no coincidence that he established exactly the same sort sympathetic relationship at the Bistro with another Toronto musician, guitarist Ed Bickert, during the 1990s.

The point is this: Mays plays on pure inspiration, that exalted level where mere technical concerns have been long forgotten. Swainson and Clarke have the skill and sensitivity to respond comfortably in kind. The result is jazz of a sophistication and sheer spontaneity that's rarely heard in any Toronto nightspot — unless, apparently, Mays is on the bandstand.

Then, anything is possible. He is an impetuous improviser, digressive and sometimes even distracted. He's also secure in the knowledge — or should be by now — that he will not lose Swainson and Clarke along the way. They'll figure out where he's heading and they'll arrive at the same place in good time.

Of course, a typical set — Tuesday's first, for example — isn't entirely without its routines. More than once, Mays and Swainson zipped in unison through a tricky bebop theme; that's not the sort of operation normally undertaken without some prior consultation.

Mostly, though, the trio simply sailed along, blue-skying its way from the opening medley of Charlie Parker's *Sippin' at Bells* and Bud Powell's *Dance of the Infidels* to the closing Cole Porter standard *You'd Be So Nice to Come Home To*. The result left much to inference and flirted frequently with abstraction but still made perfect sense. That's as close to the state of the jazz art as any three musicians could hope to get.★

November 28, 2002

"Chillun"
Scott Hamilton (2003)

There was a time when Scott Hamilton was the youngest musician on any band-stand, an early-twenty-something who looked like a teenager, fielding the tempos and tunes that the older musicians threw his way — older musicians playing in still older Swing-era styles.

The New York tenor saxophonist is a veteran 48 now and the shoe's on the other foot this week at the Top O'The Senator, where his Toronto accompanists include guitarist Lee Wallace, another twenty-something — 21, actually — who still looks like a teenager.

Perhaps mindful of his own youthful experiences, Hamilton was bringing Wallace along gently in Tuesday's opening set. The tempos were comfortable and the tunes were relatively soft lobs — *What Is This Thing Called Love, I Thought about You, Darn That Dream, Tickletoe, Jitterbug Waltz, Skylark* and *Good Bait*. Swing-era stuff, *Good Bait* aside.

For his part, Wallace handled everything well, bringing to Hamilton's main-stream stylings the sort of quietly efficient backing that characterized the work of the saxophonist's former Toronto guitarist of choice, Ed Bickert, who is now retired. Wallace's solos, in turn, were deftly melodic in their content, though under-standably still rather shy in their delivery.

But give him a night or two, as Hamilton undoubtedly will. After all, it took the saxophonist himself time to develop his own voice — to scale the larger-than-life legacy of Swing-era legends Coleman Hawkins, Chu Berry and Ben Webster

---

★ Two nights hence, Mays, Swainson and Clarke recorded the CD *Bick's Bag* (Triplet). Bick, of course, is Ed Bickert.

down to something more comfortably his own size. (He's a mere slip of a man.) As it stands now, his playing is relatively plain, his tone unadorned save for a little growl and bit of gravel.

There was nothing in his solos on Tuesday of the blowsy, fanciful exaggeration that usually accompanies Swing-era evocations. Hamilton was keeping everything simple, even the curlicued *Jitterbug Waltz*, which he soon straightened out into his most vigourous solo of the set.

His other accompanists at the Senator share his preference for the functional and fundamental, bassist Steve Wallace (Lee's father) and drummer John Sumner — the former his usual spry self, and the latter, also in character, treading the path of least resistance lightly.

If Hamilton allowed himself one indulgence in the course of the hour, it was the reference to *All God's Chillun Got Rhythm* that he slipped into *Tickletoe* — a gesture of welcome, no doubt, to the youngest musician on the bandstand. Nice.

February 20, 2003

"*Tom*-foolery"
Han Bennink (2003)

Here's a sobering thought. Han Bennink, the mad Dutch drummer, could have grown up a Canadian.

"My father had an invitation to be a drum instructor in some army bands in Canada," Bennink remembers, harking back to a period after the Second World War. "We almost went; we almost went there. I would have been Canadian. It's my favourite country anyway. For many reasons, I came to be fond of Canada. Absolutely."

In the past 10 years, Canada has taken Bennink into its heart as well. He has been a frequent visitor, beginning in 1993 with the Clusone Trio and continuing more recently with Amsterdam's ICP (Instant Composers Pool) Orchestra, which is now on the western leg of a 12-city North American tour.

Bennink is, at once, one of the great drummers and one of the great cut-ups in modern jazz, a master equally of stick and shtick. He's irrepressible, both larger and louder than life, with a penchant for finding music — and if not music, at least a good laugh — in whatever has been left incautiously lying around, onstage and off.

But here's the sobering part: would Canada have embraced such crazed creativity from one of its own? Probably not. Look no further than Guy Nadon, the

Montreal drummer who shares Bennink's predilection for general *tom*-foolery; Nadon's place on the Canadian scene is — regrettably but realistically — marginal.

So perhaps it's just as well that Bennink's family stayed put in the Netherlands, where he has become something of a local hero. Now, at 60, he lives at De Rigp, 40 kilometres north of Amsterdam. "I'm the last house on the dike," he says in a telephone interview, helpfully offering directions. There is, he adds, a windmill in the meadow nearby; he has been busy converting it into a sound sculpture — finding music, as always, where few would even think to look.

Bennink started out in this respect conventionally enough, playing along with records of American jazz musicians and, in time, with Americans themselves. He was still in his teens when he made his first trip to the U.S. as the drummer in a trio employed by a passenger ship that docked at the New Jersey port of Hoboken; he spent his three nights of shore leave prowling the jazz clubs across the Hudson River in New York.

"It was an amazing time," he remembers of the visit, reeling off the names of the musicians he heard, Ornette Coleman and John Coltrane among them. "When I came back to Holland, Misha was always saying, 'You play 10 times better even after just a week in New York.'"

Misha — that would be Misha Mengelberg, the pianist and mastermind of the ICP Orchestra. He and Bennink are the only surviving originals among its 10 current members. In fact, they've had an up-and-down working relationship for more than 40 years. (Said Mengelberg in 2001, "We are eternal enemies, of course, but at the same time I have a very big respect for Han Bennink.")

At first, they played jazz together the American way, at one point in 1964, for example, backing the visiting saxophonist Eric Dolphy on his fabled recording *Last Date* (Limelight). Soon enough, though, they — like many other Continental improvisers of their generation — broke away on their own, paralleling the events of the American avant-garde without necessarily mimicking them. The Instant Composers Pool, which floated bands of several kinds, sizes, temperaments and nationalities, was a central feature of the new European free-improv landscape.

But that was then, and the ICP Orchestra stands for something rather different now with its repertoire of compositions by Thelonious Monk, Herbie Nichols, Duke Ellington and Charles Ives — Americans all, yes — and its formal lineup of strings, reeds and brass.

"Most of the time it was total chaos," Bennink recalls of the early ICP days. "I think it's much more organized now." Of course, this change has required Bennink to make some accommodations of his own. "The first years of the big band there was always a fight between Misha and me. I was the loudest drummer in the world and I thought that when you have 10 people together, you have to play 10 times as much... Misha was always shouting to me: 'Brushes, brushes, brushes, please.' Sometimes I hated it; sometimes it was a fight. Now it's going fine."

To the suggestion that he is in fact one of the great brushmen in jazz, Bennink turns surprisingly self-effacing — almost Canadian, you might say. "It's coming," he suggests. "It's coming a bit. I do my best."

He's a little bolder, however, when he talks about the orchestra's development since its previous trip to North America. "The last time was 2001. Now it's 2003. We are two years better. And a bit older. But also better. Like wine."

March 22, 2003

"Rivers"
Essay (2003)

Very slowly, yes, but just as surely, jazz is changing. This is not news in 2003 any more than it was in 2002 or will be in 2004. Jazz is always changing, which is not the same as saying that jazz *has changed* — that whatever jazz is now has replaced whatever jazz was before. The process is infinite and it's inclusive.

A jazz fan's tastes, however, are neither. At some point, virtually everyone, no matter how open-minded, will reach a rueful state of Mouldy Figism. (Mouldy Figs were traditional jazz fans who decried, among other things, the advent of bebop in the 1940s. Bebop, you'll note, has been the *lingua franca* of jazz ever since.)

These days, the onset of Mouldy Figism might be triggered by the sound in a jazz setting of Balkan rhythms or Italian operatic arias, of bandoneons or bouzoukis, of rappers and/or turntables. The New Mouldy Fig, even one who survived the extremism of the avant-garde in the 1960s and indulged the excesses of fusion in the 1970s, will eventually harrumph, "*That's* not jazz!"

But it is. (Well, maybe not the rappers. Harrumph. But those turntables? Sure. Think of them as conga drums for the 21st century.) Jazz follows its own course, rather like a river that overflows its banks and cuts a few new channels, one or two of which continue to be navigable in their own right even after the waters recede. In time, the map is redrawn. And then it's official, whether we're talking about rivers or about jazz.

Of course, someone is always going to come along and try to dam(n) the creative flow. But let's for once leave trumpeter Wynton Marsalis out of this; he had a relatively quiet year anyway. And a few musicians will usually try to sail against the current. Among them, more trumpeters: Dave Douglas, Roy Hargrove and

Nicholas Payton, each of whom updated Miles Davis' funk-fusion from the 1970s on their most recent releases — *Freak In* (RCA/Bluebird), *Hard Groove* (Verve) and *Sonic Trance* (Warner Brothers), respectively.

If three CDs can constitute a trend, then this is one trend from 2003.

Here's another: Singers seem to be making an effort to broaden their repertoire. Cassandra Wilson's newest, *Glamorized*, features Sting, Bob Dylan and Willie Nelson songs. Norah Jones has been singing country classics lately. (Okay, when did Norah Jones ever really have anything to do with jazz anyway?). Diana Krall's next CD, now recorded, will include covers of Tom Waits, Joni Mitchell and Mose Allison titles, as well as a few new items that she has written with husband Elvis Costello. Another Canadian singer, Bonnie Brett, has released *The Elvis Costello Songbook*, a whole CD's worth of Costello material. (Does Diana know?)

Now this may just look like a marketing ploy, nothing more than an effort to break through to a mass, pop audience. But it might also be that river spilling over its banks again. Something *had* to give. As the Toronto trombonist Rob McConnell asks so waggishly in his notes to his 2003 CD, *Music from the Twenties* (Justin Time), "How many girl singers does it take to sing *Summertime*?" His answer: "All of them, apparently."

Instrumentalists are taking a similar tack, whether it's pianist Brad Mehldau playing Radiohead, the Bad Plus offering a piano-trio take on Nirvana or guitarist Pat Metheny reviving an old Gerry and the Pacemakers hit. And then there's pianist Jason Moran dallying with a Brahms étude, saxophonist Wayne Shorter looking to Villa-Lobos, and Canada's Great Uncles of the Revolution adapting Prokofiev's *Peter and the Wolf* for three stringed instruments and a trumpet. It's all part of the same process as those Balkan rhythms, those bandoneons and even those rappers, a search for something other than the same old, same old.

There's nothing wrong with the same old, same old, if you like that sort of thing, but without the search for something else, jazz would sound in 2003 just like it did in 1917 when the Original Dixieland Jazz Band made its first recordings. We wouldn't have had Louis Armstrong, Jelly Roll Morton, Duke Ellington, Charlie Parker, Thelonious Monk, Miles Davis, John Coltrane, Ornette Coleman or Cecil Taylor. We wouldn't have had Mouldy Figs either.

At this point, "something else" might be new tunes, new rhythms, new instruments or even new combinations of old traditions. This last may sound like an exercise in postmodernism, and in some hands it is, but it can also be simply the product of creative curiosity. Much of the most interesting music heard this year was made by musicians who mixed and matched with little or no concern for idiomatic uniformity or stylistic purity.

Among them, in live performance: Amsterdam's Available Jelly and Ab Baars Trio, two of several Dutch bands that toured Canada in 2003. And on CD: the

Swedish quintet Atomic (*Boom, Boom,* Jazzland), the Ottawa-born pianist D. D. Jackson (*Suite for New York,* Justin Time) and the Toronto bassist Roberto Occhipinti (*The Cusp,* Modica Music). In the same spirit, though, Jason Moran's *The Bandwagon* (Blue Note) and Wayne Shorter's *Alegria* (Verve) may have been a little *too* eclectic for their own good.

Both were nevertheless well received, although neither matched the raves given to bassist Dave Holland's double CD, *Extended Play* (ECM), which is certain to stand as the critical establishment's choice for recording of the year. While many musicians have been reaching outside the jazz tradition, the Holland quintet continues to stretch it further from within. The result, however, is still change — very slowly, yes, and just as surely.

December 22, 2003

"Bring money from home"
Marty Grosz (2004)

Many words will be written about Thomas (Fats) Waller in 2004, the centenary of his birth. Fair enough and rightly so, but Marty Grosz has been singing Waller's praises — and his songs — for years.

Waller, of course, was one of Harlem's great stride pianists, a singer of considerable charm and the composer of many songs that have become jazz classics, from *Ain't Misbehavin'*, *Squeeze Me* and *Jitterbug Waltz* to *Blue, Turning Grey over You*, *The Joint Is Jumpin'* and *Honeysuckle Rose*.

Grosz is a vastly entertaining guitarist and singer, now 73, whose affection for Waller's music, and for that of Waller's contemporaries, has stood him in very good stead with the "hot jazz" crowd alongside Art Hodes, Bob Wilbur, Dick Hyman, Dick Wellstood, Keith Ingham and others over the past 55 or so years. That's now a dwindling audience, alas, but one still large enough in Toronto to lure Grosz up from his home in Piermont, New York, for a Classic Jazz Society concert tonight and again for the Downtown Toronto Jazz Party at the end of February.

Grosz was a 13-year-old in New York City when Waller succumbed in 1943 to the effects of a good life lived just a little too well. At the time, the recording industry was in the midst of a boycott by the American Federation of Musicians; in the absence of any new music, the major companies began to reissue jazz from the 1920s and 1930s, including the work of Waller, as well as Louis Armstrong, Bix Beiderbecke, Duke Ellington and the other major artists of the classic era. Grosz was hooked. Still is.

"I really enjoy an art form when it's on the cutting edge, before it gets codified," he explains, in a telephone interview from Piermont. "My period, if I could go back in time, is the late 1920s and early 30s — up until the Swing era, when the music became in many ways formalized."

It may be hard at this late date to equate classic jazz with "cutting edge," but every new development in the music's history has been, quite logically, the avant-garde of its day. And Grosz, who is the son of noted Weimar satirist George Grosz, would know something about the avant-garde.

"Right before then," he continues, still back in the early 1930s, "when musicians recorded, they hadn't quite figured out the formula, so you have interesting combinations of instruments, interesting ways of doing things. It was a fascinating era in that way, an experimental era."

Waller, who made his first recordings in 1922, was part of it. But he was also a remarkable force in his own right.

As a pianist, for starters. Grosz marvels over Waller's "time" and his touch, specifically "the incredible precision of his playing, the weight and clarity of it" — qualities made all the more remarkable by the fact that, as Grosz puts it, "he was such a giant drinker."

Then there was his way of building a performance. "He'd often start lightly, just walking... into... it... And by the time he's finished, it's really *rocking*. That's a quality that's really lost in jazz. Performers start out now at the top and then try to push it further. Fats was a master of sneaking into things."

And there are his songs, written with Andy Razaf and other lyricists. "They're easy for jazz musicians to play," Grosz suggests. "The chords and melodies work in a way that by today's standards, I suppose, are deceptively simpleminded. But they do work, and some of them even have a built-in beat, like *Keepin' out of Mischief Now*." As proof, he sings it briefly over the phone.

For good measure, there's Waller's drollery. It's apparent, Grosz notes, in *Somebody Stole My Gal* from 1935, with its running monologue about Sherlock Holmes and Watson, and in *Lounging at the Waldorf* from 1936, which finds Waller taking a sly dig at racial attitudes of the time with this aside: "What, chitlins? No, no, you can't get none of that stuff here..."

Grosz never saw Waller perform live, but — incorrigible young jazz fan that he was — he heard just about everyone else in his teens. "When I was a kid, I went to see Cab Calloway, Duke Ellington, Benny Goodman, you name 'em. I got kicked out of school because I went to see Charlie Spivak's band. I was already on probation when they caught me."

He warms to the memory. "I remember seeing Duke Ellington about 1944 or '45. He had three girl vocalists and Ray Nance would do a tap dance, throw his horn in the air and sing a song. Duke himself had some shtick he did with the huge zoot-suit pants he wore and a big key chain; he did a monologue about standing on a street corner in Harlem, accompanied by the reed section with Harry Carney on bass clarinet playing Prokofievian fills."

But even then, the socialization of jazz was beginning to change. Grosz still sounds rankled about it. "Jazz as entertainment has disappeared," he scowls. "It has become, 'Sit there, be serious. Shhh... Be quiet!' I remember when I went to my first jazz concert in 1943 or '44, when it was something new to go to Town Hall and see a bunch of guys blowing, I wondered, 'How can everyone just sit there and not say anything, like they were all watching *Medea* or something?'"

Fear not, though, Grosz doesn't take jazz nearly so seriously. Well, the music, yes; the rest of it, no. He calls his current quartet the Wise Fools — "Wise, 'cause we're old farts; fools, because we're still doing this" — and he has made CDs with such memorable titles as *Unsaturated Fats* (Stomp Off) and *Songs I Learned at My Mother's Knee and Other Low Joints* (Jazzology). A more recent release from the Toronto label Sackville is less provocative but still very much to the point: *Rhythm Is Our Business*.

Speaking of business, though, Grosz says it "a tough haul" these days for anyone of his stylistic persuasion. "There aren't any more joints to play in." But even when the joints were jumping, he admits, life could be difficult. "There's an old axiom: 'If you're going to become a jazz musician, bring money from home.'"

That, and — like Grosz and Fats Waller before him — a sense of humour.

January 24, 2004

"Gig-wise"
Jean Beaudet (2004)

If there's a theme to the programming of the seventh annual Markham International Jazz Festival, which runs this weekend at various locations in Markham and Unionville, just north of Toronto, it's piano players.

Jamaica's Monty Alexander leads off the three-day event at the Markham Theatre on Friday, followed by the Cuban expatriate (and Toronto resident) Hilario Duran, Montreal's Jean Beaudet, Torontonian Don Thompson, Canadian-in-New-York Renee Rosnes and finally the American Benny Green in free concerts at Toogood Pond Park in Unionville on Saturday and Sunday afternoon.

It's especially good to find Beaudet in this company. He's too often overlooked when it comes to Canada's finest jazz pianists; he's an inventive improviser who has reconciled the diverse influences of Bill Evans, Herbie Hancock, Ahmad Jamal,

Thelonious Monk and Bud Powell into a personal style whose emotional intensity is in no way diminished by its incisive technical clarity.

Beaudet's latest CD, *Les Danseurs* (Elephant Records), arrived earlier this year accompanied by five pages of glowing press quotes from a 30-year career. Yet his profile remains relatively low; the Markham concert is just one of a half-dozen or so engagements to date for 2004, four of them festivals.

There are reasons for this, of course, not least that Beaudet eschews the acquiescence expected of the Canadian jazz musician. He can be outspoken. His diction — particularly when disembodied in a telephone interview from his home in Montreal — is hard. His tone often seems disaffected, his perspective a shade defensive.

Ask him about the turn of his career, for example, and he responds quite pointedly. "It's like the Jamaican bobsled team, you know? 'Canadian jazz group.' There's not a big demand for it." He catches himself quickly. "But you just can't let it get to you."

He's not alone in his thinking, even if he's alone in thinking it out loud. "The jazz business has become institutionalized with these festivals," he observes, giving voice to a concern felt by many Canadian musicians whose loyalties, like his own, are first and foremost to creative rather than commercial imperatives. "It's like a pot-smoker I know who said [about marijuana], 'Whatever they do, I hope they never legalize it.' It's the same thing with jazz. They've legalized it, they've institutionalized it, and they're killing it, man."

That's perhaps an unfair charge to raise within hailing distance of the Markham festival which, under Hal Hill's artistic direction, is offering an intelligent, if conservative lineup largely free of the non-jazz and near-jazz programming that characterizes so many Canadian festivals each summer — and that rubs so many of this country's jazz musicians raw.

But Beaudet's point about the influence of the business — not just the festivals, but also the recording industry and the commercial infrastructure more generally — stands. Suggest to him that he has conducted his career outside the business, his reply is quick and right on cue. "No, in spite of it."

In spite of it, then, he has produced four superior recordings of his own since 1987, *Jean Beaudet Quartet* (Justin Time), *Musiques interieures* (DSM), *En Concert* (DSM) and now *Les Danseurs*. He has also appeared on CDs by several other noted Montreal musicians, including guitarist Nelson Symonds, flutist François Richard and saxophonist Dave Turner.

But there he was earlier this year, working for the first time in his career on a cruise ship, plying the waters off the coast of southern California and Mexico for two months. It's the sort of job that a jazz musician will take but not necessarily talk about. Coming from Beaudet at the age of 54, the admission is doubly surprising; he has always been a hardcore, no-compromise character and this would seem to be fraught with compromise.

And then again... "It was a jazz-trio gig, six nights a week, with no objections to anything I wanted to play," he explains, adding mildly, "the only thing is, we were floating."

So, okay, a sailor he's not. But Beaudet's integrity remains high and dry. "I'd heard about these gigs before, the kind of gig where you can't leave, you know? But it surprised me that I liked it, really liked it..."

It's revealing of Beaudet's aesthetic that one of the cruise's attractions was not simply the opportunity to work, but to work hard. It took Beaudet back to his early days in Montreal when, fresh from his native Ottawa in 1979, he held an extended nightly residence at the legendary Rockhead's Paradise with the equally legendary Nelson Symonds.

"I'd rather be playing six nights a week than even be doing one concert a week," he admits now. "I haven't felt like this since I was playing with Nelson."

He points to the example of the bands that made many of the classic recordings in jazz history — the bands of John Coltrane, Miles Davis and Bill Evans, to name three, which interacted week-in and week-out. "Playing every night in a group," he notes, "the music evolves; the music we love now came from gigs that were five nights a week for a couple of months."

Unfortunately, Beaudet was at sea, so to speak, without his regular Montreal trio, so the benefits of this evolutionary process didn't accrue directly to the music closest to his heart.

"Compositions are important, I guess," he suggests, of his own trio's identity, "but they're not really what our music is all about. It's about how we play together. I'm not just towing the whole thing along, with everyone else seconding what I'm saying."

He'll be introducing a new drummer at the Markham festival, Hugo Divito, to go with the bassist from *Les Danseurs*, Marc Lalonde, and he's already looking far enough into his future with his two young bandmates that he can hear the music that they'll eventually record together for his next CD.

"More fragile," he begins, itemizing its features, "a little less left hand. The drummer, a little bit more sparse and the bass player a little more upfront."

In the meantime, there's a living to be made. Another cruise, he hopes, perhaps in January, and whatever else comes along. It's a typical jazz musician's life, even if Beaudet is not exactly a typical jazz musician.

"I don't regret anything I've done," he says plainly, "but on the other hand, if I had a million dollars at my disposal, and I'd spent 15 years promoting myself, I'd be doing better, you know? But I don't have a million dollars."

He does have something else, however, something that's clearly even more important to him. "I have the freedom to do what I want. That's what I've been wanting all along, and the price to pay is that right now it's kind of sparse, gig-wise. But I've got a long life ahead of me, man. I've no illusions, but if something comes up, I'll be ready."

August 17, 2004

"No reason to stop"
Willem Breuker (2004)

If there's a talking point to the North American tour that brings the Willem Breuker Kollektief to Toronto, Ottawa and Montreal over the next few days, it's the proclamation that greets visitors to the Amsterdam tentet's website: "30 Years on the Road!"

That's no small achievement for any musical ensemble, let alone one that typically mixes the best of the jazz and classical avant-garde with precision, irreverence and a sometimes manic sort of energy. We're not talking about Holland's answer to the Modern Jazz Quartet here, all suits and somnambulance.

Ask Willem Breuker himself about it, though, and the Dutch composer and saxophonist, who's 59, seems rather less than impressed with his band's longevity than he might be. "Well, I never had in my mind to stay 30 years on the road," he admits in a telephone interview from Buffalo, the second city of eight on the Kollektief's latest run around the United States and Canada. "It just happened. There was no reason to stop."

Simple as that. No reason to stop. How about the reason to start, then, back in 1974? That, too, is straightforward. "I've always written too many notes in my life," he explains, "and I cannot play all these notes with just a trio or quartet."

In fact, Breuker had a 23-piece orchestra in 1966, so even 10 musicians represent a fairly dramatic, yet still problematic compromise. "Actually," he says now, "a 10-piece band is hard to afford, and it's a little bit small for my ideas sometimes."

But 10 musicians it is, several of whom have been with Breuker from the outset. How has he kept them interested all this time? "I haven't the slightest idea," he replies dryly. "I just do what I do and they stay and they enjoy it. They never go away, they're on time for the rehearsals, they're on time if we are on tour. We have a lot of fun with each other."

Still, the fun doesn't necessarily extend beyond the bandstand, the tour bus and the airport. "I cannot say we are friends all the time," Breuker is quick to add, "because when we are back in Amsterdam, I never visit my colleagues, we don't see each other in bars."

As it is — to take 2004 as an example — their annual itinerary might run upwards of 70 appearances in eight countries, including a trip to China in March and a tour of Japan planned for October. They've travelled to North America roughly 15 times since 1977, though for the most part they're still playing the same sorts of small rooms that they first visited 27 years ago. Further breakthroughs have proven elusive.

"If you're not a very popular guy from TV, radio, selling records or I don't know what," Breuker observes, as someone who's none of those things on this side of the Atlantic, "then you'll always be at the same level of the system."

He's not alone in that respect. His old Dutch bandmates from the European free-jazz wars of the late 1960s, drummer Han Bennink and pianist Misha Mengelberg, face the same practical limitations with the ICP Orchestra, which returns to these shores for the umpteenth time in November.

Moreover, it's not as though they're playing jazz in a manner entirely faithful to the American tradition. That, in any event, would be a coals-to-Newcastle proposition. No, the finest of the European scene's creative minds long ago made it a point of principle to follow their own directions through, around and beyond jazz. Look at the Kollektief's recordings for Amsterdam's BHVasst label and you'll see, in addition to his own music, works by Ennio Morricone, Erik Satie, Kurt Weill and — in the form of a reworked *Rhapsody in Blue* — George Gershwin.

Breuker, for one, remembers well when he and his fellow Europeans turned away from the Americans — those tumultuous years, pre-Kollektief, when the most fearsome of free improvisation ran riot on the Continent.

"We had to do that," he suggests in retrospect, "because it was the post-war time in Europe and there was a bebop scene going on that never changed and all the musicians at that time were copying the American examples. *We* didn't want to do the same thing, and sometimes we had to use very rough methods to say what we had in mind."

These days, though, such musical manhandling is just one effect among many in the Kollektief's bag of orchestral tricks. Asked how his writing for the band has changed over its long history, Breuker offers only a cryptic remark that it is "more complex, but sounds simpler."

In that spirit, nevertheless, he has new material to present on the current tour, compositions that continue to push his musicians' limits. "We still try to go sometimes over the edge, and not to take it too easy just because a couple of the guys are in their 60s. If you say, 'Let's play the pieces that don't take a lot energy,' then you are wrong, I think. You have to go on, you know, as much as you can and not make it easy for yourself."

Of course, all the travelling isn't getting any less demanding, either. "If I have to play in Paris," Breuker remarks, "it's still from Amsterdam 500 kilometres. I cannot change that."

And so he makes the trip one more time — to Paris, to China, to Canada. It's the price he has to pay, 30 years on, to have a band that will perform his music as he would like it to be heard. "The point is that you're still the boss of your own music. Nobody can tell you what to do or what to play. And that, maybe, is an important thing."

September 25, 2004

"Just so"
Keith Jarrett (2004)

If it's not one thing with Keith Jarrett, it's another. If it's not a buzz in the sound monitor beside his piano, as it was five years ago at Roy Thomson Hall in Toronto and again this past July at the Salle Wilfrid Pelletier of Place des Arts in Montreal, then it's the chilly temperature onstage, as it was Sunday night, back at Roy Thomson Hall again.

At least he could laugh about it, blowing warm breath into cold, cupped hands. "This is not the Keith Jarrett that complains all the time," he said, rather cheekily, to the capacity Toronto crowd, having interrupted his concert just moments into his first tune in order to confer with the stage manager.

These recurring technical concerns sometimes seem like a kind of defence mechanism — clever disclaimers that ask implicitly how a great *artiste*, which the 59-year-old American pianist most assuredly is, can be expected to perform at his best under such disadvantageous circumstances. (That first tune? *It Could Happen to You.* A little sympathy please.) Yes, that might be one explanation, except that Jarrett comes pretty close to performing at his best anyway.

Those concerns might also signal this particular artist's pursuit of perfection. Everything has to be just *so*. The precision of touch and the exquisite turn of Jarrett's phrases at the piano would support this argument. But why, then, does he continue to let his drummer, Jack DeJohnette, ruin ballad performances with the loose flop of his sock cymbal? Jarrett's wistful version of *Here's That Rainy Day* was notably blighted in just this manner on Sunday.

Perhaps the truth of it is just that Jarrett's a complex man — a complex and delicate man — whose peccadilloes in performance are a small price to pay (above and beyond Sunday's $124.50 top ticket) to experience his brilliance.

And there was a good deal of brilliance in Jarrett's two-hour, 11-tune program with the unflinching DeJohnette and the resilient bassist Gary Peacock. Forget, if you will, their pedestrian, funk rendition of *God Bless the Child*, whose long, closing vamp was an exercise either in hypnosis or in indulgence, depending on a listener's power of concentration.

Remember instead their first encore, a to-die-for *When I Fall in Love*, and their inspired *Santa Claus Is Coming to Town*, offered earlier on as an off-the-cuff allusion to the wintry "elements" in the hall. (See, Jarrett does have a sense of humour, pointed though it may be.)

And marvel, too, at the pianist's marvellously deceptive de- and re-constructive *modus operandi*, as he sidled obliquely into a tune and slipped softly out the far end a little while later. His interpretation of Thelonious Monk's *Round Midnight* worked especially well this way; Jarrett was more than half done with the piece before it was clear exactly what the time was.

December 7, 2004

"Getting on"
Cedar Walton (2005)

Cedar Walton would have you believe that, at 71, he's getting on. The veteran American bop pianist played the popular standard *Old Folks* midway through his opening set with bassist Paul Novotny and drummer Barry Elmes at the Montreal Bistro on Thursday night and dedicated the tune to himself. He feigned forgetfulness when it came to identifying its composer — Willard Robison, actually — and suggested that the name was now somewhere "in the archives." Came time to start winding the performance down around the 50-minute mark, he noted, "My brain always stops at one hour."

Yeah, as the kids say these days, *right*.

Walton kept on going for another 25 minutes, taking Thelonious Monk's *Rhythm-a-ning* at a scamper and the classic *Body and Soul* at a sashay with a degree of spryness that would have done any one of the young musicians crowded in at the Bistro bar — students from Humber College and the local universities — proud. Never mind that Walton was already making history as a member of Art Blakey's legendary hard-bop Jazz Messengers 20 years before most of the kids were born.

Walton's improvisations on Thursday had an easy flow and relaxed sort of sweep, qualities achieved with absolutely no fuss and only a little nonsense. (The latter would be his penchant for quoting one tune in the middle of another, as jazz musicians are wont to do.) His movements at the piano were compact, hands working together rather than in opposition, elbows in tight and shoulders turning or leaning just slightly as he shifted back and forth through the instrument's registers.

For all of this technical economy, though, Walton still had some flashy moments, if not to the eye then certainly to the ear. Flashy, but quietly so; the dazzle in his solos was a matter of content, not delivery. He faltered a little at various points in *Time after Time*, but he had *Green Dolphin Street* and his own *Cedar's Blues* cresting on long, boppish waves that made each piece appear to be playing itself, free of resistance either from Walton or from his two Toronto accompanists.

Novotny and Elmes proved themselves the pianist's match for efficiency. No extraneous flourishes here, either. Novotny, filling in for Walton's regular Bistro bassist, Dave Young, was extensively featured on most of the set's seven tunes, summoning up a warm and methodically melodic solo each time out. Elmes, on the other hand, was limited to a handful of quick eight- and four-bar breaks. Anything more, perhaps, and the music's energy level could have started to get a little out of hand. And that's the one area where Walton — he's getting on, you'll recall — might just be taking things a little easier these days.

January 29, 2005

"Old dude"
Clark Terry (2005)

"The Golden Years," Clark Terry has taken to saying of late, "suck."

It's a quip that always gets the venerable jazz trumpeter flugelhornist and "mumbler" a laugh. He'll probably repeat it again when he arrives onstage at the George Weston Recital Hall in Toronto on Saturday afternoon with the young musicians of the Toronto All-Star Big Band — if only to relieve the tension.

"It takes me a little while to get out onstage and get settled," he explains, interrupting his breakfast for a two p.m. telephone interview from his home in New York. "People are waiting, anticipating, and saying, 'What's this old dude gonna do?'"

You can almost hear the twinkle in his eye.

This old dude, one of the true characters in jazz, is now 84. His association with the Duke Ellington Orchestra is more than 45 years behind him, his time with Count Basie's bands almost 55. He has since been a pioneering presence in the studios — the first African-American musician on staff at NBC, where he played for *The Tonight Show* — and a major force in jazz education.

"I've always been of those really macho types who's able to anything at any time for any reason," he notes, without a hint of boasting. "In recent years I've discovered that those things that were easy to come by aren't so easy to come by any more."

Indeed, three years ago he was fighting colon cancer; it's in remission now, but he will — without prompting — describe its after-effects in intimate detail. His sight, moreover, is poor, and his hearing only a little better.

Nevertheless, Terry's latest recording, *Porgy & Bess* (A440 Music Group), with Jeff Lindberg and the Chicago Jazz Orchestra, received a rare five-star review in the latest issue of *Down Beat* magazine. The CD revisits the classic arrangements that Gil Evans wrote for trumpeter Miles Davis in the late 1950s.

"It was a heck of a challenge," Terry remembers, of his sessions with the CJO, "because I can't see, you know? Jeff said, 'We'll work something out.' So he put all of my trumpet parts on big cardboard. I had a 'book' about three feet high — quarter notes as big as my fist!"

And never mind that Terry reprises a role created by Miles Davis. Any other trumpeter might be intimidated by the prospect, but not this one. "After all," Terry says, by way of qualification, "Miles was almost a student of mine when he was a little kid." The place was St. Louis, where both men grew up, Davis five years Terry's junior. The time, 1940. "I remember Miles was so thin [that] when he was in school and stood sideways, they'd mark him as absent.'"

Speaking of students, Terry has seen a lot of them over the years, as he will again with the young men and women of the Toronto All-Star Big Band this weekend. He regards the kids' attitudes toward playing jazz with a sort of good-natured impatience.

"Some of the younger players are fully prepared to work with all that's gone before, but some of them think the whole scene starts on the fifth floor; they don't know there's a basement."

And another thing: "They refer now to the 'old' music of Count Basie, but there's still nothing around swings any more than that." So who better to set them straight — about Basie and basements — than someone who worked *with* the Count, as well as with Duke Ellington, two of the legends who laid the foundation, so to speak, for so much of jazz?

"I knew both of them very well," Terry's tribute begins. "Ellington was far more knowledgeable as far as theory, harmony and counterpoint, et cetera, were concerned, but nobody in the world knew more about 'mother wit' than Basie — about what jazz was all about. He knew how, where, when and why to do whatever was being done."

Or not being done, as was often the case with Basie. The pianist, continues Terry, "offered the world something that very few people before him had offered — a total understanding of the utilization of space and time."

In real terms, that meant Basie didn't play very much piano on any given tune. He *could*, were he so inclined but, generally speaking, he chose otherwise. According to Terry, who knows a good story when he tells it (and knows plenty of them), the decision was entirely practical. There was a little club in Kansas City called the Cherry Blossom, you see...

"Basie knew everybody who came into the joint and they all knew what his 'refreshments' were. So they'd all have some of his 'refreshments' at their table. Jo Jones was in the band on drums, Walter Page on bass and the Fiddler [Claude Williams] on guitar; this was the rhythm section and they'd start swinging."

Terry mimics the sound of a walking bass line. The presence of Williams in the story dates it to 1936 or early 1937; it's not clear whether Terry, who would have been barely 16 at the time, was actually at there or not. But no matter...

"Basie'd waltz over to a table. 'Guy's got a taste for me.' Meanwhile Walter Page, Jo Jones and the Fiddler were walking right on, you know? Basie'd go back to the piano, play a little, then see someone else he knew..."

As for Ellington, well, his contributions to jazz as a composer have been justly celebrated, but Terry points to another Ducal distinction. "He taught us how to establish a rapport between the bandstand and the audience. He'd prepare a program each night, but when he went to the job, he could read the audience and know what to play and what not to play. He might change the whole program before we'd get a chance to open the book!"

That sense of rapport clearly rubbed off on Terry himself during his nine years with the Ellington orchestra. His *Mumbles* routine in particular, born in emulation of the inebriated blues singers he heard in St. Louis bars as a teenager, has been endearing him to audiences for the last 40 years.

Of course, jazz elders are a beloved breed anyway, but none more than Terry. No wonder he carries on, despite his infirmities.

"I'm still doing it," he agrees. "I can't look back now. Gotta keep steppin'."

You can almost hear that twinkle in his eye again.

February 16, 2005

"The good notes"
Pat Metheny (2005)

Celebrity is a relative concept in jazz. After Diana Krall, who? And even Ms. Krall is well down the list of the noted and notorious in the wider world of the arts and entertainment. *Well* down.

Pat Metheny is not a celebrity. So what are all these TV cameras, photographers and reporters doing, crowded into a small salon at the official hotel of the Festival International de Jazz de Montréal? Well, when the festival beckons in this city, the media respond. And there really is a story here: the always personable and currently well-tanned Missouri-born guitarist will have performed at least six times before the festival is over tomorrow, his schedule concluding on the final night with an outdoor show by the Pat Metheny Group at the corner of Ste-Catherine and Jeanne-Mance.

Actually, there's even more of a story here, if only the media knew or, perhaps, cared. Metheny at 50 is a political animal — "a more political guy than anybody I know," said his friend, bassist Charlie Haden, no political slouch himself, in an interview at this same festival last year.

Metheny has a troubled view of the world, one that forms the rationale for his latest CD, *The Way Up* (Nonesuch), whose single, 68-minute title composition was "a reaction," as he put it in an interview with *Jazz Times* earlier this year, "to a world where things are getting shorter, dumber, less interesting, less detailed, more predictable." And no, he's not a big fan of the Republicans either.

The media, however, seem to prefer fishing for compliments about the festival and about Montreal more generally. Metheny is obliging, and quite sincerely so, noting in his opening remarks, "I've said many times, and I really believe it, [this] is the best festival in the world."

To which André Ménard, the festival's artistic director, sitting to the guitarist's left, can't help but interject, "You were the first [musician] to say that we have the best jazz festival in the world. You did not change your mind. Cool."

But Metheny allows himself to be led only where he's willing to go. When asked about "music of the francophone world and what you feel about it," presumably in search of a similar endorsement, he takes a different tack.

"You know," he responds, "I don't really think about 'francophone' or 'jazz' or 'rock' or 'classical.' To me, music is one big thing. When I hear something I love, I love it, and I don't really care much about nationality or style or genre. To me, music is something that is very instructive at showing how really kind of meaningless those terms often are. It cuts right to the humanity of it."

Metheny is very much a "humanity" kind of guy. You can feel it in the sunny disposition of the music that he writes on his own and with the Pat Metheny Group's keyboard player, Lyle Mays, and you can find it in the warmth and integrity of his relationships with other musicians from around the world.

Indeed there was a perfect Metheny *tableau* to be seen in the hotel lobby a few hours before the press conference: the guitarist, just off the plane from France, balancing a Macintosh PowerBook on his knee as he called up a file to show the Italian trumpeter Enrico Rava and the Puerto Rican saxophonist David Sanchez, just two of the many players whose paths he will cross on the festival's stages this week.

The Metheny cast here also includes musicians from Belgium, Brazil, Mexico, Switzerland and Vietnam, as well as such noted Americans as Charlie Haden, tenor saxophonist Dewey Redman, guitarist Mick Goodrick, vibraphonist Gary Burton and bassists Steve Swallow and Me'Shell Ndegeocello.

Haden and Metheny will revisit compositions from their CD *Beyond the Missouri Sky* (Verve), while Redman joins the guitarist in a reprise of his album *80/81* (ECM). Burton and Swallow, meanwhile, participate in a reunion of the Burton band with which Metheny started his career in 1974.

The Pat Metheny Group, in turn, will play *The Way Up* for the final time on a tour that counted some 100 concerts in 16 countries. The piece now runs upward of 80 minutes, and the group's shows last about three hours altogether, a defiant response to the "aesthetic of reduction" that Metheny decries in contemporary culture — that trend toward making things shorter, dumber, less interesting, and so on.

Ah yes, the "aesthetic of reduction." He's talking one-on-one now. The TV cameras, the photographers and the other reporters have all left the salon, deadlines looming, and the conversation moves on to the world that so troubles him and to the effect that he, as a musician, might have on it. Ultimately, he's not sure. It's typical of Metheny, who's as thoughtful as anyone in jazz, that he can distinguish between rhetoric and reality.

"Somebody," he remembers, "wrote me an e-mail that said, 'Man, you do so much better under a Republican administration. Your music is so much better when you're on the opposition.' And I had to think: 'Well, which records were those?' I couldn't exactly remember."

In other words, whatever political subtext might be behind a particular piece or period of music may well lose its relevance to that piece or period in the course of time. Even the response to *The Way Up* on tour leaves Metheny wondering.

"As we went around from show to show, playing it night after night after night, was [the political] aspect of our efforts really what people were responding to? I'd have to say probably not. They probably were responding to the sound of it, the notes of it, the spirit of it, the *thing* of it. Then I have to ask, 'What were *we* addressing?' We were probably addressing it more from the performance aspect as well."

So what's a conscientious, politically and socially aware jazz musician of considerable international standing to do?

"I think the main thing musicians can do," Metheny offers, "is represent themselves well musically. I think there's intrinsic value in that. And not just a musician; it could be anyone doing anything. If you represent the best parts of yourself through what you do, you're on the way to offering, well, not a solution, but a component of a solution to the kinds of things we're talking about."

Not for Metheny, then, the role of musician as activist, beyond speaking his mind — when asked. "Whenever a musician finds himself in a non-musical role," he notes, "there's a certain finesse required there that most of us don't have."

Of course finesse, or the lack thereof, has never held Bob Geldof back. But Metheny is not Bob Geldof. Or Bono. Metheny is a jazz musician, well down the list of celebrity even from Diana Krall.

"In terms of musicians really feeling like they have power and impact on a social level," he suggests, "I don't think there's ever been a jazz musician who's had the platform that Bob Geldof or Bono do. Probably we're luckier for it; we're not burdened with that. It seems to be enough for us just to try and play the good notes."

July 9, 2005

Index